GERMAN WRITING
SINCE 1945

GERMAN WRITING SINCE 1945
A Critical Survey

Lowell A. Bangerter

A Frederick Ungar Book
CONTINUUM • NEW YORK

1988

The Continuum Publishing Company
370 Lexington Avenue
New York, NY 10017

Library of Congress Cataloging-in-Publication Data

Bangerter, Lowell A., 1941–
German writing since 1945.

Bibliography: p.
Includes index.
1. German literature—20th century—History and
criticism.   I. Title.
PT401.B28   1988   830'.9'00914   87-30184
ISBN 0-8044-3036-5

CONTENTS

PREFACE

It would be impossible to present as a unified whole four post-war decades of literary production in the German-speaking countries. Although commonality of language is perhaps a basis for examining together the various elements of a substantially heterogeneous body of writing, not even the shared linguistic medium can weld the experience of these nations into a true continuum. Works created by East and West German, Austrian, and Swiss writers within national frames of reference often differ as much from each other as from those of authors representing non-German origins.

In spite of such considerations, the separation of works written in German since 1945 into four clearly defined national literatures would yield an equally artificial picture of the literary situation. Particulars that reflect specific national identities are often balanced, blurred, even overshadowed by shared experience, creative interchange, cross-fertilization, and reciprocal stimulation. Even more important, many individuals have actively participated in the literary mainstream of not only a home country but also of one or more of the others. It therefore becomes impossible to draw clear lines of division that remain consistent without being forced and unnatural.

Organization of this volume into parts representing the four countries serves primarily to array conveniently the material presented about particular authors. Only in a more general way does this separation reflect patterns and relationships within the postwar history of literature written in German. Treatments of writers and their works are offered in the respective chapters mainly according to the artist's land of origin, as long as a portion of the creative work belongs to that nation's literary legacy. In a few instances, authors who have never published in the country of birth are identified with adopted homelands. It should also be noted that people treated in the Austrian section include some with origins in countries belonging geographically to the former Austro-Hungarian monarchy. Individuals born in Germany, who, living abroad, continued to publish in German after World War II without returning to one of the major German-speaking countries, are included in the West German section.

Placement of authors in the chapter on the German Democratic Republic is somewhat more complicated. Those described began their postwar writing careers in East Germany (with appropriate publications), or they eventually contributed significantly to East German literature, regardless of the country of their origin. Some of them returned from wartime exile; others came later; some grew up within the system. Among all three groups are people who have remained in the East and others who have left and now contribute to what may be termed an "East German literature in exile." Only where specific figures published nothing before leaving the Democratic Republic are they treated in the section pertaining to the new homeland.

This volume lays no claim to being complete or even definitely representative of postwar German-language writing. Except in passing, I have not dealt with the vast corpus of nonfiction that has been produced since the war. Further, since 1945 noteworthy writers have published in German in countries besides those identified here. Moreover, I have been able to treat only a small percentage of the many hundreds who have contributed to postwar literature. Perhaps I reveal enough to whet the appetites of those who care enough to taste the literature for themselves.

L.A.B.

Laramie, Wyoming
May 1988

1 ▪ THE HOUR ZERO BEFORE AND AFTER

The ceasefire in Germany in May 1945 yielded a natural opportunity for German writers to examine the recent past and contemplate the future of their art. In the early postwar years, many were drawn to the notion of a new beginning in literature. Others longed to return to traditions that seemed to have lost their efficacy. Only a few saw no need at all to alter their course. The extremists for change advocated a "clean sweep," demanding the rejection of sullied ideals and the purification of a language that had been corrupted by Nazism. Counterparts at the other end of the spectrum insisted upon dissociation from the literary mischief of the Third Reich through a retreat into the past in search of the cultural heritage of a better era. The only substantial result of the clamor for renewal was the banning of pro-Nazi authors. Neither position thoroughly dominated the ensuing creative trends.

Although there was little cohesion in German literature immediately after the war, the attempt to view 1945 as a new starting point provides a useful focus for the establishment of perspective. Examination of representative authors relative to the two suggested extremes illuminates both the overlaps and the general differences in the respective literary histories of the Germanic countries. The manner in which typical writers responded to the concept of a "new beginning" often distinguishes characteristic trends in the four nations. An au-

1

thentic starting over—to say nothing of a unified approach to postwar belles lettres—remained an illusion, however, because of divisions among the contributors. Differences in experience and attitudes existed between established artists and the new generation. Even more important was the diversity of viewpoint among the experienced writers.

In West Germany, figures who were already known to the reading public fit loosely into three groups. Their divergent wartime involvements made conflicting perspectives inevitable. Members of the first set had remained in Germany and had continued to write and publish during the Nazi period. Some had openly identified with Hitler's regime. As a result, they were given little opportunity to participate after the war. Many nationalist writers never wrote again and were quickly forgotten. Those who did not bear the stigma of active collaboration continued to publish as before, but for the most part could not claim a place in the mainstream.

Figures in a second cluster had also remained in Germany, where they had practiced "passive opposition" to the Nazi regime. Most had not published during the war years, either because their works were banned or because they voluntarily withdrew into silence. Many who belonged to this "inner emigration" continued to produce but withheld their creations from publication. Items that had waited for years in desk drawers were among the first to reach the public as these writers returned to visibility.

Established authors who became most important for postwar literature belonged to a third group. It consisted of exiles who had been driven abroad by political persecution or had left because they could neither support developments in Germany nor become mute, like the writers of the "inner emigration." For the most part, they had continued to write and publish in other countries, contributing to a literature that critically examined contemporary happenings. When they returned to Germany, they exerted powerful influence because of their political and social attitudes, and because they had not lost contact with literary developments in the world at large. So great was the impact of the returnees that works by representatives of the other two groups were often regarded as second-class art; only those who had had books banned and burned by the Nazis saw their postwar writings contribute to a perception of literary quality that endured into the 1950s.

In spite of differences in viewpoint, substance, tone, and direction, the works first published after 1945 by the older authors were largely conservative in form and approach. Timeless conventions remained valid; literary language returned to accepted norms. Some offerings, especially those of the "inner emigration" poets, were apolitical. In others, vague feelings of guilt were visible. Juxtaposed with responses to the German defeat were a few optimistic products by religious writers. Gradually the returning exiles contributed an additional richness to the new German literature because of the influence of foreign authors on them.

More than anything else, the older poets, novelists, and dramatists contributed stability and a sense of identity to postwar letters. Regardless of changes, fads, trends, and attempts to redefine artistic direction, relevance, and purpose, representatives of succeeding generations have built upon the models provided by tradition, and conventional forms have remained strong beside the experiments and innovations.

The situation at the end of the war initially made it difficult for literature to have a broad public impact. Publishing houses had to be rebuilt. Paper and other needed materials were scarce. Books were printed only in small editions.

One consequence was an increased dissemination of literature through other media. Poetry, stories, and other forms of writing appeared in newspapers. Makeshift stages were erected in cellars and other available locations and the theater attained new popularity. Limitations on the resources for printing also contributed to the development of the radio play and the literary-political cabaret.

Those affected most strongly by the changes of 1945 were writers who published their first works after the war: Very few newcomers found their way into print before 1947; they were at first overpowered by authors with proven reputations. Later, their proclaimed vision of a literary rebirth proved illusory. This postwar generation found it difficult to transcend the language of a vague traditionalism coupled with elements of neo-romanticism and popularized expressionism.

Although formal advocacy of a break with the past did not bring the "clean sweep" and "escape from the ivory tower" that eventually became slogans in 1949, it fostered the rise of an institution that had important impact on German letters for twenty years. During the first meeting of Gruppe 47 organized by Hans Werner Richter (b. 1908) and others in September 1947, the invited guests read from their unpublished writings, then discussed and criticized these. What began as a private gathering of friends soon assumed a more public character. By 1958, the loosely defined organization was at the peak of its influence. Publishers had taken definite notice of the semiannual meetings, and the group's response to a presentation could launch or destroy an aspiring writer's career. More than half of the West German authors who achieved international acclaim between 1947 and 1967 were promoted by Gruppe 47.

From 1957 to 1967, Gruppe 47 gradually became the West German literary establishment—a fact that ultimately destroyed the organization. As participants lost sight of the group's original purpose, and began to use it as a stepping stone to success, three factors caused it to collapse. First, the better writers dissociated themselves from Richter and his friends. More important, the works of new participants often lacked the quality found in those of the earlier authors. Finally, the extreme diversity of the members' interests, together with the old leadership's inability to identify with new attitudes, caused irreparable divisions. The final meeting of Gruppe 47 was disrupted by political demonstrations and the organization disintegrated, a victim of internal polarization.

The conflicts that destroyed Gruppe 47 reflect again the one characteristic of postwar German literature that has remained constant since 1945: its disunity. A month after Hans Werner Richter first called his friends together in Allgäu, approximately two hundred people assembled in Berlin at the First German Writers' Congress. In spite of a manifesto that declared the participants' intention to work together for peace, the result of the gathering was not harmonious collaboration. The dominant theme of the meeting was the East–West conflict, and discussions degenerated into debates about phenomena such as the "inner emigration." What began as an assembly of individuals with seemingly shared concerns ended as the first step toward separation of German authors into major political and ideological camps. When the Second German Writers' Congress was held the following spring in Frankfurt am Main, representatives from East Berlin and the Soviet Occupation Zone refused to attend.

On a different level, the internal lack of common direction in West German literature was already apparent in the disparate approaches of individual writers to real contemporary problems. Attempts to deal with life in a changed world varied from the mournful quest for a lost "better Germany" to the sharp retrospective declaration of "Never again!" Proponents of "pure" literature clashed with advocates of politically committed writing. Aggressive, critical satire became a popular medium for expressing disillusionment, distrust of everything from language to traditional ideals, dissatisfaction with slow and false change, and frustration at the inability to cope with overwhelming realities of the past. In short, the new creative works represented a painful, often chaotic beginning of a search for redefinition of self.

During the 1950s, the ascendancy of Gruppe 47 was paralleled by the continued strong influence of more traditional writers, especially the returned emigrants. At the beginning of the decade, many new authors began to find publishers. At the same time, the older generation was bringing out both new works and new editions of old ones. The result was a new richness, pluralism, and an independence of literature. Around 1950, authors gave renewed attention to style, transformation, manner of presentation, imagination, and the development of personal tone. To some extent, realism was suppressed in favor of the earnest examination of subjective memories, feelings, ideas, and play of moods. Creations emerged that emphasized exploration of images, impressions, and emotions more than they did perception and the articulation of reality.

Among the works that were especially visible after 1950 were treatments of the recent past. War novels and eyewitness accounts became popular as they permitted ex-soldiers and others to rediscover their own identities. Some productions countered the reminders of a dark and evil legacy with portrayals that fostered and strengthened the idea of middle-class humanity. Others focused on the contemporary problems that had emerged as the products of destruction, defeat, and the need to build a different society.

By the end of the 1950s, West German literature had attained to an internationally recognized maturity. In 1958, Günter Grass received the annual literary prize of Gruppe 47 for his novel *Die Blechtrommel* (1959; *The Tin Drum,* 1962). Two days after it was given to him, Grass was the talk of the literary world. The publication in 1959 of both *Die Blechtrommel* and Uwe Johnson's *Mutmaßungen über Jakob* (1959; *Speculations About Jakob,* 1963) signaled the advent of a new era of quality, depth, and innovation in German Literature.

The increased visibility of German letters coincided with a period of intellectual unrest. At the turn of the decade to the 1960s, the general atmosphere in the Federal Republic was one of self-satisfaction and complacency. Tension existed between reconstruction-era politicians and writers alarmed by the materialistic orientation of the society. While political leaders condemned literary productions that discussed public issues, committed authors increased their attacks on the middle class. Motivated by growing revolutionary impatience, intellectuals moved toward the ideological left. Heavy emphasis was placed on such concepts as emancipation and shared governance. One typical manifestation of this political and social agitation was the demonstration that disrupted the final meeting of Gruppe 47 in 1967, when leftist students and their supporters tried to force it to take a stand against the Springer newspapers.

The gradual decline of Gruppe 47 during the 1960s encouraged authors to move in new directions. Some of them experimented with radical forms of expression. The questions of function, meaning, and communicative viability of language stimulated alternatives that led toward such phenomena as concrete poetry and nonlinear prose.

Besides the literary experiments and the trend toward committed political literature, two other tendencies became especially strong during the 1960s. The first was a product of the reaction against the middle class. It focused on the world of industry and work. The second movement promoted the cultivation of a new, penetrating realism. In March 1961, the Dortmunder Gruppe 61 was organized as a small regional group of writers. Its stated purpose was the promotion of an artistic treatment of the industrial world, particularly of the Ruhr district. At public meetings the members imitated their counterparts in Gruppe 47 by reading and discussing their manuscripts. Important concerns were not literary aesthetic questions but socially critical nearness to reality, general intelligibility, and clarity of presentation. For the most part, the involved authors had difficulty in finding a personal language. The inclination was to reject an ego-centered, esoteric approach to writing in favor of a new brand of socialist realism.

As the activity of Gruppe 61 received more publicity, for some of its members socialism grew more important than literature. A division caused the forming of the Werkkreis Literatur der Arbeitswelt in 1970. The literature of work then became the focus of conflict between the two rival factions.

The resurgence of realism was fostered by advocates of the use of simple, clear language and readily available themes in all genres. The French New Novel became a model for the Cologne School of New Realism; other writers used the debates of the 1930s between Bertolt Brecht (1898–1956) and Georg Lukács (1885–1971) as a basis for rejecting plots and style that were only superficially realistic. The strongest manifestation of this deepening focus on reality was a surge in the publication of memoirs, family novels, autobiographical and biographical writings.

The literary tendencies of the 1960s had strong impact on developments of the following decade. Some paths that opened in the earlier period were rejected, others were modified or expanded. Negative reaction to specific thrusts was catalytic to changes in direction that took place as West German literature became more diverse.

The often violent literature of political commitment remained strong during the first years of the 1970s. It also influenced less revolutionary authors. Governmental measures directed against leftist tendencies gave rise to treatments by members of the literary establishment of problems such as freedom of conscience. Newer writers focused on protest and the dichotomy of liberty and terror.

Two factors soon contributed to a tendency to depoliticize literature. Lack of public support for the revolutionaries sent them underground, where some became terrorists whose deeds provoked a "law and order" reaction. Also, with the end of the Vietnam War, leftist writings lost part of their market. Not until later in the decade, when the German Democratic Republic expelled the poet Wolf Biermann (b. 1936), did the attention of authors in the Federal Republic gain a new political focus as the division of Germany again entered the foreground of interest.

One trend that steadily grew stronger during the 1970s was the literary treatment of work. The activities of the Werkkreis Literatur der Arbeitswelt quickly expanded into several industrial cities. Workers were encouraged to write. The first products of these efforts appeared in 1970 in anthologies of stories. Some writers directed their attention to the development of anticapitalist themes, while others wrote eyewitness reports about the conditions and problems of industrial laborers.

The New Realism of the 1960s now evolved along two main tracks. The stronger thrust was inward. Autobiographical writings and memoirs grew more popular and formed the nucleus of a new subjectivism. Almost as intense was a less ego-centered reawakening of interest in the past.

Post-1970 literature devoted to the individual penetrated a broad range of personal concerns. Although the major focus is an analysis and interpretation of the relationship between the self and society, political and social questions are substantially displaced by treatments of existential and psychological problems. Important themes include love, the conflict of the sexes, the connection between parent and child, personal sexuality, the difficulties of communication, isolation and its accompanying loneliness, sickness, death (with special emphasis on suicide), mental disturbance, and self-destruction through drugs and alcohol.

An interesting subcategory of this kind of writing emerged in the women's literature that was stimulated by the rapid growth of the feminist movement. The accent on sexuality is particularly vivid. There is a programmatic examination of lesbianism, individual eroticism, and the politics of sex. Feminine psychology plays a significant role in the creations of writers who explore women's fears, longings, complexes, emotions, and experiences in the search for personal identity.

Superficially the creations of subjectivists founder all too often in a sea of bleakness, despair, anxiety, and helplessness. Nevertheless, the vitality of these works lies in their projection of a hope for happiness and for healing the emotional, mental, and spiritual illnesses that threaten the individual, as well as in an unyielding search for harmony between self and the world. Moreover, healthy color forces its way through the grayness and gloom in a rejection of documentary reality in favor of the full literary possibilities of fantasy and feeling.

To some extent, the concerns of introspective authors overlap those of artists who turn their attention to the past. One form of preoccupation with self emphasizes nostalgia. Similarly, a renewal of the demand to grapple with the reality of the Nazi period exposes the past as one nurturing ground for the malaise of the present. On the other hand, much of the recent literature that focuses on earlier times is writing of renewal, rather than despair and recrimination. There has been a revival of older genres, an awakened interest in classicism and romanticism, a return to more positive, less violent forms. Among the more significant products of these developments are the resurgence of the historical novel and the propagation of biographical narratives, especially fictionalized presentations of artists' lives.

During the first half of the 1980s, most of the literary tendencies of the preceding decade have continued. Some have intensified. Especially visible is a magnification of subjectivism that focuses on problems of alienation, confusion, and fear. Among the most consistent themes are insanity, death, surrender, injury, distance, desolation, coldness, and a distinct farewell to hope. The writings of young authors reflect a sense of helplessness in facing the threats of a malevolent future.

Representations of the present often depict contemporary man as a wounded, injured, disabled creature who exists in a world nearing collapse. Distrust and inability to communicate are major characteristics of a life full of crisis, falseness, and hostility. Missing are believable goals and viable traditions. Stress is placed on the individual's lack of influence upon institutions such as government. The response to these conditions is a literature that seeks for escape into alternate worlds.

Increased preoccupation with the past continues as one avenue of retreat from the present. The search for safer worlds within the self is another. Too often the interior realm appears as bleak and desolate as the external one, and German writers are now exploring other possibilities for spiritual refuge from the icy landscapes that confront even the inner eye.

One new tendency is the attempt to reintroduce the dream of a true national identity. Authors now offer their own ideas about what "homeland" can and should be, responding to a hunger within the society for things German. An important outgrowth of this longing is a significant increase in literary regionalism. The other escape direction that is typical for recent West German writing inclines toward fantasy. Creations of the past five years are particularly rich in fairy-tale elements, magical realism, and other manifestations of a creative spirit that releases itself from the strictures of physical, social, political, and even historical reality. That in itself is an encouraging sign of a self-renewing vitality.

The German Democratic Republic might well have offered the intellectual environment most conducive to a radical "new beginning" in literature after 1945. Conditions in the Soviet Occupation Zone were different from those in the West. The attitudes of writers were more uniform. Political and social factors seemed to favor a clean break with the past. Nonetheless, 1945 was no more an "hour zero" for East German authors than it was for their counterparts across the Elbe.

The established novelists, poets, and dramatists who continued their careers in East Germany could not be classified in the same three groups as those of the Federal Republic. For one thing, there was no significant representation of the "inner emigration" among them. Almost all of the major figures were former exiles, and the one or two who were not had been prisoners of war. Fewer older authors returned to the Soviet Zone than to areas occupied by the Western Allies. Nevertheless, those who chose the East dominated the literary scene there almost completely. Only a very few important new writers began to publish in the East during the late 1940s.

For a brief period after the war, the cultural picture remained somewhat clouded for two reasons. Initially, writers experienced a large measure of artistic freedom. This contributed to a delay in conforming their works to the specific standards and models that were formally established as the country moved toward politically programmed literature. The other cause of a sense of ambiguity, especially among returning emigrants, was their difficulty in dealing with socialist goals from the new perspective of positive regime support, rather than the accustomed opposition to an existing capitalist establishment.

Uncertainty caused intellectuals to look for a rallying point beyond immediate political and social conditions. The result was not a new literary focus but, rather, reestablishment of ties to traditions and political motivations of the anti-fascist struggle of the 1930s. Adaptation of Popular Front attitudes, concerns, and approaches to the new national situation finally served as a starting point for a rather ragged consolidation of cultural/intellectual effort.

The most influential leftist authors had belonged to the old League of Proletarian Revolutionary Writers. Many had also been together abroad. For these reasons, the writings they published between 1945 and 1949 were somewhat more homogeneous than Western literary production during the same period. This aesthetic and political uniformity reflects a one-dimensional continuity with earlier leftist middle-class and socialist literature, a continuity that limited the possibilities of artistic perception and learning for younger authors.

At first, writers in the East openly promoted works by other anti-fascists who settled elsewhere after the war. Acceptance of middle-class humanists and critical realists, however, did not prevent them from rejecting modernism as decadent. By resisting modernist influence, the East German literary establishment cut itself off from major international currents. In con-

trast to West Germany, the emerging Democratic Republic
followed a cultural policy that was essentially isolationist.

The product of these attitudes was a duality of emphasis. On
one level literary artists encountered an official doctrine of
progression between tradition and postwar writing. The working class became executor of the classicists' estate and perfector
of their goals and ideals. Writers were also expected to follow
the patterns of socialist realism and Marxist-Leninist aesthetics. In reality, forced cultivation of the classical heritage had
only superficial impact, while the East German brand of socialist realism became the doctrinary basis for programmed
literature.

As practiced in the German Democratic Republic, socialist
realism is a modified version of the artistic dogma that was
codified in the Soviet Union at the first Soviet Writers' Congress in 1934. Features characteristic for the literature produced in East Germany after 1945 include: a specific focus on
the party's role in the evolution of the new society; deemphasis
of form in favor of content; treatment of substance from the
proletarian world; reduction of psychological, erotic, and mythical components of human experience; separation of the concepts of "truth" and "reality," such that truth is tied to the
process of revolutionary progress; creation of a revolutionary
romanticism in which an attractive aura is given to manipulated reality; development of a "positive hero" who furthers the
cause of socialism through consistent exemplary action. The
primary goal of writings with these characteristics was ideological education or reeducation toward the unconditional subordination of the individual to society.

East German literature that adheres strictly to the prescribed patterns is shallow and uninteresting. It portrays life
as black-and-white, with stereotyped characters and superficial conflicts that are easily resolved. Artificial feelings, such
as desexualized love, sentimentality, and pure hate are typical.
The treatment of political matters is saturated with optimistic
mood, agitation content, and byzantine reverence for historical
leaders, current functionaries, and the party as an institution.
Milieu descriptions move the background into the foreground

with detailed representation of work procedures and landscape.

Although substantial amounts of such writing have appeared, the more imaginative authors have paid lip service to
the dogma while deviating from the prescribed norms. A dynamic tension exists in their efforts to walk the fine line between politically acceptable and ideologically intolerable literary utterances. Over the years, this condition has produced
some of the most fascinating documents of modern German
letters.

The official programming of writing did not begin until 1949.
At that time, the creative focus shifted somewhat. The propagation of anti-fascist substance remained a dominant force, but
a new dimension was added. Stress was placed on the description and promotion of the new society's development as *the*
critical factor in postwar reconstruction. Immediate political
reality then caused the building of socialism to emerge as a
primary general theme of East German literature in the 1950s.

Integration of artistic creation into the nation's social/polit-
ical program resulted in reconstruction literature that was
functionalistic by decree. Externally, writers were pressured to
regard their art as a stimulus to industrial production. Accordingly, they were to focus on making their products part of a
major social force. To some extent functionalization retarded
the writing process, because politicians stressed the importance of writers immersing themselves in the society, gathering information, and then presenting the results in their
works.

The directions of programmed literature during the early
1950s are reflected in the triple focus of a writers' initiative of
1952. Specific themes targeted for elucidation included life in
the rural sector, construction of industrial centers, and the
reconstruction of Berlin. Many new books contained artificial,
weak, and trivial plays, stories, and novels about life in the
factories, on the farms, and at the building sites. The process of
agricultural collectivization gave special impetus to writings
about the rural situation. These productions often degenerated

into a romanticism built around figures like tractor drivers and young girls who tend geese. At the same time, works about urban workers seldom transcended schematicism and the whitewashing of contradictions and failures.

In the 1950s, variations in direction, literary thrust, and the general creative atmosphere were usually a direct function of external and internal political developments. Stalin's death in 1953 inaugurated a "thaw" in the restrictions imposed on authors. A relaxing of censorship took place during liberalization that peaked in January 1956, when the Fourth East German Writers' Congress rejected administrative patronizing and doctrinization of literature. Shortly thereafter, the reins were sharply tightened because of the uprising in Hungary. Other factors that promoted changes included the official campaign for an increase in political partiality, which began in 1957, and the Fifth Convention of the Socialist Unity Party in 1958. At that meeting participants emphasized overcoming both the division between life and art and the alienation of the artist from the people.

The culmination of the effort to integrate the writer into the immediate realities of the new society, and the peak of emphasis on reconstruction literature, were reached at the first Bitterfeld Conference in April 1959. Participants developed a two-pronged initiative for bridging the gap between intellectuals and workers. Established writers were told to go into the factories, work in the brigades, and study the conditions, situations, and concerns of the laborers, while the workers were encouraged to write about their experiences, problems, and lives.

Most authors rejected the challenge, but some members of the middle and younger generations obediently entered the world of work. Only a few significant books were produced as a result of their experiences. Writing workers, on the other hand, became quite visible. Hundreds of support groups were established. The result was the production in collectives of literature about and for the proletariat. Opportunities were provided for promising candidates to study at special schools at government expense. It was hoped that the quality of works created by the workers would thereby be improved. Little of worth resulted from these efforts, and they were relatively short-lived. Although the Bitterfeld Movement remained a part of the official cultural plan through the 1960s, a second Bitterfeld Conference in 1964 failed to revive the dying program.

In spite of its failings, the Bitterfeld initiative had a strong influence on East German letters during the 1960s. With its emphasis on the context of postwar reality, it served as the point of departure for the younger generation's change of focus to the future. Movement in that direction after 1961 was based on the premise that socialist society was an accomplished fact, not an unrealized goal.

The primary difference between this literature of arrival and earlier writing lies in the treatment of fictional characters. Unlike their predecessors, figures portrayed by the younger generation are subject to action and growth as individuals. Nevertheless, the focus remains narrow, with heroes who move to some turning point where they acquire socialist consciousness. Their progress is dictated by stereotyped perception, even though it is a product of changing social conditions.

Politically, East German literary trends of the 1960s reflect the hardening of anti-Western policies that began with the erection of the Berlin Wall. The wall placed pressure on authors to focus more strongly on local living conditions and relationships. One result was increased tension between the government and writers. The latter became more critical of the society and its situation. More and more manuscripts were rejected by publishers; more and more plays were kept from performance. Many East German authors wrote about and for their own country but could publish and be read only in the Federal Republic.

Until the wall was built, East Germany had officially supported the concept of a unified German culture. During the 1960s, political decisions emphasized the separation of East and West, declaring the German Democratic Republic's status as the only legal and humanistic German state. Harsh measures were taken against promoters of cultural coexistence. In 1963, Walter Ulbricht vocally assailed the representatives of "so-called modernism." The struggle reached a high point in 1965 with the ostracism of writers who represented "skeptical," "anarchistic," "nihilistic," "liberalistic," and "por-

nographic" currents. Such individuals were accused of violat-
ing the basic norms of ethics and morality, propriety and
manners, while avoiding contemporary reality and its problems.

As a result of the continued hardening of the political line,
the relationship of writer to state began to crumble. The new
society's failure to keep its promises of universal emancipation
and improvement of conditions caused intellectuals to reassess
their positions. Many turned away from political faith and
toward reflection and the security of identity without ideology.
They also began to question the ideas of political enlighten-
ment and the Marxist concept of the future. Even writers who
professed allegiance to Marxism were subjected to new political
harassment. The conflict eventually became intolerable for
many of them. During the following decade, numerous writers
left the Democratic Republic and were welcomed in the West,
where they began to contribute to a viable East German exile
literature.

Ironically, the same period was also an era of visible liberalization and revitalization of cultural endeavor. Indeed, without the easing of restrictions that occurred, the exodus could
not have achieved the dimensions that it did.

The turning point came in 1971, when Erich Honecker suc-
ceeded Walter Ulbricht as First Secretary of the Socialist
Unity Party's Central Committee. Action taken at the Eighth
Party Convention in June and the Fourth Plenary Session of
the Central Committee six months later granted the arts an
almost general license that facilitated the development of a
lively, albeit controversial, literary life. Honecker declared that
the establishment of socialism signaled an end to taboos in art
and literature. Many writings that had previously been suppressed or restricted were allowed to reach a broader audience.

One remarkable basis for a healthier approach to writing
was a change in official perceptions of the country. The Democratic Republic was no longer described as an established socialistic community, but rather as a non-antagonistic class
society. By admitting that classes still existed, the regime and
its policies no longer compelled writers to portray nonexistent

harmonious social relationships. Authors could now describe real conflicts and offer realistic criticism of conditions.

In spite of the apparent return of the responsibility for art and literature to artists and writers, not all conflicts were resolved. Some authors were still not permitted to publish. Others remained significantly restricted. Two key factors contributed to this situation: Liberalization had not extricated scholars and critics from the tangle of dogma and strictures that kept them from responding positively to younger writers; at the same time, continued exclusion of East German literature from an international context precluded many possible developments.

The mixture of liberalization on some levels and rejection of change and criticism on others magnified tensions during the first half of the 1970s. Works such as Ulrich Plenzdorf's *Die neuen Leiden des jungen W.* (1973; *The New Sufferings of Young W.*, 1979) broke with socialist realism and invoked the wrath of critics who objected to subjectivism, animosity toward production quotas, and criticism of the model culture concept.

Conflicts between authors and the state peaked in the canceling of the poet Wolf Biermann's citizenship while he was in the Federal Republic in 1976. More than seventy writers openly protested, but the outcry availed nothing. The regime instituted new repressions and sanctions while permitting intellectuals who irritated it to leave the country.

In the literature of the 1970s, the central theme is the relationship of the individual to society. Human demands are plain and loud. Awareness of conflict is clearly visible. Mistakes, failures, and guilt of specific persons, collective, state, and party are presented more frequently than before. Fictional characters no longer progress toward a concrete socialistic image of man. They are therefore more alive, more sensual, more real. Frequent motifs include the need for personal happiness, experiences of sadness, mourning, and failure, and confrontation with death. This new literature describes the threatened, harried individual and his flawed life, portraying the conditions that have made him what he is.

The manifestation of increased concern for the problems of

the self parallels literary currents in the Federal Republic. That fact is especially visible in the accelerated development of women's literature in the East. During reconstruction, female figures were presented working beside men in the factories and on the farms. In the 1960s they appeared more frequently as doctors, teachers, and scientists, achieving emancipation by following the male pattern in a masculine world. By the next decade, women had begun to demand self-realization according to their specific needs. New works stressed the acquisition of a personal, human nature in the area of sexuality. Portrayals of liberation from masculine models and norms offered fairy-tale, surrealistic visions and many-sided subjective experiments that often deviated from the demands of socialist realism.

In the late 1970s and early 1980s many authors focused on the theme of "real socialism" and its tendency to subordinate and instrumentalize the human being. The common direction of such writers is an attack on East German reality and its rituals of self-portrayal, varnishing over, conformity, and subjection without compromise. Even the previously inviolate world of work becomes questionable. Planners and leaders are scrutinized in the performance of their social responsibilities. The real world is now treated specifically and in local detail.

The most important recent rend is the magnification of the writers' feelings of alienation from their time and country. A sense of not belonging is reflected in several phenomena: a negative relationship to the German cultural heritage, where preoccupation with earlier artists and their legacy stresses insanity, ill-health, suffering, self-destruction, and the like; the fostering of nightmare visions of reality; increases in fear, insecurity, and withdrawal into the self; an emphasis on the inability to communicate; and experimentation with escapes from reality into worlds of fantasy and dream.

The prevailing mood of uncertainty reflects the real situation of writers in the Democratic Republic. Although what can be said in literature is less restricted since the beginning of the 1970s, freedom of expression remains limited. That truth was hammered home once again when Volker Braun's (b. 1939) *Hinze-Kunze-Roman* (Hinze-Kunze novel) was published in 1985. Its appearance seemed to signal a new relaxing of cen-

sorship, but the ensuing controversy brought closer official
scrutiny of manuscripts and a return to tighter restraints.

In 1945, Austria's spiritual/intellectual atmosphere was less
conducive than Germany's to a complete break with the literary past. Austrians shared with citizens of the emerging German states the dreadful experiences of the war, the con-
sequences of defeat, the challenges of reconstruction, and the
problems of overcoming the Nazi past. Nor were the immediate
backgrounds represented in the respective groups of writers
significantly different. What was not the same was the dis-
tribution of the three groups of previously established authors
among active postwar contributors to Austrian letters.

Only a few of its exiles returned to Austria. For that reason,
writers who had remained behind had a stronger voice than
the comparable group in the Federal Republic. Even some Nazi
supporters managed to regain a degree of stature after 1945.
As a result, the Austrian response to the opportunity for reex-
amination and renewal of literary endeavor differed markedly
from that of either East or West Germany.

Besides the composition of the literary establishment, other
factors contributed to a diversity of activity during the early
postwar years. The voices supporting a fresh beginning for
literature, based on new criteria and premises, were substantially weaker than those in West Germany. Much stronger were
advocates of a national cultural isolationism and a return to
the ideals and models of Austrian tradition. These individuals
were determined to negate the impact of the Nazi period by
excising the wounds and establishing a connection to the
legacy of a more humane past. This approach favored the total
dissociation of Austria from German influences of any kind.
The push for nationalistic traditionalism became another force
dividing Austrian writers, because it favored the older generation and alienated younger talent.

Tensions between the generations were not the only causes of
disaffection during the late 1940s. Another important problem
was the fact that Austrian publishers printed very little new
literature. As a result, some of the best young authors left
Austria for the more receptive Federal Republic, thereby con-

tributing to a polarity between pure nationalists and Austrian participants in the West German literary establishment.

The focus on "Austrianness" had important meaning for both the traditionalists and the innovators. For the former, the special situation of Austria as a multi-national, multi-ethnic, multi-lingual community was worthy of preservation in literature. Accordingly, one of their major concerns was revival of awareness of the Slavic, Hungarian, Italian, Spanish, and even Burgundian influences on public institutions, bureaucracy, church, and art. Supporters of a fresh start, on the other hand, created works that expressed doubt and mistrust. Their directions led to productive questioning of motivations, institutions, political actions and attitudes, and cultural productions—as to their validity, value, and even their mirroring of the "true Austrian spirit."

A dichotomy between writers seeking continuity with the past and younger ones who left Austria is especially pronounced in the differing themes of their creations. The conservatives often produced social criticism of the prewar Austrian world, rural and peasant life, and examined fundamental universal human problems such a guilt and suffering. Authors who exposed themselves to international trends were more inclined to treat the conflicts encountered in modern society and to involve themselves in experimentation and movements like surrealism.

Some emerging polarities in Austrian literature came into sharper focus as a result of political and cultural developments in 1947. One pivotal event was the currency reform. It ended an initial period of uncertainty, new freedom that lacked real direction, heroic steps forward, and optimistic plans for a flowering of culture. In its wake came a stabilization of conditions and a clarification and sifting of the separate groups that had formed, especially in the avant-garde. Members of the younger generation began to gather around the periodical *Theater der Jugend,* the voice of surrealism that became *Neue Wege* in 1948, while the attention of older writers was drawn to the Austrian PEN Club's return to Vienna. Establishment of Gruppe 47 in the Federal Republic also had important signifi-

cance for individuals who began to leave Austria in search of a
more favorable intellectual climate.

Two directions in Austrian literature became especially visible after 1947. The first was a proliferation of writings based on
personal experience of the war. To some extent authors reflected moral purpose in their creations, although they felt
neither guilty nor committed to atone for Nazism and its
effects. What concerned them was illumination of the human
condition as mirrored in their own confrontations with armed
conflict, injury, imprisonment, persecution, exile, and danger.
By coming to grips with such things, they hoped to transcend
the evils of the past and move toward a more positive future.

The other trend that had impact was the new interest in
surrealism. Progressive writers aligned with the journal *Neue
Wege* fell into three categories. An artistic right wing, represented by Herbert Eisenreich (b. 1925) and others, was open to
modernism but opposed to uncontrolled surrealism. At the
other end of the spectrum were authors like René Altmann
(1929–78) and Hans Carl Artmann (b. 1921), whose works
promoted an extreme feeling of life and genial but unpredict-
able judgment. They employed playful, alogical elements that
legitimized their claims to being surrealists. Between the two
poles a middle group remained critical of both extremes but
regarded surreal elements as valid devices of expression.

By 1951, open division had occurred in the ranks of the
surrealists. Andreas Okopenko (b. 1930), representing the
moderates, founded a new periodical, *publikationen,* in opposition to *Neue Wege.* He was joined by a loosely formed Wiener
Gruppe junger Autoren in promoting a generally realistic literature that rejected destructive surrealism but accepted surrealistic mechanics as an attractive component of reality. From
these origins eventually emerged the Wiener Gruppe that contributed to Austrian literary and cultural life during the late
1950s and early 1960s.

Although the sharp separation of Austrian writers into two
literary camps was not finalized until the 1970s, there were
already movements in that direction in the 1950s. On one level
there was an increasing political polarization of authors. More

important was the competition for dominance between the conservatives and the avant-garde. Prior to 1955, an ambivalent identity of literature permitted new experimentation to run parallel to the continuation of tradition, without substantial conflict. Although various political forces opposed the avantgarde, it was not really taken seriously by the press, the public, or the more established writers. Events in the middle of the decade shifted the balance sharply in favor of traditionalism. Even the younger writers gained a stronger voice in literature by focusing on specifically Austrian forms and substance.

Two factors weighed heavily in this pronounced emphasis on "Austrianness." The first was the signing of the *Staatsvertrag.* The second was the emergence of the Wiener Gruppe as a significant literary force.

The *Staatsvertrag,* the international treaty that ended the occupation of Austria and made it a neutral nation, strengthened the supporters of continuity in literature by magnifying the political focus on awareness of things Austrian. The idea of heritage translated during the late 1950s into literary emphasis on stability, preservation of established values, moderation and balance, rejection of dialectic and extremes, aversion to force and change. Stress was placed on personal origins, ties to the homeland and its people, and a timeless Austria that could be equated to a healthy world with man at its center.

Beginning in 1952, Hans Carl Artmann, Friedrich Achleitner (b. 1930), Konrad Bayer (1932–64), and others became involved in processions, demonstrations, proclamations, and other forms of clamor. Although they founded a club in 1954, it was not until 1956, when they composed their first joint works, that they began to achieve public recognition as the Wiener Gruppe.

From 1956 to 1964, the Wiener Gruppe had profound influence on Austrian letters in two areas: literary experimentation and writings in dialect. The group's program included a comprehensive probing of poetic possibilities, elements, and techniques. Its members experimented with linguistic and extralinguistic devices in various combinations. They used concrete forms, baroque, expressionistic, and even dadaist patterns to create works aimed at provoking and reorienting their readers.

Among their major concerns were changes in language caused
by new forms of expression, modifications in world view, and
criticism of language.

The focus on language was most productively manifested in
dialect literature. Artmann and his cohorts wanted to make
their art accessible to a broader readership. By using regional
dialect, provincial props, local forms, and traditions, they
sought to break open specific patterns of thought. A collection
of Viennese dialect poems that Artmann published in 1958
became extremely popular and breached part of the barrier
between modernists and traditionalists. The result was an avalanche of dialect poetry, radio and television plays, and mini-
dramas that had models in the writings of Johann Nepomuk
Nestroy (1801–62), Ferdinand Raimund (1790–1836), Karl
Kraus (1874–1936), and other earlier authors.

Austrian literature of the 1950s, whether created by conservatives or the avant-garde, highlighted the perception of
reality and its interpretation at all levels. The range of themes
treated in satires and monologues of the blossoming cabaret-
theater, for example, included the cruelty and cynicism of the
lower classes, dread, violence, sexual perversion, political corruption, bureaucratic ineptitude, and the country's unresolved
connections to the fascist past. Portrayals of contemporary
moral indifference, opportunism, treachery, exploitation of
women, and aesthetic insensitivity were juxtaposed with the
praise and glorification of tradition as a timelessly valid model.
In the process, skepticism and mistrust became visible as Austrian virtues.

The formal influence of the Wiener Gruppe continued until
1964. By 1960, however, other groupings were beginning to
form that would mold the literature of the coming decade.
Although the less formally defined Kärntner Gruppe should
also be mentioned in this context, the most important of the
new associations was in Graz.

Using as its center Forum Stadtpark, a cultural club founded
in 1959, the Grazer Gruppe quickly evolved into a potent literary force. It began conservatively and was influenced by older
members of the Wiener Gruppe. One initial emphasis was the
rejection of authorial provincialism. As new writers gained

more influence, polarities and diversity in the interests of the membership became more visible.

Many authors focused on connections between language and such problems as cultural manipulation and domination of the individual. Their concern was the influence of language on life, and their works reflect a literary reduction of events and relationships to linguistic elements. Other figures proceeded in the opposite direction. Manifestations of expansionism include Okopenko's "encyclopedia" novel form and the so-called "possibilities novel," in which the reader creates a private narrative. These productions represent the final extremes of the encyclopedic literary tendencies of the twentieth century.

Because of its openness to innovation, Forum Stadtpark became the promoter of virtually all Austrian literary talent that appeared in the 1960s. To some extent it combined various impulses to produce a general movement away from traditionalism and toward an intensified social criticism. Writers born around 1940 were especially visible, with their projections of a sense of danger in a one-sided fixation on the past. Their attacks on tendencies that fostered provincial narrowness drew stronger attention as older traditionalist authors died.

The most important critiques of Austrian society appeared in novels. Sentimental regional narratives were employed to examine the important problems confronting the nation and its people. During the early 1960s, the spiritual/political landscape of the country was a key factor in the representation of reality. A typical work of the period features the picture of a "healthy" province illuminated in simple prose. The closed microcosm becomes a context for developing the idea that modern Austrian society leans toward provincialism and can best be depicted and criticized in a village or small-town model. Characteristic themes include illness, agony, death, deformation, isolation, fear, and insanity. Their treatment is sometimes expanded from the local frame, and they are given the dimensions of universal symbols.

Another kind of commentary about Austrian society occurred in works that continued the experimentation with language that had been popularized by the Wiener Gruppe. General social criticism is communicated in the rejection of established linguistic patterns and the provocative departure from familiar models, meanings, and usages. The focus of many such experiments was an attempt to change society through the creative alteration of self-expression and its interpretation.

By the late 1960s, the previously dominant emphasis on traditionalism was essentially gone. The authors who had remained at home, separated themselves from foreign influences, and stressed the universality of the Hapsburg past had mostly retreated into provincial isolation. Those who were endeavoring to eradicate the old Austrian idea had moved into the international literary mainstream.

The success of the avant-garde in the 1960s did not reflect progressive Austrian political/cultural policy. No members of the Wiener Gruppe or Graz's Forum Stadtpark received governmental support. Although the Austrian Society for Literature was charged with the task of promoting the full spectrum of literary directions and writers, only the officially accepted traditional literature was given strong assistance. Only worldwide recognition of the modernists eventually forced the political establishment to take note of important younger authors.

During the early 1970s, the separations between Austrian literary groups became sharper and more pronounced on a number of levels. As the government took broader notice of literature, groupings began to take place based on national, regional, and local institutional support.

By that time, the avant-garde included representatives of three distinct artistic directions. One division was made up of experimental extremists who employed concrete, visual, and auditive devices to focus on the problems of language. Another concentrated on the sociological, political, and ideological aspects of social reality, emphasizing literature that was useful to the Austrian people. Members of the third group were also concerned about social reality, but they promoted a revival of naturalism to deal with problems related to the generation gap—to tradition and parents on one side and youth and pop culture on the other. Ironically, the generation gap was, on a larger scale, also a major focus of division among the writers themselves.

The polarization of Austrian authors reached its climax in 1973. At that time a body of young progressive writers responded to the continuing antagonism of important older figures by refusing to associate themselves with the Austrian PEN Club. As a counter-action, they founded the Graz Authors' Assembly, which was promptly given the nickname Anti-PEN. Since then, a constant tension has existed between the two organizations.

Although relegated to a secondary role, tradition-oriented patterns remained alive in Austrian literature of the next decade. Their typical characteristics include a dwelling on the past, a commitment to the cultivation of language, style, and form, a strong sense of irony, and a feeling for the possibilities of an orderly world. To some extent such tendencies are complemented by works of the younger authors who left Austria because of frustration and dissatisfaction with the Second Republic and its society. Even though their creations are clearly anti-authoritarian and anti-parochial, their experience of international literary currents has retarded the craving for something politically and aesthetically new and promoted a partial return to the more traditional forms and genres.

In many respects Austrian literature of the last ten years parallels that of the Federal Republic. There has been an increase in subjectivism and the accompanying inward focus, with a dampening of linguistic and sociological denial of the individual. Fictionality, aesthetic sensitivity, and literary fantasy have all become popular again. Other similarities include a new involvement with the world of work and the growth of women's literature.

In spite of these points of coincidence, recent writings of representative authors maintain a definite Austrian flavor. The cultivation of the individual and his inner concerns, the subjective mediation of social experience, the emphases on both the present and previously taboo areas of the past all reflect a coming to grips with new dimensions of Austrian reality. Writers who treat women's problems focus on questions of emancipation, isolation, and self-concept from the perspective of traditional Austrian role restraints. Even literature that examines the world of work does so from the perspective of labor as a manifestation of Austria's provincialism in modern reality.

The most significant trend in Austrian writing during the first half of the 1980s has been an increased awareness of modern international problems. One result is a sense of community with other countries, especially the Federal Republic. The latest works of the younger generation share the heavy mood of cultural pessimism so strongly visible in West German creations. The same fears are there, the same reflections of failed and broken relationships, the same emphasis on sickness, coldness, isolation, and death, the same visions of a nightmare future.

The German-language writers of Switzerland were affected by the end of World War II far less than their fellows in other countries. There was no clearly defined "hour zero" for Swiss authors, because their production had not been interrupted or changed significantly by the war years. They had neither lost contact with major international literary movements nor encountered breaks in the continuity of their political or cultural development. Experiences of the immediate past imposed no strong feelings of guilt, no substantial pressures for change. For these reasons the new tendencies that emerged after 1945 did so more slowly and were less sharp, less radical than those generated elsewhere.

Although the war's end did not immediately impact Swiss writing, it did have meaning for the international visibility of Swiss authors. Prior to 1945, the twentieth-century German literature of Switzerland had rarely been acknowledged as important. Several factors had contributed to this situation. Swiss writers were even more provincial than the Austrians. They were also heavily tied to tradition and less inclined to respond productively to innovations. Most important was the fact that standard German was not a natural medium for those accustomed to the Swiss dialect. This circumstance invited negative foreign criticism about the quality of literary creations.

To some extent the war had magnified these problems. The

advent of the Nazis had ended cultural exchange with Germany, denied Swiss authors access to German publishers and the associated market, and effectively isolated them from the rest of German-speaking Europe. As a result, many who published in the late 1930s and early 1940s never achieved the exposure and renown that members of the younger generation attained. In that respect, the termination of hostilities did alter the condition of Swiss writers. It freed them from their isolation and permitted them to take advantage of the otherwise healthy and stable conditions of the cultural/intellectual establishment.

Postwar Swiss letters claimed new recognition for a number of reasons. Authors experienced a unique creative fruitfulness during the late 1940s because they could identify with an uninterrupted tradition. Direct exposure to German-exile literature during its genesis and to wartime currents in other countries provided models and stimuli that were not as quickly available in Austria and Germany. A lack of direct involvement in the war also permitted the Swiss to approach weighty problems more rapidly, more objectively, and with greater conceptual energy. By dealing with immediate German matters, they gave their national literature new validity and incentive. The decisive innovation was the introduction of a strong political element that had not been present in earlier writings.

Developments that stimulated international interest in Swiss literature were primarily visible in the works of a few exceptional personalities. In the immediate postwar period, progress in fiction and drama was promoted by two men who then overshadowed virtually all other Swiss dramatists, novelists, and storytellers for decades. They were Max Frisch (b. 1911) and Friedrich Dürrenmatt (b. 1921). With regard to concrete consideration of contemporary global concerns, Frisch provided major treatments and models for emulation. His contributions were complemented, especially in drama, by Dürrenmatt's tragicomic parables on guilt, justice, punishment, and social responsibility. These two writers share the overwhelming responsibility for introducing socio-political and socially critical themes into modern Swiss literature.

The ascendancy of Frisch and Dürrenmatt had a dampening

effect on other Swiss authors, who found it difficult to compete
with them. For that reason, during the late 1940s and early
1950s, most Swiss writers addressed themselves to local and
regional audiences, concentrated on personal problems set in
Swiss surroundings, produced traditional forms, resisted modernistic trends, maintained a sense of historic continuity, and
promoted a general attitude of spiritual/intellectual defense of
the homeland. In spite of inroads made by isolated exceptions,
the literary establishment remained largely under the control
of the traditionalists.

The conservative power of Swiss literature in the 1950s lies
in its commitment to heritage and milieu. Attempts to transcend localized background and point of view were not well
received within the country, since cultural perceptions were
inseparably connected to Switzerland's small-town nature. The
Swiss experience informs the writings of this period such that
the town or village becomes symbolic for life and problems in
the broader world context.

Aside from exceptions in the works of figures such as Frisch
and Dürrenmatt, the strongest themes of the 1950s are closely
tied to provincial regionalism. They color almost all consideration of Switzerland as a social and political entity, determining
especially the definition and analysis of the individual's roles
and responsibilities. Only gradually did the perspective
broaden to include examination of the nation's relationship to
other countries. Not until about 1955 did Swiss authors seem
to understand the need to examine negative aspects of the
immediate past, including concessions made to the Third Reich
in supplying weapons and turning back Jewish refugees. Even
then, little attention was given to such matters for another
decade.

An especially visible feature of postwar Swiss literature is a
lack of balance among the genres. There is a heavy dominance
of narrative forms, with special emphasis on shorter prose.
Even many novels might more accurately be viewed as expanded short stories rather than broad epics. Swiss drama
remained somewhat more visible than prose until the
mid-1960s, but only because of the genial efforts of Frisch and
Dürrenmatt. Production of lyric poetry has been perfunctory at

best, primarily because Swiss conservatism has warded off most modernistic influences.

One major exception to the weak performance of Swiss poets occurred in the 1950s with Eugen Gomringer's (b. 1925) establishment of the concrete poetry movement. In that single instance Swiss poetry moved to the forefront of experimental literature, exerting substantial influence on developments in West Germany and Austria.

An important factor for the Swiss response to progressive ideas was the modernists' preoccupation with language. Writers in Switzerland were more inclined toward skepticism about the validity of language than toward linguistic acrobatics. That fact is especially critical to an understanding of the changes that began to take place in Swiss fiction around 1959. A new generation of authors based the formation of narrative structures on a systematic questioning of the standard language's capacity to transmit meaning. As Swiss literature moved into the 1960s, it became more and more receptive to the influence of the French New Novel and other trends.

Because of the strength of traditionalism, tension between generations of writers was not an important factor in the development of Swiss literature until the 1960s. At that time, clashes began to occur between writers who could still remember a more healthy existence and those who had experienced childhood or youth during the Depression, Nazi era, and war. Members of the latter group were able to separate themselves from the inherited concepts and values to which their fathers remained faithful. During the second half of the decade, conflicts led to open confrontations concerning artistic approaches to the homeland and literary attitudes regarding its social structure. Among the more consequential of these struggles were the so-called "Zurich Literature Dispute" of 1966 and the division of the Swiss Writers' Union in 1969.

Another kind of division was the increased association of individual literary artists with specific regional groupings. Three of the more notable distributions included the writers of the Jura Mountain area, a smaller number in Rapperswil, and a group in Aargau. The significance of such connections lies in the fact that novels and other productions continue to derive their life from the milieus in which their respective creators moved. Many of the works produced under these conditions lack broad global ramifications. Nevertheless, successful penetration of local surroundings and problems brought a measure of international acceptance and admiration to regionalist authors.

Provincialism and a pervasive commitment to "Swissness" prevented rapid or abrupt alterations in writing patterns during the 1960s. Discernible changes were hampered by the difficulty that specific writers encountered in coming to grips with feelings of inferiority caused by a sense of nonparticipation in the active international world. Gradually, however, two major developments gave new dimensions to Swiss writing. The first was a continuing increase in political awareness. The second was an advancement in dialect poetry that gave special individuality and identity to Swiss literature in the international context.

Magnified sensitivity to politics was a product of the attitude of spiritual/intellectual defense of the homeland. The same influence that caused many authors to retreat into provincialism now enabled members of the younger generation to achieve a world perspective. Fluidity in the political situation moved them to be more active in public matters. One manifestation of intensified political concern was the emergence of the political diary as a literary form. Another was the progress toward intense examination of Switzerland's wartime past; this particular trend accelerated during the 1960s and reached its peak in the next decade.

Until 1967, Swiss dialect literature had failed to win acceptance abroad. In that year, Kurt Marti's (b. 1921) successful publication of his dialect poetry in West Germany opened the way for vernacular writers to have greater impact on literature. Within a short time, dialect authors progressed from treatment of traditional folk material to examination of contemporary themes and problems. The most important effect of this development was the new literary freedom that it gave to individuals for whom standard German was a "foreign" language.

Authors who became prominent in the 1960s contributed significant diversity to modern Swiss letters. In addition to works that examine Switzerland as a social and political entity, they produced strong treatments of the contemporary individual and his problems. Traditional themes of romanticism, exploration of antiquity, involvement with nature, religion, and the relationship of the artist to society are balanced by modern psychological presentations of the search for identity, questioning of social roles, establishment of personal responsibility, and determination of motivations for action. Specific writers examined broad social problems including the situation of foreign workers and the conflicts of urbanization. Others focused attention on the world of work. Still others created precisely analytical descriptions of human processes, perceptions, interactions, and movements. At once building upon and transcending established models, these voices enabled Swiss literature to go from the external acceptance and recognition of only a few outstanding figures to international acknowledgment of some newer talent.

Young Swiss writers were strongly influenced by the political events of 1968. Their experience of the student revolts and related social unrest led them to fruitful elaboration of political themes. The individual perspectives of these authors differed from those of the preceding generation for at least two reasons: Their perceptions were not colored by conscious experience of the war, and they had no real awareness of the cold war's impact on Swiss culture during the early postwar period. As a result, they could examine present-day life and its situations with freshness and objectivity.

Aside from its heightened political intensity, the strongest characteristic of Swiss literature in the 1970s is its renewed preoccupation with aspects of national identity. This search for "Swissness" offsets the perpetuated influence of social and cultural ties to Germany. Unique perspectives come from the deep involvement of writers in endeavors apart from their craft. Most of them are not full-time artists, but rather teachers or intellectual professionals in other areas. For that reason, their works often reflect social commitment and a sense of current reality, but a lack of formal aesthetic ambitions in approaching the object: Switzerland. Visible characteristics that amplify the impression of concern for the homeland include a cultivation of aspects of dialect and colloquial Swiss usage and an emphasis on a realism that is tied to strong moralism. A major focus of attention is the tension between representation of Switzerland as it is and depiction of what it should be. One goal of Swiss authors appears to be portrayal of a land and people that *are* what they claim to be.

In other respects, tendencies in Swiss writing of the 1970s and early 1980s parallel trends in West Germany and Austria. The literature of the workplace and feminist productions have grown more popular. Since 1970, several women writers have gained prominence with explorations of home and family interactions. Many authors have also been influenced by the new subjectivism. Alienation is emphasized in works depicting the isolation of the intellectual, the generation gap, the demoralizing effect of mass media, and the response of individual to environment. After Frisch and Dürrenmatt turned away from the theater in the early 1970s, new dramatists emerged, stressing inner conflicts, problems of communication and guilt, mental crises, and anxieties. Their creations have complemented prose narratives with similar themes of death, malaise, retreat from reality, and society's victimization of the individual.

Contemporary Swiss literature is a diverse and peculiar blend of tradition and innovation, convention and experimentation, national particularity and cosmopolitan tendency. It has its own unique identity. At the same time it also belongs to a literary community that is inextricably bound together by language, elements of cultural heritage, and shared visions of past, present, and future. These factors will continue to define the nature of German writing during the decades ahead.

2 ▪ THE FEDERAL REPUBLIC OF GERMANY

FICTION

Novels and stories produced by West German authors immediately after the war reflect diverse responses to the Nazi era. Some individuals focused on personal encounter with banishment, flight, confinement, and the return home. Others were more concerned with finding themselves within the context of a world in tatters. An especially popular object of contemplation was the concept of a more positive, spiritual Germany.

Aside from books published abroad, including Thomas Mann's (1885–1955) *Adel des Geistes* (1945; *Essays of Three Decades,* 1947) and Theodor Plievier's (1892–1955) *Stalingrad* (1945; *Stalingrad,* 1948), the first hour of postwar prose belonged to representatives of the "inner emigration." Characteristic of their initial productions was an autonomy that separated the author from the ruins and confusion and facilitated entry into a realm outside of reality that somehow remained healthy and sane.

Very few books were published in West Germany in 1945. Among the exceptions was the first volume of Ernst Wiechert's (1887–1950) *Die Jerominkinder* (2 vols., 1945–47; *The Earth Is*

Our Heritage, 1950), which describes the intrusion of Nazi terrorism into an East Prussian village. Melancholy resignation and optimism about the possibility of human progress are juxtaposed in this document of Wiechert's commitment to the renewal of religion and morality. *Der Totenwald* (1946; *The Forest of the Dead,* 1947), based on Wiechert's four-month confinement at Buchenwald in 1938, magnifies that commitment even further. It was one of the first German narratives to deal directly with life in the concentration camps.

Werner Bergengruen (1892–1964) was a herald of the intact world. His collected works made clear the eternal systems of order and the inextricable interweaving of German culture and Christian heritage. Known especially for his exemplary novellas, he achieved new recognition after the war when *Der Groβtyrann und das Gericht* (1935; *A Matter of Conscience,* 1952) was republished and discussed thoroughly for the first time. Bergengruen's most important postwar narratives reflect a preoccupation with nature and history as the two great manifestations of organic life. *Das Beichtsiegel* (1946; the seal of confession), *Das Tempelchen* (1950; the little temple), and the anthology *Räuberwunder* (1964; robber miracle) all offer variations on the allegorical essence of individual destiny. A particularly engaging version of the escape into a more natural existence is *Pelageja* (1947; Pelageja), the account of a Russian woman who is captured by Alaskan Eskimos and chooses not to be rescued. Bergengruen reached the peak of his narrative career in *Der Letzte Rittmeister* (1952; *The Last Captain of Horse,* 1953), *Die Rittmeisterin* (1954; the horse captain's wife), and *Der dritte Kranz* (1962; the third wreath), books that are remarkable for their originality, humor, and fullness in portraying a lost European era.

History as shaping force and allegory for modern life is also a central focus of Kasimir Edschmid's (1890–1966) most significant postwar novels. Edschmid, a pioneer of expressionist prose, dealt with the past on an intimate personal level in *Das gute Recht* (1946; good justice), which describes how National Socialism made a shambles of justice as it invaded the family. Although his later books, from *Der Zauberfaden* (1949; the magic thread) to *Drei Kronen für Rico* (1958; three crowns for

Rico), do not have the literary importance of his prewar writings, they demonstrate an unflagging ability to present a thoughtful dissection of the past.

Stefan Andres (1906–70) depicted man's relationship to eternal principles of order and the inexhaustible forces of nature. The dominant characteristic of his novellas and novels is the preoccupation with life's polarities. Although they are clearly conceived and make strong statements about Andres's perceptions of the Nazi past, his novels *Ritter der Gerechtigkeit* (1948; knights of justice), *Das Tier aus der Tiefe* (1949; the animal from the depths), *Die Arche* (1951; the ark), and *Der graue Regenbogen* (1959; the gray rainbow) are not as successful as *Der Knabe im Brunnen* (1953; the boy in the well), a semiautobiographical novel that is one of the best early postwar expositions of childhood memories.

One of the clearest tendencies in the search for a healthy spiritual framework is a return to religious values. The ethics of Christian humanism provided answers to critical contemporary questions for Elisabeth Langgässer (1899–1950) and Reinhold Schneider (1903–58).

Langgässer's two novels, *Das unauslöschliche Siegel* (1946; the indelible seal) and *Märkische Argonautenfahrt* (1950; *The Quest,* 1953), reflect a new prose style that mixes realistic, surrealistic, and magico-religious elements. Her theme is the cycle of life. Its course is a pilgrimage that leads back to basic human origins. *Das unauslöschliche Siegel* forms an important complement to her final cycle of poetry.

The novellas of Reinhold Schneider are more meaningful for their masterful use of language than their realization of artistic form. The novella *Der Tod des Mächtigen* (1946; the mighty man's death) set the tone for his postwar creations. It exemplifies his preoccupation with the antinomy of worldly power and divine mercy. Schneider's strongest attribute was an analytical perspective that made his critical essays at least as significant as his works of narrative prose.

Ernst Kreuder (1903–72) offered escape into a different world through romantic and surrealistic visions. In *Die Gesellschaft vom Dachboden* (1946; *The Attic Pretenders,* 1948), he rejected historical precision in favor of artistic substance.

His critics condemned his flight from the hard conformity of present-day life into the irreality of a deceptive poetic realm, but he was awarded the Georg Büchner Prize in 1953 for having the courage and ability to defend the sovereignty of art. Kreuder reached the peak of his career with *Die Unauffindbaren* (1948; the untraceable ones), a novel about an anarchistic group of individuals who occupy an imaginary America. His subsequent novels and stories failed to maintain the literary quality of their predecessors.

Two of the most influential women writers of the "inner emigration" were Luise Rinser (b. 1911) and Gertrud von Le Fort (1876–1971). Besides their common Catholic background, they shared an interest in problems of human order, decision-making, and the connections between history and contemporary life.

Luise Rinser eventually made notable contributions to modern women's literature. She explored problems of the Nazi era and various existential questions. She was primarily concerned about the difficult role of women in society. Her novella *Jan Lobel aus Warschau* (1948; Jan Lobel from Warsaw) portrays with sensitivity the tragic situation of a Polish Jew who flees from the Nazis but eventually perishes. In Nina, the central character of *Mitte des Lebens* (1950; *Nina*, 1956) and its sequel *Abenteuer der Tugend* (1957; adventure of virtue), Rinser presented her vision of a new type of woman who can deal with complex challenges in establishing her own identity. Later works have been greeted with mixed criticism. Some approach the power and effectiveness of *Nina* and *Abenteuer der Tugend*. Others bog down in triviality and artificiality.

The writings of Gertrud von Le Fort are more strongly informed by religious faith than those of Rinser. Le Fort reached the peak of her career during the 1930s with such creations as *Die Letzte am Schafott* (1931; *The Song at the Scaffold*, 1961) and *Die Magdeburger Hochzeit* (1938; the Magdeburg wedding). Later narratives, including *Am Tor des Himmels* (1954; *The Gate of Heaven*, 1962) and *Die Letzte Begegnung* (1959; the last encounter) among others, reveal an increased inclination to present experience symbolically. Le Fort's strength was the ability to present the inner development and tragic conflicts of her female characters with clarity and precision.

An extraordinary document of the search for order is Hermann Kasack's (1896–1966) masterpiece of magical realism, *Die Stadt hinter dem Strom* (1947; *The City Beyond the River,* 1953). This portrait of a city of the dead is a utopian projection of a final judgement of European society in ruins, a metaphysical allegory for the senselessness of mass existence in an absolute dictatorship and a diagnostic interpretation of the institutions, ethics, ideologies, and emptiness of Western civilization as a whole. Kasack's less successful books, especially *Der Webstuhl* (1949; the loom), *Das Große Netz* (1952; the great net), and *Fälschungen* (1953; counterfeits), dwell on the questionableness of modern existence.

In general, authors who continued their careers in Nazi Germany and did not belong to the "inner emigration" made few significant contributions to West German fiction after the war. Among the scattered exceptions were Wolfgang Weyrauch (1907–80), Gerd Gaiser (1908–76), Ina Seidel (1885–1974), and Wolfgang Koeppen (b. 1906).

The importance of Wolfgang Weyrauch lies in his successful combination of aggressive moral and political activism with modernist tendencies in form and style. In *Auf der bewegten Erde* (1946; on the moving earth), he cultivated internal monologue as a means to bring new dimensions to the themes of army life, war, imprisonment, and the return home. Rejecting traditional aestheticism, he defended the idea that everything an author writes should become a barb in his reader's flesh. Especially typical for his continuing experimentation are the stories in *Mein Schiff das heißt Taifun* (1959; my ship is called typhoon).

Gerd Gaiser employs the techniques of magical realism in his critiques of modern life. The narratives in *Zwischenland* (1949; between land) and *Eine Stimme hebt an* (1950; a voice is raised) focus on the misery, suffering, and frustration that plague his characters. Gaiser's most successful works are novellas like *Gianna aus dem Schatten* (1957; Gianna from the shadow) and *Ariela* (1958; Ariela), in which he effectively employed a device of dream-associative arrangement. Other significant creations include *Die sterbende Jagd* (1953; *The Last Squadron*, 1956), one of the best early German books based on the war, and *Das Schiff im Berg* (1955; the ship in the mountain), a powerful example of Gaiser's ability to illuminate present-day conditions through the use of myth.

Ina Seidel's fiction is permeated by a strong Protestant humanist ethos coupled with a penetrating yet sensitively sympathetic feminine psychology. She wrote her best novels and stories before the war, but her later treatments of human decision-making show great depth of insight into the workings of the mind. *Die Geschichte einer Frau Berngruber* (1953; the story of a Mrs. Berngruber) offers a compelling portrayal of the inner struggle of a foster mother faced with having to return a child to its natural mother. The psychology of personal judgment also governs depiction of a confessionally mixed marriage in *Das unverwesliche Erbe* (1954; the incorruptible legacy) and Seidel's interpretation of collective German guilt in *Michaela* (1959); Michaela).

Although not a representative of the "inner emigration," Wolfgang Koeppen experienced a break in his career between 1935 and 1950. His three novels *Tauben im Gras* (1951; doves in the grass), *Das Treibhaus* (1953; the greenhouse), and *Der Tod in Rom* (1954; *Death in Rome,* 1956) are products of a second phase in his creative development. Like Weyrauch, he responded constructively to modernist influences. *Tauben im Gras* demonstrates his mastery of internal monologue while offering a combination of melodic fullness and optical clarity in its descriptions. The result is a powerful political, sociological, and existential cross-section of the times. Koeppen's most successful work is *Das Treibhaus,* a political satire about the founding of the Federal Republic and the subsequent conservative restoration.

By 1947 the creations of exiled authors had begun to attract considerable attention and gain importance in determining postwar literary directions. Although political emigrants rapidly combined to become the loudest voice in the mainstream of German fiction, other artists had left Germany before the rise of Hitler. At least one of them had a strong impact on postwar prose.

Hermann Hesse's (1877–1962) most substantial works were published before 1945, but his final masterpiece, *Das Glasperlenspiel* (1943; *The Glass Bead Game,* 1969), with its vision of a state of culturally ordered existence based upon spiritual austerity, was greeted enthusiastically as a model for interpreting the immediate past, when it appeared in Germany.

Most of the political exiles had reached or passed their prime by war's end. Nevertheless, they contributed to the development of postwar fiction in at least two ways. The works they had published abroad had tremendous impact when they finally began to appear in Germany, because they mediated the influence of contemporary international trends. In addition, some of these figures did produce significant later works after they had returned home.

Theodor Plievier, a representative of the "new factuality" movement of the 1920s, published his best novel just as the war ended. Based on documentary materials obtained from the Red Army, *Stalingrad* (1945; *Stalingrad,* 1948) is a brutal mosaic of the German Sixth Army's destruction on the Eastern Front. It is also a symbolic representation of the existential collapse of Germany as a whole. With *Stalingrad* Plievier achieved immediate international recognition. Unfortunately, his subsequent novels—including *Moskau* (1952; *Moscow,* 1953) and *Berlin* (1954; *Berlin,* 1956)—failed to sustain the literary quality of *Stalingrad.*

Unlike Plievier, Alfred Döblin (1878–1957), whose epic masterpiece, *Berlin Alexanderplatz* (1929; *Alexanderplatz, Berlin,* 1931), had made him famous, produced nothing after the war that compared with his earlier achievements. *Hamlet* (1956; Hamlet) was greeted as the best work of his late period, but its fanatically realistic depiction of a physically and mentally crippled soldier is more oppressive than convincing.

One or two of Erich Maria Remarque's (1898–1970) postwar novels are almost as good as *Im Westen nichts Neues* (1929; *All Quiet on the Western Front,* 1929). This is especially true for *Arc de Triomphe* (1946; *Arch of Triumph,* 1946), the powerful story of a German doctor who escapes from the Gestapo into the Paris underworld. The work achieves its narrative success through an immediate realism arising from the intense psychological penetration of a restricted cast of characters. Later books, such as *Der Funke Leben* (1952; *Spark of Life*, 1953), enjoyed only a limited popularity.

Some really gifted political emigrants remained abroad after the war. The most important of them was Thomas Mann. He influenced developments in narrative prose through the deeply perceptive psychological realism of his wartime creations and his later masterpieces. The four-volume cycle *Joseph und seine Brüder* (1933–42; *Joseph and His Brothers*, 1934–45) established the basis for a successful magnification of typical, universally human elements. Combining mythical, psychological, and religious substance into a monumental portrait of life, Mann produced a new model for the exploration of human motivations and interrelationships.

In *Doktor Faustus* (1947; *Doctor Faustus*, 1948) Mann created his most complex and powerful treatment of modern man's self-destructive struggle with the problems of guilt and responsibility. The story of the musician Adrian Leverkühn is the culmination of Mann's projection of the conflict of spirit and art as a major symbol for the illness and decadence of contemporary society.

Another novelist who refused to return permanently to Germany was Hermann Kesten (b. 1900). His first postwar novel, *Die Zwillinge von Nürnberg* (1947; *The Twins of Nuremberg*, 1946), is little more than an obligatory presentation of the bright and dark spots in German history after 1918. It has neither the literary quality not the bitter humor of his later satires, *Abenteuer eines Moralisten* (1961; adventure of a moralist), *Die Zeit der Narren* (1966; the time of the fools), and *Ein Mann von sechzig Jahren* (1972; a man of sixty years).

Kesten also made important contributions to the short story. The tragicomic tale "Oberst Kock" ("Colonel Kock," 1943), contained in *Mit Geduld kann man sogar das Leben aushalten* (1957; with patience one can even endure life), is typical of his socially critical fiction. It attacks the spiritual weakness of the middle class as represented by a figure whose attitudes always coincide with those of the current government.

The most innovative and enigmatic of the political emigrants was Hans Henny Jahnn (1894–1959). His monumental trilogy *Fluß ohne Ufer* (river without banks), consisting of *Das Holzschiff* (1949; *The Ship,* 1961), *Die Niederschrift des Gustav Anias Horn* (2 vols., 1949–50; Gustav Anias Horn's written narrative), and *Epilog* (1961; epilogue), combines fullness of thought, complicated spiritual processes, surrealistic descriptions, and autobiographical reflections about the struggling artist, in an allegorical representation of man's inevitable submission to evil. Reminiscent of Franz Kafka's writings in their nightmarelike transcendence of reality and their focus on the confrontation of the individual with a hidden inner self, *Fluß ohne Ufer* and *Die Nacht aus Blei* (1956; the night made of lead) are among postwar German fiction's most unusual attempts to arrive at the true essence of man's nature.

During the early postwar years, the dearth of materials and publishing facilities combined with the competition of established authors to limit the number of new writers whose works made their way into print. Only the strongest voices of the rising generation were heard at all.

In spite of the brevity of his career, Wolfgang Borchert (1921–47) quickly established himself as an important spokesman for the younger generation that had returned to a homeland in ruins. His books of short stories, *An diesem Dienstag* (1947; on this Tuesday), *Die Hundeblume* (1947; the dog-flower), and *Die traurigen Geranien* (1962; *The Sad Geraniums,* 1972) decry with extreme sensitivity the senselessness of war, the betrayal of human values, and the stark contradictions between traditional ideals and the horrors of a chaotic reality.

Walter Jens (b. 1923) made his debut with the pacifistic novella *Das weiße Taschentuch* (1947; the white handkerchief), the fictional confession of a conscripted student. In his later writings, Jens concentrated on themes related to disrupted reality and the changing world. Among his most important novels are *Nein. Die Welt der Angeklagten* (1950; no. the world of the accused), a story about the last individualist in a totalitarian state, and *Herr Meister* (1963; master), a pointed dialogue between an author and a critic. The significance of Jens's narrative prose lies in its consistent questioning of both conventional and experimental style models through the magnification of essayistic and critical devices.

The early works of Hermann Lenz (b. 1913), including *Das stille Haus* (1947; the quiet house) and *Das doppelte Gesicht* (1949; the double face), exhibit a dreamlike quality in responding to the problems of the times. *Das stille Haus* juxtaposes a demonic world of destruction, hatred, and insanity with a quiet realm of inner order, offering a substantial contrast to the sharp characterization of figures and the concrete emphasis on reality in his mature novels. *Der russische Regenbogen* (1959; the Russian rainbow) is notable for its successful combination of simplicity and lyrical language with penetrating psychological insight. Beginning with *Spiegelhütte* (1962; mirror cottage), elements of a strong magical realism appear in Lenz's writing. They contribute a poetic tone to his introspective observation of the decaying middle class.

The most important writer of fiction to emerge in the late 1940s was Heinrich Böll (1917–85), who eventually received the Nobel Prize for Literature in 1972. His solidly realistic depictions of the war's horrors and chaotic aftermath in *Der Zug war pünktlich* (1949; *The Train Was on Time*, 1956), *Wanderer, kommst du nach Spa* (1950; *Traveller, If You Come to Spa*, 1956), and his best early novel *Haus ohne Hüter* (1954; *Tomorrow and Yesterday*, 1957) are presented with terse vividness that is weakened only by excessive sentimentality.

In his mature novels, Böll revealed his mastery of interior monologue, flashbacks, and shifting narrative perspectives. His bitingly satirical analyses of German history and postwar reconstruction in *Billard um halbzehn* (1959; *Billiards at Half Past Nine*, 1962) and *Ansichten eines Clowns* (1963; *The Clown*, 1965) offer profound commentary on persisting social and political problems in the Federal Republic. *Gruppenbild mit Dame* (1971; *Group Portrait with Lady*, 1973) is regarded by many critics as Böll's best novel. A subtle social satire, it depicts the author's vision of possibilities for new, humane kinds of interpersonal relationships.

The major narratives of Böll's late period emphasize his perceptions of particular recent problems in West Germany and continue to develop the basic themes of corruption and compromise as the essence of postwar society. The culmination of these works is his final novel, *Frauen vor Flußlandschaft* (1985; women before a river landscape), an interesting prose drama written in monologues and dialogues that rehearse forty years of history within the event frame of a single day.

Hans Werner Richter, the "father" of Gruppe 47, is more important for his promotion than his creation of politically committed literature. His early novels include *Die Geschlagenen* (1949; *Beyond Defeat*, 1950), *Sie fielen aus Gottes Hand* (1951; *They Fell from God's Hands*, 1956), and *Du sollst nicht töten* (1955; thou shalt not kill). They belong in the solid mainstream of fiction dealing with the immediate German past, but they are not outstanding works of art. The same can be said of his later efforts. Only the autobiographical novel *Spuren im Sand* (1953; tracks in the sand) forms an exception, with its personally toned yet objective descriptions and its compelling illumination of the common man's political narrowness.

The most radical and controversial new writer of the late 1940s was Arno Schmidt (1914–79). He was recognized for the power of his language, his nonconformity, his experiments with form, daring motifs, and vocabulary, and his creative diversity. Schmidt's first collection of stories, *Leviathan* (1949; Leviathan), features highly individual language and a surrealistically visual presentation technique. His novels *Aus dem Leben eines Fauns* (1953; *Scenes from the Life of a Faun,* 1983), *Das steinerne Herz* (1956; the stone heart), and *Die Gelehrtenrepublik* (*The Egghead Republic,* 1979) enhanced the picture of an author who was master of various narrative approaches. Schmidt reached the pinnacle of his career with *Zettels Traum* (1970; Zettel's dream), a monumentally complex work that employs conversations about the life and works of Edgar Allan Poe to produce a world model based on the history of literature, theory of language, and the psychoanalysis of literary artistry.

Only a few significant novelists and storytellers emerged in the Federal Republic during the early 1950s. Those of lasting impact were Wolfdietrich Schnurre (b. 1920), Siegfried Lenz (b. 1926), Wolfgang Hildesheimer (b. 1916), and Hans Bender (b.

1919). Each is an observer of the world, an analyst of its history and weaknesses, and a critic of its falseness and façades.

The early publications of Wolfdietrich Schnurre set a pattern of radical anti-ideological moralism. From the beginning, his works documented a forceful rejection of war and the things that make it possible. In *Die Rohrdommel ruft jeden Tag* (1950; the bittern calls every day), the first of many anthologies, he established himself as a master of sharply honed satire, carefree parody, unforced humor, and conciliatory irony. He has also written three novels, the most successful of which is *Das Los unserer Stadt* (1959; the fate of our city), an apocalyptic, surrealistic vision of Berlin that criticizes the internal and external events of the times.

Like Schnurre, Siegfried Lenz employs his stories and novels to mediate perceptions of the social and political conflicts of Germany's past and present. His first two works, *Es waren Habichte in der Luft* (1951; there were hawks in the sky) and *Duell mit dem Schatten* (1953; duel with the shadow), are not entirely successful in their parabolic interpretation of confrontations with dictatorship. During the 1950s and early 1960s, Lenz produced books of varying literary value. *Deutschstunde* (1968; *The German Lesson,* 1972) was his first truly superior novel. It makes an outstanding contribution to the literature devoted to grappling with the Nazi past. *Das Vorbild* (1973; *An Exemplary Life,* 1976) and *Heimatmuseum* (1978; *The Heritage: The History of a Detestable Word,* 1981) are less successful than *The German Lesson,* but *Exerzierplatz* (1985; exercise yard), with its unique presentation of an East Prussian refugee household, rivals the earlier masterpiece in literary power.

Lenz has also produced several good collections of short stories. Among them are *Jäger des Spotts* (1958; hunter of ridicule) and *Der Spielverderber* (1965; the spoilsport). His short prose is diverse in theme and artistic approach. Representative examples range from profound existential investigations to humorous commentaries on modern life.

Wolfgang Hildesheimer has committed his stories and novels to satirical exposure of social clichés. His writings combine irony and satire with grotesque and surrealistic elements in a strong play of fantasy. The anthology *Lieblose Legenden* (1952; loveless legends) brought him quick recognition as a master of style, but he did not receive international acclaim until the novel *Tynset* (1965; Tynset) was published. This curious collection of reflections about the past makes a profound statement about the postwar individual's hopeless inner isolation.

One of the most consistent themes of Hildesheimer's writing is the mystery of artistic creativity. It is given interesting treatment in the fictional biography *Marbot* (1981; *Marbot,* 1983), the story of a young Englishman who "invents" Freudian art analysis decades before Freud.

Recognized more for his short prose than his ability as a novelist, Hans Bender specializes in narratives that stress clarity and honesty in their portrayal of modern reality. His collections, from *Die Hostie* (1953; the host) to *Die halbe Sonne* (1968; the half sun), are remarkable for the sharpness and sensitivity with which they describe landscape and human interactions. Especially representative for his art is "Die Wölfe kommen zurück" (the wolves are returning) from the collection *Wölfe und Tauben* (1957; wolves and doves), in which a prisoner of war and his overseer share a moment of danger and human closeness.

By the mid-1950s, the stability of reconstruction had produced a climate more favorable to young authors trying to get into print. As result, the second half of the decade witnessed a sharp increase in the number of novelists and storytellers who published their first books.

Ingeborg Drewitz's (b. 1923) anthology *Und hatte keinen Menschen* (1955; and had no human being) was important only as a prelude to her novels about individual loneliness in the big city. *Der Anstoß* (1958; the impact) set the pattern for her consistently realistic analyses of everyday conflicts. Berlin as a symbol for emptiness is a major focus of her mature novels. In *Oktoberlicht* (1969; October light), Drewitz plays off German history from 1933 to the present against the day's activities of a divorced woman. Later successful novels examine such problems as the inability of good people to adjust to a corrupt reality, and the banality of life for the average residents of a Berlin apartment house.

Like Drewitz, Martin Walser (b. 1927) writes about the alienation and dehumanization of the individual. The somewhat Kafka-like stories of *Ein Flugzeug über dem Haus* (1955; an airplane above the house) offer less successfully the themes of his mature novels. Especially typical for Walser's fiction is his trilogy, *Halbzeit* (1960; half-time), *Das Einhorn* (1966; *The Unicorn,* 1971), and *Der Sturz* (1973; the fall). The protagonist's progress from traveling salesman to successful, but unfulfilled, author is Walser's model for the inability to resolve the internal conflict between desires for social success and isolation. Similarly, the central characters of *Die Gallistl'sche Krankheit* (1972; the Gallistl illness), *Jenseits der Liebe* (1976; *Beyond All Love,* 1983), and *Ein fliehendes Pferd* (1978; a fleeing horse) are frustrated by inability to escape from a hostile world. The development of this type of character reaches its temporary culmination in *Meßmers Gedanken* (1985; Messmer's thoughts), a puzzling, confusing narrative that is the least satisfying of Walser's recent creations.

Alfred Andersch (1914–80) combined elements of personal experience, moral concern, and narrative simplicity in emphasizing the need for individual freedom. In *Sansibar; oder, Der Letzte Grund* (1957; *Flight to Afar,* 1958) he depicted the flight of refugees from Nazi Germany. Escape is also the theme of *Die Rote* (1960; *The Redhead,* 1961), a novel about a German woman who goes to Venice and becomes a factory worker. Both *The Redhead* and *Efraim* (1967; *Efraim's Book,* 1970), Andersch's most important novel, are significant documents of the young generation's search for identity.

Personal experience and the threat to individual freedom also inform the works of Horst Bienek (b. 1930). The prose pieces in *Traumbuch eines Gefangenen* (1957; prisoner's dream book) and *Nachtstücke* (1959; night pieces) emphasize confinement and the resulting human indignities. The same problems are given metaphysical dimensions in his first novel, *Die Zelle* (1968; *The Cell,* 1972), the portrait of a prisoner who experiences the decay of his body through the lenses of fever dream and insanity.

Bienek developed a second set of symbols for universal experience in novels about his Upper Silesian homeland. *Die erste Polka* (1975; *The First Polka,* 1978), *Septemberlicht* (1977; *September Light,* 1986), *Zeit ohne Glocken* (1979; time without bells), and *Erde und Feuer* (1982; earth and fire) employ events in the town of Gleiwitz as background for the relatively successful depiction of the general human condition.

Gabriele Wohmann's (b. 1932) fiction resembles that of Ingeborg Drewitz in its focus on everday life, but Wohmann is more at home in the short story and more inclined toward experimentation. She favors devices that permit her to explore a character's inner world directly. Her important anthologies, beginning with *Mit einem Messer* (1958; with a knife), have given her a reputation as a weaver of subtle psychology in depicting vulnerable outsiders. The stories of *Einsamkeit* (1982; loneliness) feature almost plotless projections of female characters caught in conflict with an oppressive society. *Der kürzeste Tag des Jahres* (1983; the shortest day of the year) offers sensitive glimpses into the fear-filled private lives of the elderly and other inhabitants of an empty existence.

Wohmann's novels have never received as much critical attention as her short stories, but some of them, such as *Schönes Gehege* (1975; pleasant enclosure), *Frühherbst in Badenweiler* (1978; early autumn in Badenweiler), and *Das Glückspiel* (1981; the game of chance), are quite effective in elucidating the minute details of domestic conflicts and identity crises.

The most important author to enter the German literary scene in the late 1950s was Günter Grass (b. 1927). His first novel, *Die Blechtrommel* (1959; *The Tin Drum,* 1962), quickly became an international sensation. The first part of his Danzig trilogy—which also includes *Katz und Maus* (1961; *Cat and Mouse,* 1963) and *Hundejahre* (1963; *Dog Years,* 1965)—*The Tin Drum* presents the dwarf Oskar Matzerath as a symbol for the petit-bourgeois essence of Nazism. Oskar and the central characters of the other volumes are outsiders whose lives illustrate the criminality and postwar rehabilitation of Nazis.

Grass's later novels are more controversial. They reflect his increased involvement in West German politics. *Örtlich betäubt (1969; Local Anaesthetic,* 1969) offers a carefully orchestrated dialectical discussion about the student revolts of the late 1960s. In *Aus dem Tagebuch einer Schnecke* (1972; *From the Diary of a Snail,* 1973), he documented his own support of the Social Democrats in the 1969 election campaign. The peculiar novel *Der Butt* (1977; *The Flounder,* 1978) employs a framework of research on cooking to present ideas on male and female social roles. Grass's least successful novel is *Kopfgeburten oder Die Deutschen sterben aus* (1980; *Headbirths; or, The Germans Are Dying Out,* 1983), a somewhat disorganized picture of worries about disarmament, overpopulation, big industry, and the threat of war. A possible realization of his worst fears forms the background for *Die Rättin* (1986; the female rat), an allegorical doomsday novel that brings Grass's prose full circle with its elaborations on the further career of Oskar Matzerath, the unpleasant, alienated dwarf of *The Tin Drum.*

The lyrically artificial, playful novel *Im Schein des Kometen* (1959; in the glow of the comet) brought Peter Härtling (b. 1933) no significant recognition, but publication of *Niembsch oder Der Stillstand* (1964; Niembsch; or, the standstill) established him as a promising narrative artist. His theme in *Niembsch,* and *Janek* (1966; Janek), is man's confrontation with time. *Das Familienfest oder Das Ende der Geschichte* (1968; the family celebration; or, the end of the story) is a transitional work that links the preoccupation with time to the question of the nature of history—the major concern in the fictional biography *Hölderlin* (1976; Hölderlin). One of Härtling's most successful novels is *Eine Frau* (1974; a woman), the portrait of a figure whose memories convince her that she has always been the victim of external forces. *Das Windrad* (1983; the wind wheel) reflects a deterioration of Härtling's style to hollow woodenness and monotony. He redeems himself somewhat in *Felix Guttmann* (1985; Felix Guttmann), but the peak of his career is probably behind him.

Like Günter Grass, Uwe Johnson (1934–84) achieved instant success with his first novel. He became acclaimed as one of Germany's most important analysts of the tensions, pressures, adjustments, and contradictions that mold everyday life in the two German states. *Mutmaßungen über Jakob,* an analytic fable about the death of an East German railroad dispatcher, is something of a judicial inquiry in which witnesses illuminate the case from different perspectives. *Das dritte Buch über Achim* (1961; *The Third Book About Achim,* 1967) is a search for an East German bicycle racer's inner self. The author's clearest treatment of the typical German citizen's passivity and inability to see beyond meaningless superficiality is *Zwei Ansichten* (1965; *Two Views,* 1966). It describes the impact of the Berlin Wall on two unlikely lovers who have nothing in common. The monumental *Jahrestage: Aus dem Leben von Gesine Cresspahl* (4 vols., 1970–83; partially translated in *Anniversaries: From the Life of Gesine Cresspahl,* 1975), Johnson's most demanding work of fiction, combines expansion and summation of events and impressions of his encounter with New York City between 1966 and 1968, and a personalized history of Germany from the 1920s to the postwar era. Although the never-completed mosaic often bogs down in endless minutiae, it is a powerful climactic document of the real force of history that is backbone and substance of all of Johnson's novels.

Both Uwe Johnson and Gerhard Zwerenz (b. 1925) left East Germany before establishing themselves as writers. Unlike Johnson, Zwerenz has never developed stylistic polish or literary balance. His writings are more popular for their direct political activism than for their artistic quality. After *Aufs Rad geflochten* (1959; broken on the wheel) and *Die Liebe der toten Männer* (1959; the dead men's love) failed to reach a wide audience, the controversial bestseller *Casanova oder Der kleine Herr in Krieg und Frieden* (1966; *Little Peter in War and Peace,* 1970), with its pornographic satires on contemporary bourgeois life, propelled him into the public consciousness. Gradually, works such as *Kopf und Bauch* (1971; head and belly) and the autobiography *Der Widerspruch* (1974; the contradiction) brought him wider acknowledgment. The grotesque novel *Die Erde ist unbewohnbar wie der Mond* (1973; the earth is uninhabitable like the moon), an attack on West German capitalism, is perhaps his best book, although critical response has not been uniformly positive. *Der Bunker* (1983; the shelter), a satire about the possibilities of atomic war, exemplifies current West German prose's preoccupation with imminent doom.

During the 1960s, West German fiction grew increasingly more diverse. Younger authors began to question the effectiveness of traditional novels as mediators of ideas. Parallel to conventional approaches, there emerged a tendency to permit the play of thoughts, dreams, and memories to focus on important moments rather than on a continuity of events. There was also an increase in grotesque literature, an emphasis on a new realism with very differing branches, and a renewed experimentation with language.

For Jürgen Becker (b. 1932), the creative process yields an open, indefinite, free prose that combines lyrical, dramatic, and essayistic elements with narration. The result is a hybrid that magnifies "fields" of encounter. Becker established his unique artistic pattern in *Felder* (1964; fields). There he employed changing voices filled with humor, irony, and parody to combine the events and processes of a single morning with those of a three-year period in an open demonstration of the transformation of individual consciousness into language. *Ränder* (1968; borders) and *Umgebungen* (1970; surroundings) offer new experiments with language and form, placing emphasis on problems of cliché or reality as a function of time. In *Erzählen bis Ostende* (1981; storytelling until Ostende), there is less experimentation than in earlier works, but the succinct episodes and blocks of experience reflect more than ever the author's success in bridging the gaps between the genres.

The writings of Hannelies Taschau (b. 1937) are dominated by the situations of individuals who are at odds with the social norms. Taschau does not produce language experiments, but she is concerned with basic problems related to perception of reality. Her first novel, *Kinderei* (1960; childishness), went almost unnoticed, and *Taube auf dem Dach* (1967; dove on the roof) was dismissed by critics as shallow reading. Not until *Strip und andere Erzählungen* (1974; strip and other stories) and the novel *Landfriede* (1978; country peace) did she prove her ability to employ simple realistic devices effectively to illuminate the vain search for valid forms of existence. Her most effective treatment of the tension between suffering individual and society is *Erfinder des Glücks* (1981; inventors of happiness).

Among the more important documents of perceptionist fiction are the early narratives of Peter Weiss (1916–82). His experimental "micro-novel" *Der Schatten des Körpers des Kutschers* (1960; *The Shadow of the Coachman's Body,* 1970) deemphasizes plot and action in favor of description and visualization. The object of his subsequent prose is the search for self. *Abschied von den Eltern* (1961; *The Leavetaking,* 1962) is an attempt to come to grips with the author's own childhood. It served as a preliminary study for the autobiographical novel *Fluchtpunkt* (1962; *Vanishing Point,* 1968), a work of magical realism that describes the process of declaring independence from one's personal origins. *Vanishing Point* is Weiss's best narrative. In contrast to the early autobiographical novels, the political and aesthetic confession *Die Ästhetik des Widerstands* (3 vols., 1975–81; the aesthetics of resistance) defines a life that Weiss wished he might have had. Its essayistic tone makes it very tedious.

In the works of Thomas Valentin (1922–80) authenticity is the product of a precise observation of language patterns and character types. Valentin uncovers the timeless aspects of everyday existence by portraying reality directly and clearly. *Hölle für Kinder* (1961; hell for children) is a deep penetration of psychological and environmental conditioning as determining forces in human action. Much of his later writing is devoted to realistic confrontation with the Nazi era. In *Die Unberatenen* (1963; the unadvised ones) he offers a diagnostic illumination of the relationship between educating rebellious youth and the older generation's failure to communicate the truth about the past. The anthology *Der Fisch mit dem roten Halstuch* (1969; the fish with the red neckerchief) examines the general problem of the oppression of the individual from a variety of perspectives. One of Valentin's most powerful narratives is *Jugend einer Studienrätin* (1974; youth of a female instructor), a psychological investigation of the Third Reich's spiritual deformation of a young girl. Like earlier works, *Grabbes letzter Sommer* (1980; Grabbe's last summer) reflects the power of evocative language, although the portrayal of

Christian Dietrich Grabbe (1801–36) is not particularly convincing.

Ernst Augustin (b. 1927) is a disciple of Franz Kafka. His surrealistic novels, *Der Kopf* (1962; the head), *Das Badehaus* (1963; the bathhouse), and *Mamma* (1970; Mamma), demonstrate his ability to illuminate human schizophrenic tendencies, although *Mamma*, with its often monstrous descriptions, is brutally jarring. *Raumlicht: Der Fall Evelyne* (1976; space light: the case of Evelyne) is Augustin's most compellingly realistic work. It describes with extreme sensitivity, poetic mastery, and intellectual grace the psychiatric treatment of a schizophrenic woman.

Two notable defenders of the working world are Max von der Grün (b. 1926) and Angelika Mechtel (b. 1943).

Von der Grün's novels *Männer in zweifacher Nacht* (1962; men in double night) and *Irrlicht and Feuer* (1963; will-o'-the-wisp and fire) were the first in a long series of books that elaborate the workers' condition in capitalistic industrial society. Although saturated with realism and social commitment, his productions lack any significant aesthetic quality and are often stylistically weak. The popularity of *Späte Liebe* (1982; late love), a practically oriented story about "romance" between two seventy-year-olds, simply shows that von der Grün maintains mass appeal in spite of his triteness and sentimentality.

In *Die feinen Totengräber* (1968; the fine gravediggers), Angelika Mechtel offered several refined, effective, and somewhat daring stories about flaws in contemporary consumer society. The artistic promise suggested by her short stories remained unrealized in the novels *Kaputte Spiele* (1970; broken games), *Friß, Vogel* (1972; eat, bird), and *Das gläserne Paradies* (1973; the glass paradise), in which she employed the black-and-white perspectives of pulp literature. More important are *Die Blindgängerin* (1974; the blind woman) and *Ein Plädoyer für uns* (1975; a speech in our defense), two strongly convincing contributions to the feminist novel. Her best work to date is *Gott und die Liedermacherin* (1983; God and the songwriter), an outrageous, irreverent, but effective satire that attacks the foundations of masculine power structures.

Like Thomas Valentin, Hubert Fichte (b. 1935) emphasizes precise reproduction of language and milieu. The central focus of his art is the outsider in Hamburg. The stories of *Der Aufbruch nach Turku* (1963; departure for Turku) underscore his sympathy for neglected youth. *Das Waisenhaus* (1965; the orphanage), his first novel, reflects an extraordinary mastery of the child's perspective while offering a unique approach to the insecure world of the humiliated and persecuted outsider. Hippies, anarchists, and other asocial elements populate the respective worlds of *Die Palette* (1968; the palette) and *Detlevs Imitationen "Grünspan"* (1971; Detlev's imitations "verdigris"). They are the objects of Fichte's precise observation of Hamburg reality and preliminary studies for the autobiographical *Versuch über die Pubertät* (1974; essay on puberty), an almost vivisectionist attempt to define the author's own identity. *Versuch über die Pubertät* is Fichte's most provocative work, because of its precise analysis of alternate lifestyles, but it lacks the artistic intensity of *Die Palette*.

Social criticism is magnified to the point of grotesqueness in the harshly sarcastic writings of Gisela Elsner (b. 1937). Her bitter stories are directed against philistinism on all levels. In *Die Riesenzwerge* (1964; *The Giant Dwarfs,* 1965) she presents the inhumanity and bestiality of the narrow-minded middle class from the perspective of a four-year-old child. Both *The Giant Dwarfs* and *Der Nachwuchs* (1968; the progeny) rely heavily on perspective distortion for their effect, but *Das Berührungsverbot* (1970; the touch ban) unmasks sexual perversity in precisely realistic descriptions of details, gestures, and reflections. Elsner's ironic indictment of the new German upper class in *Der Punktsieg* (1977; the point victory) is less interesting than her earlier narratives, but *Abseits* (1982; *Offside,* 1986), a novel about the progressive spiritual disintegration of a suburban housewife, is extremely readable.

The prose sketches and novels of Günter Herburger (b. 1932) stress the mediocrity and dullness of everyday life, without irony or satire. His first collection of stories, *Eine gleichmäßige Landschaft* (1964; *A Monotonous Landscape,* 1968), illustrates a commitment to traditional realistic methods. The novels *Die Messe* (1964; the fair) and *Jesus in Osaka* (1971; Jesus in

Osaka) demonstrate an inner rejection of traditional forms and doctrines, but they are not as jarring as other social criticisms of the period. Grotesque aspects of society are present in *Die Messe* but remain passive and powerless. The most disappointing of Herburger's novels are *Flug ins Herz* (1977; flight into the heart), *Die Augen der Kämpfer* (1980; the eyes of the fighters), and *Die Augen der Kämpfer: Zweite Reise* (1983; the eyes of the fighters: second journey). They are interesting for their symbolism and the use of psychedelic images, but they lack coherence and bog down in tedious relationships.

Rolf Dieter Brinkmann (1940–75) was more successful than Herburger in portraying real experience. In *Die Umarmung* (1965; the embrace) he combined perceptionist techniques with objectification of emotions and inner tensions to produce extremely plastic and immediate descriptions. The narratives in *Raupenbahn* (1966; caterpillar track) are less personal and more formalized. Their strength lies in the author's attention to detail. Brinkmann's only novel, *Keiner weiß mehr* (1968; nobody knows more), is less satisfying than his short stories. It documents in disturbing fashion the absence of perspective in modern marriage.

The initiator of "new realism," Dieter Wellershoff (b. 1925), advocated novels that explore only "objective" situations by combining action and reflection to yield a consistent personal penetration of reality. His first major work of fiction, *Ein schöner Tag* (1966; *A Beautiful Day*, 1971), is artistically unsuccessful because it loses direction amid a barrage of details. *Die Schattengrenze* (1968; the shadow border), a subjective, psychological criminal novel, is somewhat more readable, but it suffers from a lack of coherence. The central figures of *Einladung an alle* (1972; invitation to all) and *Die Schönheit des Schimpansen* (1977; the chimpanzee's beauty) are murderer symbols for the individual whom society has mentally and spiritually crippled; their preoccupation with violence becomes tedious and even repellent. *Die Sirene* (1980; the siren) and *Der Sieger nimmt alles* (1983; *Winner Takes All*, 1986) are even less satisfying. *Die Sirene* lacks resolution, and *Winner Takes All* belabors predictable processes interminably.

Peter O. Chotjewitz (b. 1934) created a new kind of novel

based on unrestricted language experimentation. *Hommage à Frantek* (1965; homage to Frantek) illustrates his idea that the act and manner of writing are important, but the substance is not. The circular pursuit of the title figure's identity explores the possibilities of language while ironically placing the creative process in question. Chotjewitz's early short prose writings are also dominated by experiments with form and the rejection of traditional narrative norms. In *Die Insel* (1968; the island) and *Vom Leben und Lernen* (1969; on life and learning) he attempted unsuccessfully to relate an ironic toying with aesthetic and moral aspects to the concept of revolution. Only in his more serious later anthologies did he finally establish himself as a writer worthy of note. *Abschied von Michalik* (1969; farewell to Michalik), *Die Trauer im Auge des Ochsen* (1972; the sadness in the ox's eye), *Reden ist tödlich, schweigen auch* (1974; speaking is deadly, remaining silent is the same), and *Durch Schaden wird man dumm* (1976; through injury one becomes stupid) reveal a productively diverse crystallization of talent.

The approach of Herbert Achternbusch (b. 1938) reveals that he also regards art as an open revolt against reality, ideology, and restricted, formally managed life. His narrative technique is consciously anarchistic and formless. The stories in *Hülle* (1969; hull) and *Das Kamel* (1970; the camel) exemplify his rejection of artistic regulation and the absolute role of consciousness in his determination of theme. Achternbusch's first major narrative accomplishment was *Alexanderschlacht* (1972; the battle of Alexander), a contourless product of creative fantasy. Later novels, beginning with *Der Tag wird kommen* (1973; the day will come) and *Die Stunde des Todes* (1975; the hour of death), reflect the increased influence of his screenwriting activities. The most recent text of this kind, *Die Olympiasiegerin* (1982; the olympic victress), demonstrates Achternbusch's continued rejection of logical, linear narration of reality.

The subjectivism of the 1970s informs all of the novels of Karin Struck (b. 1947). *Klassenliebe* (1973; class love) is simultaneously an act of inner liberation and an analytical treatment of specifically feminine experiences. Struck's two subsequent novels, *Die Mutter* (1975; the mother) and *Lieben* (1977;

loving), are almost offensively direct and exhibitionistic in their revelation of her search for identity in personal sexual encounter. Following her early novels, Struck wrote several shorter prose works that intensified the general autobiographical tone of her writing. *Finale* (1984; finale) and *Glut und Asche* (1985; fire and ashes) continue both her penetrating introspection and her feminist themes, but they reflect a degeneration into banality and dull conventionality.

Social realism is clearly present in the prose works of Ludwig Fels (b. 1946). His major literary concern is reproduction of the hopeless poverty and misery of the working class. Representative stories in *Platzangst* (1974; place fear) emphasize humiliation and isolation. His first novel, *Die Sünden der Armut* (1976; the sins of poverty), depicts the laborer's realm as a miserable prison from which there is no escape. *Ein Unding der Liebe* (1981; a monstrosity of love), his most impressive work, shows considerable strength in its sensitive portrayal of the problems of youth and puberty. Fels's ability to develop fresh approaches is effectively demonstrated in the lyrically poetic sketches of *Betonmärchen* (1983; concrete fairy tales).

One of the most successful, most controversial writers of the 1970s is Botho Strauß (b. 1944). His first prose publications, *Schützenehre* (1975; sharpshooter's honor) and *Marlenes Schwester* (1975; Marlene's sister), placed him in the mainstream of subjectivism. The problem of identity crisis is treated successfully in *Die Widmung* (1977; *Devotion*, 1981). In *Rumor* (1980; *Tumult*, 1984), an intense treatment of modern neuroses, Strauß equates the spiritual/mental decay of his nonhero with the collapse of his society, skillfully tying the malaise to its origins in the Nazi years. Although *Der junge Mann* (1984; the young man) exhibits a degree of unevenness and imbalance in its structure, its penetrating criticism and analysis of culture attest to Strauß's increasing maturity as a novelist.

Among the strongest manifestations of inwardness and alienation in the fiction of the late 1970s is a nearly pathological emphasis on illness and death. Important examples are found in the writings of Paul Kersten (b. 1943) and Bodo Kirchhoff (b. 1948).

Kersten's *Der alltägliche Tod meines Vaters* (1978; the everyday death of my father), *Absprung* (1979; jump), and *Die toten Schwestern* (1982; the dead sisters) focus on the morbidity of modern existence and the necessity for self-analysis. *Der alltägliche Tod meines Vaters* effectively and sensitively grapples with the problems of sickness and dying, while *Die toten Schwestern* successfully links the spiritual disease of the present with the Nazi past.

Psychological depth is characteristic for Bodo Kirchhoff's explorations of man's confrontations with his own frailty. *Ohne Eifer, ohne Zorn* (1979; without zeal, without anger) and *Body-Building* (1980; body-building), brought him little critical attention, but they are notable for their intense subjectivism. *Die Einsamkeit der Haut* (1981; the solitude of the skin) associates the skin symbol with sexuality and mortality in peculiar variations of the idea that love and death are closely linked. Kirchhoff's first novel, *Zwiefalten* (1983; Zwiefalten), maintains the mixture of narcissism and narrative distance that gave *Die Einsamkeit der Haut* its particular flavor, but the story is somewhat disjointed and often fails to transcend banality in presenting confrontation with dull reality.

The search for identity is given less pathological illumination in the novels of Hans-Josef Ortheil (b. 1951). In *Fermer* (1979; Fermer), a prizewinning novel about a young military recruit who flees from an unacceptable, threatening system of values, the author gives a romantic flavor to the unraveling of personality and inner self. Subsequent novels have made him one of the most promising novelists of the new generation. *Hecke* (1983; hedge), in particular, reflects unusual balance, maturity, and sophistication in both style and content, and makes a strong contribution to recent fiction that grapples with the Nazi past.

The authors who produced their initial works during the first half of the 1980s mirror the increasing diversity of approaches to individual isolation in a threatening, depressing world. Maria Beig (b. 1920), with her novels *Rabenkrächzen* (1982; raven's cry) and *Hochzeitslose* (1983; unmarried women), has established herself as a writer whose succinct authenticity enables her to transform individual fates clothed in the trappings of her Swabian origins into potent symbols for universal feminine suffering. The narratives of Brigitte Kronauer (b. 1940), including *Frau Mühlenbeck im Gehäus* (1980; Mrs. Mühlenbeck in the shell), *Die gemusterte Nacht* (1981; the patterned night), and *Rita Münster* (1983; Rita Münster) are mediocre examinations of modern women whose alienation from mundane existence generates a subtle longing for anarchy. In *Die Berliner Situation* (1983; the Berlin situation) and *Blende* (1985; shutter) Bodo Morshäuser (b. 1953) offers a sometimes grotesque and trivial record of the chaos, alienation, and illusion of life. One of the most artistic feminist works of the 1980s is Karin Reschke's biographical novel *Verfolgte des Glücks* (1982; fugitive from happiness), the painful story of Henriette Vogel, who committed suicide with author Heinrich von Kleist (1777–1811). Reschke's second novel, *Dieser Tage über Nacht* (1984; of these days by night), is a surrealistic, sensitive treatment of a prostitute's punishing, hunted solitude.

POETRY

Most established lyric poets who published during the first postwar years followed traditional patterns. In elegiac, morally oriented poems, they conveyed a strong mood of literary self-sufficiency and muted hope for the future. These creations were rooted in Christian humanism and in conservative, often mystical, nature and landscape verse. There was little attempt to confront contemporary developments and the catastrophes of the war. Rather, poets emphasized form, style, and distance, while avoiding the nationalistic models promoted by the Nazis. Writers of the "inner emigration" led the forces of restoration.

Like his fiction, the poetry of Werner Bergengruen stresses humane order and man's relationship to nature. *Dies irae* (1945; day of wrath) set the tone for his subsequent verse creations. The poems form a lyric confession that proclaims the healing power of Christian faith. They contain realistic, expressionistic, and neo-baroque elements of style. Devoted to preservation and renewal of healthy human existence, later

books, from *Lobgesang* (1946; song of praise) and *Die heile Welt*
(1950; the healthy world) to *Figur und Schatten* (1958; figure
and shadow) and *Herbstlicher Aufbruch* (1965; autumn departure), exhibit an extraordinary fullness of musicality, imagery,
and poetic substance.

The late lyrics of Rudolf Alexander Schröder (1878–1963)
complement those of Bergengruen in their Christian humanism. Schröder is especially important as a preserver of traditional classical forms. He wrote odes, distichs, elegies, terza-
rima, sonnets, and hymns. After the war he published several
collections, the most important of which are *Auf dem Heimweg*
(1946; on the way home), *Gute Nacht* (1947; good night), *Die
geistlichen Gedichte* (1949; the religious poems), and *Fülle des
Daseins* (1958; fullness of existence). His poems are less melodic than those of Bergengruen, but they are significant for
their plastic imagery. Schröder is justifiably recognized as the
most important renewer of the German Protestant hymn in the
twentieth century.

Another notable contributor to the poetry of Christian humanism was Reinhold Schneider. He published four major lyrical anthologies: *Apokalypse* (1946; apocalypse), *Die neuen
Türme* (1946; the new towers), *Herz am Erdsaume* (1947; heart
on earth's seam), and *Die Sonette von Leben und Zeit, dem
Glauben und der Geschichte* (1954; the sonnets on life and
time, on faith and history). His basic theme is the realization of
Christian existence during mortal life. The poems are uncomfortably ascetic in tone, but they are important for their exemplary mastery of form.

Erich Kästner (1899–1974) is best known for moralistic
verse that focuses on the effects of social indifference, militarism, and perverted nationalism. To achieve his effects, he
successfully employed the devices of irony, criticism, mockery,
accusation, and humor. The new creations in *Der tägliche Kram*
(1948; the everyday stuff), *Kurz und bündig* (1948; short and to
the point), *Die kleine Freiheit* (1952; the little freedom), and *Die
13 Monate* (1955; the 13 months) are somewhat less militant
than earlier lyrics, although they still maintain a tone of warning. They reflect a strong preference for concise, sensitive apho-

risms and epigrams. *Kurz und bündig* is the best of his efforts in that direction.

One of the most important nature poets of the "inner emigration" was Wilhelm Lehmann (1882–1968). His highly individual magical realism dominates poems inclined toward rational coolness and terseness. Lehmann's greatest strength lay in an incomparable precision in dealing with individual natural manifestations. In *Entzückter Staub* (1946; enraptured dust), *Noch nicht genug* (1950; still not enough), *Ruhm des Daseins* (1953; fame of existence), and *Meine Gedichtbücher* (1957; my poetry books) he developed a natural mysticism that has sensual experience of the world as its point of departure. His lyrical treatments of nature are often intertwined with motifs from fairy tale, legend, and myth. The resulting art is rich in symbolism and powerful imagery, and illustrates an enormous ability to integrate nature and the rational human world poetically.

In contrast to Erich Kästner, Gottfried Benn (1886–1956) had initially supported the Nazis. For that reason, he found it difficult to reestablish his literary reputation after the war. Nevertheless, his poetic theories, as presented in *Probleme der Lyrik* (1951; problems of poetry), became a major guide for younger poets during the 1950s and 1960s. The most important aspects of his lyric approach include a rejection of models provided by Rainer Maria Rilke (1875–1926), the avoidance of subjectivism, and the elimination of faded devices.

Benn's important postwar anthologies are *Statische Gedichte* (1948; static poems), *Trunkene Flut* (1949; drunken flood), *Fragmente* (1951; fragments), *Destillationen* (1953; distillations), and *Aprèslude* (1955; afterlude). Although there is a degree of continuity between these late works and his prewar mythical visions, the new poems reflect an increase in pessimism and despair. His symbols emphasize a duality of light and mourning as building blocks of modern life. The result is a lyrical retreat into darkness, silence, and alienation.

Although he had published his first volume of poetry in 1932, Ernst Meister (1911–79) did not hit his lyric stride until after the war had ended. His poetry is known for its terse, pointed, hermetic style and its surrealistic visionary quality. *Unterm schwarzen Schafspelz* (1953; beneath the black sheepskin) illustrates his predilection for that which perishes. The poems of *Zahlen und Figuren* (1958; numbers and figures) are full of death, suffering, and prophetic darkness. Despite the sharpness of Meister's visions and the softness of his descriptions, many of his symbols are accessible to the reader only with great difficulty. In *Zeichen um Zeichen* (1968; sign after sign) he presented meditations and reflections that combine physical reality with abstraction, while *Es kam die Nachricht* (1970; the news came), *Sage vom Ganzen den Satz* (1972; say the sentence about the whole), and *Im Zwiespalt* (1976; in conflict) contain some of the most effective existential lyrics of the postwar era.

There were only a few significant poets whose careers continued without major interruption during the Nazi period. Among those who made important contributions to postwar poetry are Friedrich Georg Jünger (1898–1977), Oda Schaefer (b. 1900), Günter Eich (1907–72), and Karl Krolow (b. 1915).

Friedrich Georg Jünger was another traditionalist whose works reflect a magical approach to nature and strong formal ties to classical antiquity and German classicism. He published several volumes of verse after the war, including *Der Westwind* (1946; the west wind), *Gedichte* (1949; poems), *Iris im Wind* (1952; iris in the wind), *Ring der Jahre* (1954; ring of the years), *Schwarzer Fluß und windweißer Wald* (1955; black river and wind-white forest), and *Espocht an der Tür* (1968; there's a knock at the door). These collections display a consistent strictness of form, but the language is remarkably austere and often cold in spite of occasional flashes of brightness and serenity.

The works of Oda Schaefer reflect her rejection of realism and her belief that the poem is a product of lyrical magic based upon strict form, rhyme, and artistic inspiration. *Irdisches Geleit* (1946; earthly escort) established her as a renewer of ballad and folk-poetry forms. A deep sensitivity for nature is combined with an optimistic worldview in productions that are notable for their colorful flow of melodic language. In her later books, *Kranz des Jahres* (1948; wreath of the year), *Grasmelodie* (1959; grass melody), and *Der grüne Ton* (1973;

the green tone) her optimism remains constant in lyrics of strong personal consciousness.

Günter Eich combined depressive pessimism and pregnant, cultivated language in melodic nature lyrics and poetic descriptions of simple things. *Abgelegene Gehöfte* (1948; remote farmsteads) and *Untergrundbahn* (1949; subway) established him as one of the most important poets of the early postwar period. Eich saw himself as a warner against complacency. *Botschaften des Regens* (1955; messages of the rain) is his most important poetic accomplishment. Its poems attempt to translate from the magical language and symbols of nature the information that will wake the reader from the slumber of imperception. *Zu den Akten* (1964; for the records) and *Anlässe und Steingärten* (1966; occasions and rock gardens) are dominated less by the earlier natural magic and messages of warning, and more by sadness, resignation, and hopelessness. Next to Benn, Eich was the most influential figure in the shaping of early postwar German poetry.

Karl Krolow's works exemplify the changing directions of West German lyrics from the late 1940s to the present. His first postwar nature and landscape poems were published in *Gedichte* (1948; poems), *Heimsuchung* (1948; visitation), and *Auf Erden* (1949; on earth). Krolow's verse combines graphic precision with visual sensitivity and keen images. *Die Zeichen der Welt* (1952; the signs of the world) was the first manifestation of a trend toward fresh techniques, forms, and themes. It contains songlike long poems, hymns, and odes that document a transition to free rhythms. In *Wind und Zeit* (1954; wind and time) the poet intensified his focus on the rigid artificiality of modern society. *Tage und Nächte* (1956; days and nights) introduced a third, surrealistic, phase in Krolow's development, triggered by influences from modern French and Spanish poetry, Dadaism, and the writings of Hans Arp (1887–1966). The poems of the late 1950s and 1960s are marked by laconic, dry language and a tendency toward anecdotal narration. More recent volumes, from *Zeitvergehen* (1972; the passing of time) to *Zwischen Null and Unendlich* (1982; between zero and infinity), combine in tempered synthesis many elements of earlier phases. They are marked above all by resignation and gloom, and some poems show a degeneration into triteness, insipidness, and shallowness.

Known especially as one of the founders of Dadaism and as a strong contributor to surrealism, Hans Arp was a singularly important stimulus toward poetic experimentation. He was not a shatterer of language but, rather, a believer in its magic. In his most important late collections, *Auf einem Bein* (1955; on one leg), *Worte mit und ohne Anker* (1957; words with and without anchor), *Mondsand* (1960; moon sand), *Sinnende Flammen* (1961; thinking flames), and *Logbuch des Traumkapitäns* (1965; the dream captain's log), he played with the meanings of words and recombined them in unexpected ways. Although his productions are often the offspring of dream experiences, their richness comes from the artist's powerful imagery.

Only a few noteworthy West German poets produced their initial volumes of verse during the latter half of the 1940s. Even those who did publish were not newcomers to the literary scene. The most visible first-time lyricists were Rudolf Hagelstange (1912–84), Wolfgang Weyrauch, Marie Luise Kaschnitz (1901–74), and Nelly Sachs (1891–1970), but fiction by each of them had already appeared earlier.

Rudolf Hagelstange was essentially unknown until the appearance of *Venezianisches Credo* (1945; Venetian creed), which grapples directly with the Nazi past. The sonnets of this cycle are remarkable for their purity of form. Hagelstange's later collections reflect a consistent optimism about mankind's ability to find a positive future, although they also respond directly to postwar conditions. One of his most interesting works is the allegorical *Ballade vom verschütteten Leben* (1952; *Ballad of Buried Life*, 1962), which was stimulated by reports about six German soldiers who were buried alive in a supply bunker. *Stern und Staub* (1953; star and dust), *Lied der Jahre* (1962; song of the years), and *Gast der Elemente* (1972; guest of the elements) document progress away from formal, ornamental lyrics to a calmer, yet artistically melodic, poetry.

The first new openly political lyricist was Wolfgang Weyrauch. His most important lyric works are *Von des Glücks Barmherzigkeit* (1946; on the compassion of happiness), *Lerche und Sperber* (1948; lark and hawk), *An die Wand geschrieben* (1950; written on the wall), *Gesang um nicht zu sterben* (1956; songs to keep from dying), *Nie trifft die Finsternis* (1956; darkness never strikes), and *Die Spur* (1963; the track). Weyrauch's initial purpose was to strike against the protective taboos that still sheltered the political causes of human misery. This accounts for the restlessness and directness of his language and his rejection of conservative aestheticism. His *2 Litaneien* (1978; 2 litanies) and *Das Komma danach* (1978; the comma after it) reflect his continuing magnification of earlier developments in political poetry.

The poetry of Marie Luise Kaschnitz is more traditional than progressive. It exhibits a strong orientation toward Christian humanism. *Gedichte* (1947; poems) established Kaschnitz as an author with an intuitive power of language and a sure sense of classical form. Its poems depict her homeland and southeast European landscape, but also her experience of an inner world. In the free rhythms of *Zukunftsmusik* (1950; future music) her theme shifted, striking out against the fears of the individual who must live in the present. The creations in *Neue Gedichte* (1957; new poems) turn inward again, illuminating a background of memory and subconscious experience. The important collections, *Dein Schweigen—meine Stimme* (1962; your silence—my voice), *Ein Wort weiter* (1965; one more word), *Kein Zauberspruch* (1972; no magic spell), and *Gesang vom Menschenleben* (1974; the songs of human life), mirror her consistent search for hard inner truth and a viable position regarding contemporary human conditions.

The haunting poems of Nelly Sachs are the product of her deep personal ties to the Jewish people. Her verse is masculine in tone, its language dry yet rich in metaphors. *In den Wohnungen des Todes* (1947; in the dwellings of death) brings her basic themes—flight and persecution, the horrible wartime situation of the Jews—into sharp focus. Subsequent collections, especially *Sternverdunklung* (1949; eclipse of the stars) and *Flucht und Verwandlung* (1959; flight and metamorphosis), established her as the most important German-language poet to write about the Holocaust. Her poetry is a starkly beautiful monument to the suffering and degradation of man and to a paradoxical confidence, based in religious faith, that enables human beings to survive amid misery and death. The late anthologies, *Glühende Rätsel* (1964; glowing puzzles) and *Späte Gedichte* (1965; late poems), among others, present in condensed elliptical verse an absolute mastery of language and complex symbolism.

Strong emphasis on traditional substance and approaches remained a determining factor in lyrical works by a number of new poets who began to publish their first collections during the 1950s. Two writers who became especially visible with their nature poems were Wolfgang Bächler (b. 1925) and Heinz Piontek (b. 1925).

Bächler's poetry reflects the influence of Gottfried Benn and Georg Trakl (1887–1914). Its tone is often magical and heavy, but an extraordinary belaboring of detail sometimes encumbers the poems and makes them difficult to understand. In *Die Zisterne* (1950; the cistern), *Lichtwechsel* (1955; change of light), *Türklingel* (1962; doorbells), *Türen aus Rauch* (1963; doors made of smoke), and *Ausbrechen* (1976; breaking out) two dominant factors inform the individual creations: magnification of personal experience and voluptuous descriptions. Bächler's best lyrics are those in which he returns to natural scenes, as in *Türen aus Rauch* with its portraits of French landscape.

In contrast to Bächler, Piontek offers simplicity and lightness in his nature poems. His early verse, contained in *Die Furt* (1952; the ford), *Die Rauchfahne* (1953; the plume of smoke), and *Wassermarken* (1957; watermarks), is similar to that of Wilhelm Lehmann. It is notable for its rustic, fresh imagery and its melodic lyricism. In later collections, such as *Mit einer Kranichfeder* (1962; with a crane's feather) and *Klartext* (1966; clear text), Piontek moved toward existential themes. His poetry became an expression of his view of life as temptation and hopeless struggle with death. *Tot oder lebendig* (1971; *Alive or Dead*, 1975) is the creative high point of his poetic career. It combines clarity and precision with expansion of theme to form poems that are more laconic, more sharply reflective, more pointed than his earlier efforts.

Although traditional poetry held its own during the 1950s, it was overshadowed by tendencies toward experimentation and expansion of lyric opportunities. The influences of surrealism, playful Dadaism, and concrete poetry led to shifts in poetic structure and content that had far-reaching impact. During the 1950s, German poetry began to free itself from national narrowness, one-sidedness, and stagnation, and to explore diverse new possibilities for articulation. The period derived its specific artistic character from a general inclination toward experimental individualism.

For Peter Härtling, poetry leads into a world of unlimited playfulness. In contrast to his fiction, his collections of verse, from *poeme und songs* (1953; poems and songs) through *Yamins Stationen* (1955; Yamin's stations), *Unter dem Brunnen* (1958; beneath the fountain), *Spielgeist—Spiegelgeist* (1962; play spirit/mirror spirit), and *Anreden* (1977; addresses), explore the idea of lyrically transforming substance and form into new constructs, things, and figures in endless variety. *Spielgeist—Spiegelgeist,* with its revelation of life in peculiar nursery-rhyme imitations, is especially typical for Härtling's art. Unfortunately, the lyrical peak that Härtling achieved in *Anreden* was followed in *Vorwarnung: Gedichte* (1983; early warning: poems) by less satisfying creations that degenerate into repeated statements of emptiness with overtones of hollow pathos.

The lyric experiments of Helmut Heißenbüttel (b. 1921) are directed toward reduction of emotional word content to a bare minimum. Heißenbüttel employs a skeletal language that is often free of specific meaning. In *Kombinationen* (1954; combinations) and *Topographien* (1956; topographies) he illustrated his ability to produce unique language combinations, phrase parodies, and playful provocations in the transitional area between reality and nonsense. The abstract picture poems in *Das Textbuch* (1970; *Texts,* 1977) present newly calculated forms of word play, in which language is a tool for the investigation of reality, and criticism of language becomes criticism of the times and interpretation of self. *Ödipuskomplex Made in Germany: Gelegenheitsgedichte, Todestage, Landschaften 1965–1980* (1981; Oedipus complex made in Germany: occasional poems, death days, landscapes 1965–1980) contains all of the elements that have bewildered readers for years, but also interesting signs of mellowing in texts that are more traditionally poetic.

Günter Grass also made important contributions to experimental lyrics. *Die Vorzüge der Windhühner* (1956; the advantages of wind fowl), *Gleisdreieck* (1960; track triangle), and *Ausgefragt* (1967; interrogated) reveal a poetic playfulness that is undermined by suspicion. This factor makes the linguistic game negative and uncomfortable. At the same time, Grass's poems take a realistically direct approach to questions of the times. They are products of external stimuli rather than programmed toying with the creative act. More recent collections, including *Liebe geprüft* (1974; love examined), *wie ich mich sehe* (1980; how I see myself), and *Ach Butt, dein Märchen geht böse aus* (1983; oh flounder, your fairy tale ends badly), suggest that his poetry has been reduced to a supplemental art. While some of the poems are witty, mordant, or poignant, others, such as a poem about human excrement, simply form a sad commentary on the decline of a creative genius.

Christoph Meckel's (b. 1935) surrealistic poetry is another outgrowth of experimentation. His early anthologies, *Tarnkappe* (1956; cloak of invisibility), *Hotel für Schlafwandler* (1958; hotel for sleepwalkers), and *Nebelhörner* (1959; foghorns) document progression from expressionistic tendencies to playful language and bizarre fairy-tale themes. In *Wildnisse* (1962; wildernesses) the dream world becomes more somber, and the later volumes, *Bei Lebzeiten zu singen* (1967; to be sung while alive), *Lieder aus dem Dreckloch* (1972; songs from the dirt hole), and *Wen es angeht* (1974; whom it concerns), show Meckel's final transition from happy, positive tones and moods to darker, harder irony and pathos. The laconic "love" poems in *Säure* (1979; acid) and *Souterrain* (1984; underground) are among Meckel's best works to date. In their illumination of degenerating human relationships, they exhibit extraordinary richness, variety, and subtlety.

The influence of surrealism is also visible in the lyrics of Hilde Domin (b. 1912). *Nur eine Rose als Stütze* (1959; only a rose for support) is strongly akin to French and Spanish surrealist poetry of the 1920s and 1930s. Especially typical is a tendency toward strongly associative, independent, and autonomous metaphors that dominate the specific texts. In *Rückkehr der Schiffe* (1962; return of the ships) there remains a strong element of personal experience, but it is coupled with emphasis on the power of individual words and their articulation possibilities. *Hier* (1964; here), *Höhlenbilder* (1968; cave pictures), and *Ich will dich* (1970; I want you) mirror the poet's progress, through phases of melancholy, skepticism, and longing, to fear and depression. The highly successful poems of *Ich will dich* claw at the reader, demanding attention and seemingly impossible action.

The most important West German representative of the concrete poetry movement is Franz Mon (b. 1926). His *Artikulationen* (1959; articulations) and *Sehgänge* (1964; visual excursions) feature collages of quotations, letter graphics, the delineation of lexical fields, and the employment of language clichés as such. Mon's poems have more visual aesthetic value than literary power, because they contain no clearly definable statements but only the suggestion of possible messages.

Unlike the works of other experimenters, the satirical poems of Peter Rühmkorf (b. 1929) are distinctly political. *Irdisches Vergnügen in g* (1959; earthly pleasure in g) is the product of a powerful but rebellious facility with language that is used to underscore the need for political and social change. The poet parodies and satirizes common lyric forms, combines elements from different levels of usage, and creates new relationships between words by refining and intensifying shades of meaning. His creations usually verge on insolence, but they reflect a mastery of language that is seldom matched by his contemporaries. *Haltbar bis Ende 1999* (1979; durable until the end of 1999) is more relaxed, mellower than earlier writings; it reflects a new combination of serenity, activism tempered by resignation, and suspicion of all ideologies.

Other writers who began to use poetry for political and social commentary were less experimental than Rühmkorf. Among the most representative observers of the times are Horst Bienek, Hans Magnus Enzensberger (b. 1929), and Hannelies Taschau.

Horst Bienek's verse serves as a thematic point of reference for his prose narratives. *Traumbuch eines Gefangenen* (1957; partially translated in *Poems,* 1969) and *Was war und was ist* (1966; partially translated in *Poems,* 1969) emphasize the individual's power to survive the threats of the times. Simultaneously, they reject experiments that deprive poetry of its clearly defined message. In *Was war und was ist, Vorgefundene Gedichte* (1969; poems found at hand), *Die Zeit danach* (1974; the time afterward), and *Gleiwitzer Kindheit* (1976; Gleiwitz childhood) he achieved a renewal of everyday language that gave his works fresh clarity and simplicity.

The strongest new contributor to political verse in the 1950s was Hans Magnus Enzensberger. His *verteidigung der wölfe* (1957; defense of the wolves) is a provocative, harshly satirical assault on the bureaucratic establishment, supporters of rearmament, and other manifestations of passive and exploitive extremes. In *landessprache* (1960; the country's language) he continued to offer his material in nontraditional forms that exhibit carefully orchestrated diction while suggesting multiple levels of meaning. His later collections, especially *blindenschrift* (1964; braille) and *Mausoleum* (1975; *Mausoleum,* 1976), are products of increasing maturity. In these works, the mode of expression has become simpler and more subtle, the politics more subdued. *Die Furie des Verschwindens* (1980; the fury of vanishing), with its subtle projection of the mood of the 1970s, is an extremely effective lyrical appraisal of that decade.

Hannelies Taschau's poems are harsher and politically more direct than those of Enzensberger. *Verworrene Route* (1959; confused route) and *Gedichte* (1969; poems) present hard, aggressive, sharp-edged criticism of the consumer society and its human and political problems. *Luft zum Atmen* (1978; air to breathe), with its socio-political "mind photographs" of environmental pollution, and *Gefährdung der Leidenschaft* (1984; endangerment of emotion), which comments on issues such as capital punishment and rearmament, are particularly characteristic of her more recent works. They reveal a remarkable combination of distance, sober diction, sensitivity, and emotional depth.

The decade of the 1960s was a time of increasing diversity in poetry. The movement toward strong, even vitriolic social and political criticism entered its most powerful phase. At the same time, there was also an increase in poetic radicalism that concentrated on subjective, fragmented, personal experience. Other poetic phenomena of the 1960s included a calculated reduction of the metaphysical dimension, a renewed focus on practical interpretation of the world, and the appearance of some documentary lyrics late in the period.

Among the more radically subjective figures was Rolf Dieter Brinkmann. He is best known as a discoverer and mediator of American pop poetry. Although he published his first book in 1964, his most important collections are *Was fraglich ist wofür* (1967; what is questionable for what), *Die Piloten* (1968; the pilots), *Gras* (1970; grass), and *Westwärts 1 und 2* (1975; westward 1 and 2). His poems are very personal and mirror a distinct sensitivity of perception. They illustrate a unique technique of drawing external things into the inner world, where they are made part of the poet's identity. Their strength lies in Brinkmann's ability to describe in detail momentary events in the outside world, but their illustration of pop culture's influence is also significant.

Another subjectivist is Margarete Hannsmann (b. 1921). Her early poems, in *Tauch in den Stein* (1964; dive into the stone) and *Maquis im Nirgendwo* (1966; Maquis in nowhere), describe experiences with landscapes and nature. In the anthology *Zwischen Urne und Stier* (1971; between urn and steer) she combined mythology, landscape, politics, and social consciousness in autobiographical interpretations of conditions encountered in Greece. Later poems and collections give her responses to immediate political and social problems: confrontation between East and West in *Der andere Ufer vor Augen* (1972; the other shore before my eyes), the economic miracle, student unrest, and the grappling with her own Nazi past in *Spuren* (1981; traces). Some of her creations are serious, others ironic. Although her examination of the present in light of the past is not always convincing, the processing of personal experience contributes authenticity to her writings.

The poetry of Friedrich Christian Delius (b. 1943) is especially typical for the movement toward more intense social and political consciousness. *Kerbholz* (1965; tally) emphasizes in short, rhymeless, laconic verse the unsatisfactory relationship between the individual and modern society. Political activism and revolt form the bases for aggressively militant creations in *Wenn wir, bei Rot* (1969; if we, with red). *Wenn wir, bei Rot* is particularly significant as a strong manifestation of Bertolt Brecht's influence on the evolving political poetry of West Germany. *Ein Bankier auf der Flucht* (1975; a banker on the run) is more subjective than earlier works. Personal skepticism regarding the political development of the Federal Republic determines the tone of most of these poems. In *Die unsichtbaren Blitze* (1981; the invisible lightning bolts), Delius offers some of his finest poems about the continuing legacy of history and the necessity to cut through clichés and stereotypes that conceal underlying truths about reality.

The specific focus of Helga M. Novak's (b. 1935) verse is socialistic activism in the cause of the oppressed. The relationship between private and public spheres is especially important in the harsh *Ballade von der reisenden Anna* (1965; ballad of traveling Anna) and *Colloquium mit vier Häuten* (1967; colloquium with four skins). Like Delius, Novak favors the political and street-ballad forms employed by Brecht, but she also uses other old and new approaches, including coarse—even obscene—images and language. Her most convincing creations are succinct love poems. *Ballade vom kurzen Prozeß* (1975; ballad of the short trial) is an interesting example of agitation and propaganda poetry. Novak's most personal poems are contained in *Margarete mit dem Schrank* (1978; Margarete with the cabinet), a mixture of impressions from encounters in East and West Germany, recent years, and childhood.

Yaak Karsunke (b. 1934) is another agitation and propaganda poet. The strong influence of Brecht is visible in the precise, clear offerings of *Kilroy und andere* (1967; Kilroy and others), *reden und ausreden* (1969; speeches and excuses), and *Da zwischen* (1979; between them). Karsunke's poems are notable manifestations of political and social unrest, but they have little artistic value.

Unlike the works of Novak or Karsunke, Nicolas Born's (b. 1937) political lyrics are free of agitation and propaganda elements. Born combines in his writings an illusionless realism and strong elements of subjectivism. *Marktlage* (1967; market situation) features terse, laconic poems that reduce contemporary reality to cold hard facts, using the vocabulary of everyday language. His subsequent collections, *Wo mir der Kopf steht* (1970; where my head is) and *Auge des Entdeckers* (1972; eye of the discoverer), reflect his belief that poetry cannot create measurable changes in society, but that it can be subversive.

The masterful political epigrams of Arnfried Astel (b. 1933) are among the best productions of literary activism. In *Notstand* (1968; state of emergency) and *Kläranlage* (1970; clarification apparatus) he presented unrhymed provocative aphorisms that hammer away at both the Nazi past and the capitalist present. Documents of Astel's personal political feud with the establishment accompany the poems in *Zwischen den Stühlen sitzt der Liberale in seinem Sessel* (1974; the liberal sits between the two stools in his armchair). Later collections, including *Die Faust meines Großvaters* (1979; my grandfather's fist) and *Die Amsel fliegt auf* (1982; the blackbird flies up), are especially successful in their employment of words that convey different layers of meaning.

Although the epigrammatic didactic poem remained popular during the early 1970s, the death of the political student movement caused a gradual decline of activist lyrics. Political poets remained fashionably leftist but their themes shifted toward the past, and increasing banality rendered much of their work aesthetically questionable. As political verse declined, the lyric emphasis shifted. New subjectivist poetry highlighted the writer's everyday life. Its substance became movies, travel, friendship, love affairs, still pictures of the ego and its surroundings. There was a trend toward formally and linguistically simple creations that border on rhythmic prose. The poets became skeptical about the validity of reason, science, technology, ideology, state. Their philosophy began to emphasize the deserter, the unknowing, the indifferent, the vagabond individual as a peculiar model of the new sensitivity.

The poems of Ludwig Fels, in *Anläufe* (1973; approaches), *Ernüchterung* (1976; sobering up), *Alles geht weiter* (1977;

everything continues), *Ich war nicht in Amerika* (1978; I was not in America), and *Zeitgedichte* (1979; poems of the times), reflect the influence of Brecht, Brinkmann, American underground poetry, and pop music. Although the themes are often taken from the world of work, the resulting productions are isolationist in tone. They attack exploitation of the individual and the broad social and political threats to personal survival. The real strength of Fels's works lies in their lack of artificiality.

Jürgen Theobaldy (b. 1944) is another writer who was strongly influenced by American pop lyrics. Especially characteristic of his works is colloquial language that varies through the spectrum from romantic to sloppy. His collections, from *Sperrsitz* (1973; seat in the orchestra) through *Blaue Flecken* (1974; blue spots), *Zweiter Klasse* (1976; second class), and *Schwere Erde. Rauch* (1980; heavy earth. smoke), are products of subjective interpretation of the private mundane world. They incline toward lyrical autobiography but also offer ideas that are readily accessible to the reader, presented in simple, direct language. *Die Sommertour* (1983; the summer tour) contains some of his best poems, but the quality of the collection as a whole is mixed.

The declared purpose of Jürgen Becker's carefully calculated poetic "walks through the self" is the awakening of suppressed memories within the reader. His most representative books of poems include *Das Ende der Landschaftsmalerei* (1974; the end of landscape painting), *Erzähl mir nichts vom Krieg* (1977; tell me nothing about the war), and *In der verbleibenden Zeit* (1979; in the remaining time). In them he employs simple, clear diction to produce a new lyrical factuality. Using personal experiences of nature, but also memories and historical background, he describes everyday modern life with its dying nature, industry, and apartment buildings. Becker's more recent works, in *Gedichte 1965–1980* (1981; poems 1965–1980) and *Fenster und Stimmen* (1982; windows and voices), suggest a decline in his lyric creativity. While the poems are often more laconic and less contrived than earlier efforts, they are also extremely flat and trite.

For Gabriele Wohmann, poetry is a secondary literary form,

but *So ist die Lage* (1974; that's the way it is) and *Grund zur Aufregung* (1978; reason for excitement) are strong complements to her fiction. Like her prose, they present clear evidence of the writer's ceaseless observation of self in the context of the external world. The strongest characteristics of Wohmann's lyrics are their reproduction of complex individualization and their reflection of her ability to capitalize on detail and nuance. In *Komm lieber Mai* (1981; come, dear May) and *Passau, Gleis 3* (1984; Passau, track 3) the emphasis on gesture, petty emotion, meanness, and insensitivity fail to move beyond superficiality. As a result, many of the poems are insipid and lacking in artistic fascination.

Rainer Malkowski's (b. 1939) poetry projects reactions to a coldness lying hidden beneath the surface of things. The short, clear, melodic offerings in *Was für ein Morgen* (1975; what a morning) and *Einladung ins Freie* (1977; invitation into the open) mediate inner grapplings combined with responses to nature and everyday objects. Malkowski's lyrics are especially interesting for their discreet, yet disciplined, irony of self-interpretation. In *Vom Rätsel ein Stück* (1980; a piece of the puzzle) he continued to use evocative images to emphasize a keen awareness of small things. Although *Zu Gast* (1983; as a guest) lacks affirmation of life, its subtle poems contain no cynicism and avoid triviality.

In *Von beiden Seiten der Gegenwart* (1976; from both sides of the present), Karin Kiwus (b. 1942) demonstrated an interesting ability to process descriptions of personal experience through a filter of sensitive registration. The resulting lyrics document the poet's illusionless search for her own identity and the discovery of a divided self existing in a world of potential insanity. With *Angenommen später* (1979; assumed later) and *Gedichte* (1981; poems) Kiwus exhibited her strong facility to manipulate mood and tone, yet remain clear and direct, without generalizations or pretentions of abstract-truth content.

Problems of self-discovery peculiar to feminist literature form the basis for Ursula Krechel's (b. 1947) writings. *Nach Mainz* (1977; to Mainz) is the product of a complex intellect. Its poems are decisive in tone. They concern themselves with shattered illusions in a world dominated by men. In *Verwundbar wie in den besten Zeiten* (1979; vulnerable as in the best times) she evokes an inner reality that is tangled in deception, suffering, and hypocrisy. The verse here is less successful than that of her first book. While individual pieces mirror the destruction of habitual language as a symbol for the modern world's condition, the presentations lack vitality. In spite of a wealth of images and a demonstration of Krechel's continued social commitment, *Vom Feuer lernen* (1985; learning from fire) suggests that she has nearly exhausted her themes.

Among the most compelling subjectivist poems of recent years are those of Gerald K. Zschorsch (b. 1951), an East German refugee with an enthusiastic following. His lyric treatments of the divided-Germany question, the problems of exile, and the difficulties of adjusting to West German reality, in *Glaubt bloß nicht, daß ich traurig bin* (1977, expanded 1981; just don't believe that I'm sad), successfully convey the poet's misery. The strong artistic expression of his first collection and *Die Duft der anderen Haut* (1981; the scent of the other skin) is also present in many offerings in *Klappmesser* (1983; switchblade), but other items lack the force and edge that the title seems to promise.

The intense pessimism, coldness, and alienation of West German literature in the first half of the 1980s are readily visible in *Trotz alledem* (1980; in spite of all that) and *Liebe Grüße* (1982; fond greetings) by Kristiane Allert-Wybranietz (b. 1955), West Germany's most popular young poetess. Threatening images of unprotected children playing in the streets, the destruction of landscape, personal "propellers" that break on cliffs of fear, and hearts lost in fogs of insecurity dominate poems that convey anxieties, wishes, and feelings in clear, simple words.

The coldness of the external world is sharply juxtaposed with subjective inner warmth in the first poem of Richard Exner's (b. 1929) *Fast ein Gespräch* (1980; almost a conversation). Other offerings present an interesting, mature balance between images of silence, cold, distance, loneliness, and death, and contrasting elements of speech, heat, proximity, love, and life. Exner's successful maintenance of artistic tension between simplicity and complexity, laconicism and detail, optimism and pessimism in *Mit rauchloser Flamme* (1982; with a smokeless flame) have brought him justified recognition as one of the most effective, most sensitive poets currently writing in West Germany.

DRAMA

With few exceptions, the state of West German drama during the early postwar years was extremely weak. Most playwrights were unsuccessful in dealing effectively with contemporary material. For one thing they lacked contact with recent international trends. For another, their production was adversely affected by the relationship between the theater and the state. To have their works performed, authors had to accept the dictated tasks of education, forming the new society, and consolidation of the community. Most programmed drama lacked imagination and vitality, and not much of it was staged because the theaters initially did not promote new pieces.

Two factors shaped dramatic literature immediately after the war. The first was the influence of Bertolt Brecht, whose didactic approach and concepts of staging and style had profound and lasting impact on theater across Europe. The other force was a sharply recognized need to come to grips with the immediate past in an effort to combat the possibilities of renewing the experienced horrors. This second element gave substance and dramatic power to new creations.

Established writers had considerable difficulty in reclaiming a place in the repertoires of the rebuilt theaters. Very few of them made substantial contributions to the renewal of drama after the war.

Günther Weisenborn (1902–69) was the only truly successful representative of the "inner emigration." Upon his return to the theatrical scene, he proclaimed the political purpose of the theater. His involvement in the founding of the Hebbel Theater was part of a strong initial movement toward renewal of the stage in Berlin. Later, the city's division and isolation prevented it from becoming the West German theatrical capital.

Die Illegalen (1946; the underground) reestablished Weisenborn's dramatic reputation and rapidly became a symbol for the new political dramaturgy. Much of its artistic strength derives from the author's effective processing of personal experience.

Although Weisenborn continued to write successful satires and social criticisms, few of them achieved the stature of *Die Illegalen*. Some, including *Babel* (1946; Babel) and *Ballade vom Eulenspiegel, vom Federle und von der dicken Pompanne* (1949; ballad of Eulenspiegel, Federle and fat Pompanne), exhibit the strong influence of Brecht, but others exemplify the timeless, placeless pieces that were Weisenborn's most important contribution to the theater in his later years. Among the more representative plays of this kind are *Drei ehrenwerte Herren* (1951; three honorable gentlemen), a comedy about three released criminals who are mistaken for newly appointed city fathers, and *Zwei Engel steigen aus* (1954; two angels disembark), a satirical science fiction farce about two alien girls who come to earth to study love.

Of the exile dramatists, only Carl Zuckmayer (1896–1977) regained a measure of his prewar popularity. Zuckmayer is best remembered for *Der Hauptmann von Köpenick* (1931; *The Captain of Köpenick,* 1932), a satire on military culture in Imperial Germany. *Des Teufels General* (1946; *The Devil's General,* 1962), his first postwar play, was enormously successful on the German stage. It is meaningful for its effective use of substance from the Nazi era as a frame for treatment of individual guilt in the historical context. Zuckmayer's later dramas deal with crises, guilt, and confusion of beliefs as basic tragedies of modern existence. Aside from *Der Gesang im Feuerofen* (1950; the song in the fiery furnace), a tragic piece about the French Resistance, none of them enjoyed the popularity of *The Devil's General.*

Fritz von Unruh (1885–1970) failed to regain even a modest measure of his previous artistic stature. After World War I, he had won wide acclaim with his pacifistic plays, but new creations of the late 1940s and the 1950s failed to find significant public resonance. Although he attempted to deal with contemporary themes in *Der Befreiungsminister* (1948; the liberation secretary), *Wilhelmus von Oranien* (1953; William of Orange), *Duell an der Havel* (1954; duel on the Havel), and *17. Juni* (1954; the 17th of June), he no longer had the official patronage that had kept his earlier works on the stage. More important, his new works tended to bog down in faded generalities, ambiguity, and triviality.

From a different perspective, one of the most important continuing writers was Günter Eich. He had written one comedy and a radio play before the war. After 1945, he became the best radio playwright in the field. The enormous success of *Träume* (1950; dreams) helped establish the radio play as a powerful genre. Eich's contributions included developments in sound effects and a particular mastery of spoken language. *Träume,* with its demonic revelation of the postwar world's nightmares, set the pattern for his later creations. In *Die Andere und ich* (1952; the other woman and I), from the collection *Stimmen* (1958; voices), a carefree American woman experiences a transformation that lets her live the miserable life of an Italian fisherman's wife. Other plays deal with existential searches for self, problems of coping with the past and future, and criticism of social, political, and personal dilemmas and contradictions.

With isolated exceptions, the West German stage really belonged to dramatists who produced their first creations after 1945. Three writers who began their dramaturgical careers between 1945 and 1949 are Wolfgang Borchert, Reinhold Schneider, and Peter Weiss.

Wolfgang Borchert wrote only one dramatic piece, *Draußen vor der Tür* (1947; *The Man Outside,* 1952). First presented as a radio play, later on the stage, the creation made its author famous immediately. *The Man Outside* gave impetus to what became known as "Literature of the ruins." Its production history, on makeshift stages in bombed-out cellars and school gymnasiums, symbolizes the physical situation of drama until reconstruction was finally completed with the reopening of the Darmstadt Theater in 1972. A depiction of the internal and external tragedy of a young returning soldier, the play complements Borchert's prose as a powerful document of the spiritual rape of an entire generation.

Although Reinhold Schneider belonged to the "inner emigration," before 1945 he had published only prose and a small amount of poetry. His first drama, *Der Kronprinz* (the crown prince), appeared in 1948. It was quickly followed by *Das Spiel vom Menschen Belsazar* (1949; the play about Belshazar), *Der große Verzicht* (1950; the great renunciation), *Der Traum des Eroberers. Zar Alexander* (1951; the emperor's dream. Czar Alexander), and other plays. Like his fiction, Schneider's plays are based in Christian humanism and emphasize a variety of spiritual, cultural, ethical, and political questions. Unfortunately, most of them do not make the artistic transition from heavy prose to viable drama.

The early plays of Peter Weiss, including *Der Turm* (1948; the tower), *Die Versicherung* (1952; the insurance policy), and even *Nacht mit Gästen* (1963; night with guests), established him as an existential innovator, but they were not very successful on the stage. During the 1960s, Weiss achieved international fame with *Die Verfolgung und Ermordung Jean Paul Marats dargestellt durch die Schauspielgruppe des Hospizes zu Charenton unter Anleitung des Herrn de Sade* (1964; *The Persecution and Assassination of Jean Paul Marat as Performed by the Inmates of the Asylum of Charenton Under the Direction of the Marquis de Sade,* 1965), a dialectical drama that combines elements of Brecht's epic theater with aspects of Antonin Artaud's (1895–1948) Theater of Cruelty, and *Die Ermittlung* (1965; *The Investigation,* 1966), a documentary "oratorio" that focuses on the Frankfurt Auschwitz trials of 1963–65. The strength of *Marat/Sade* lies in its powerfully theatrical juxtaposition of ideas from Marxist-Leninism with pre-Freudian nihilistic aestheticism. In *The Investigation* Weiss effectively transformed the realistic trial situation into an indictment of the capitalistic system. His later plays, such as *Gesang vom Lusitanische Popanz* (1967; *Song of the Lusitanian Bogey,* 1970) and *Diskurs über die Vorgeschichte und den Verlauf des lang andauernden Befreiungskrieges in Viet Nam* (1968; *Discourse on the Progress of the Prolonged War of Liberation in Viet Nam,* 1970), are strongly marked by socialistic propaganda—to the detriment of artistic quality.

Many new dramas written by young authors around the turn of the decade to the 1950s were quickly forgotten. The writers had difficulty in responding effectively to international influences and the demand for contemporary substance. The result was decadence and eclecticism. External social and political uncertainties caused many playwrights to move toward generalization, allegory, and parable.

Leopold Ahlsen (b. 1927) established himself during the 1950s as a promising radio and stage dramatist. Although his first major work, *Zwischen den Ufern* (1952; between the shores), was panned by critics for its hazy mysticism, *Pflicht zur Sünde* (1952; duty to sin) was received quite positively. The latter play offers a compelling treatment of moral and ethical questions about individual guilt and responsibility. Ahlsen's first overwhelming theatrical success was *Philemon und Baucis* (1956; Philemon and Baucis), a clever play that combines tragedy and humor in depicting the problems and death of an old Greek couple. Later works, such as *Sie werden sterben, Sire!* (1964; you will die, sire!) and *Der arme Mann Luther* (1964; poor Luther), were less successful on the stage, but they are good illustrations of Ahlsen's technique of "dissecting souls" to interpret historical substance from the perspective of the present.

The works of Richard Hey (b. 1926) attempt to transform current events and conflicts into timeless allegories. Even Hey's satirical farce *Revolutionäre* (1953; revolutionaries) exhibits aspects of symbolic realism. *Thymian und Drachentod* (1956; thyme and dragon death) is especially representative of his plays. It transports the conflict of divided Germany into a parabolic world where a young man flees from a totalitarian land of dragons into a weak anti-dragon nation. The generalization of the real world problem weakens its presentation and renders the play banal. Subsequent creations have encountered division among critics. *Der Fisch mit dem goldenen Dolch* (1958; the fish with the golden dagger) and *Wehe dem, der nicht lügt* (1962; woe to him who does not lie) illustrate that Hey's talent as a satirist and his sharp sense of dialogue are often undermined by an excess of theatrics and failed transitions from real to surreal domains.

Legends and parables are also a central element of Wolfgang Hildesheimer's dramatic works. Beginning with *Das Ende einer Welt* (1953; the end of a world) and *Prinzessin Turandot* (1953; Princess Turandot), which was later staged by Gustaf Gründgens (1899–1963) as *Der Drachenthron* (1955; the dragon throne), Hildesheimer produced many pieces devoted to the shattering of social clichés through the use of combinations of irony, satire, grotesque and surreal elements, and bizarre fantasy. Among his best creations are the short plays of *Spiele, in denen es dunkel wird* (1958; plays in which it gets dark) and *Die Verspätung* (1961; the delay). The successful use of plays on words, visual tricks, and other representative techniques have made him the most important German contributor to the Theater of the Absurd.

Another dramatist who wrote absurdist plays in the 1950s is Günter Grass. His first dramas, from *Hochwasser* (1957; high water) and *Onkel, Onkel* (1958; uncle, uncle) through *Die bösen Köche* (1961; the evil cooks), employ the standard techniques of the Theater of the Absurd without attempting any sort of social analysis. They simply make banal statements about the world's craziness. Grass's later plays, such as *Die Plebejer proben den Aufstand* (1966; *The Plebians Rehearse the Uprising,* 1967) and *Davor* (1969; *Max: A Play,* 1972), are somewhat more successful, but they primarily confirm the fact that drama is not his best medium.

The strong development of the radio play facilitated a new depth of penetration into the workings of the mind. This tendency is particularly visible in the successful productions of Peter Hirche (b. 1923). In *Die seltsamste Liebesgeschichte der Welt* (1953; the world's strangest love story) he presented two young strangers having an imaginary dialogue about love and loneliness. This work demonstrated a mastery of radio's possibilities through its effective use of music. *Die Heimkehr* (1954; the homecoming) revealed extreme linguistic sensitivity in reproducing human consciousness. Inner dialogues, monologues, and collages are employed effectively in portraying a dying woman's visionary return to her home area. Hirche's most successful radio play is *Miserere* (1965; misery). Its precise composition, pointed psychology, and use of multiple voices combine to produce a powerful exposure of the evil and threatened state of the world as exemplified in the lives of several apartment house dwellers.

Wolfgang Weyrauch also had a strong influence on radio drama. Like Hirche, he used monologue to combine elements of reality and dream. Weyrauch leans toward aggressive, experimental social criticism in his plays. One of the better examples of his creative diversity is *Die Minute des Negers* (1953; the Negro's minute), a peculiarly musical incantation in ballad form. In it the listener is confronted with the vision that a condemned black man has during the final minute of his life.

Der blaue Elefant (1959; the blue elephant) was the first of a series of plays by Dieter Waldmann (1926–71), in which substance is presented on two levels: reality and fairy-tale dream world. Waldmann emphasizes the incompatibility of the two realms in the story of an old woman and a foundling whose shared fantasy existence sets them at odds with their real environment. *Von Bergamo bis morgen früh* (1960; from Bergamo until tomorrow morning) employs the devices of the Commedia dell'arte to attack the senselessness of modern society from a different perspective. Later plays, such as *Atlantis* (1963; Atlantis) and *Die Schwätzer* (1965; the windbags), offer other forms of the dream realization theme but remain flat because they lack any satisfying resolution of their central problems.

Although Siegfried Lenz's development as a playwright is a chronological product of the 1960s, his theatrical works belong to the earlier parabolic theater. *Zeit der Schuldlosen* (1961; time of the guiltless), the first of three allegories dealing with the problems of guilt, power, and human corruption, was the only one to be successful on the stage. Its strength depends on the penetration of human types and the contemporary appeal of its moral message. The other two pieces, *Das Gesicht* (1964; the face) and *Die Augenbinde* (1970; the blindfold), did not attract much attention, because the parabolic approach divorced them from new theatrical trends, and because the flat development of trite themes rendered them unviable.

The most important developments in West German drama during the 1960s moved in the direction of renewed realism.

One especially visible extreme was the documentary theater. Some writers continued to work with parabolic, grotesque, surreal, and romantic elements, but dramatists who insisted on clinging to outmoded approaches quickly faded into obscurity.

One defender of poetic theater was Konrad Wünsche (b. 1928). His early one-act plays, *Über den Gartenzaun* (1962; over the garden fence) and *Vor der Klagemauer* (1962; in front of the wailing wall) are variations on the theme of the expulsion from paradise, while *Der Unbelehrbare* (1963; the unteachable man) is a parody of Shakespeare's *Hamlet*. Wünsche's later surrealistic experiments share with the early works a weakness of language that is not offset by strong plotting or theatrical development.

Tankred Dorst's (b. 1925) first plays were notable for their diversity, from romantic fantasy to grotesque satire, from Commedia dell'arte style to parables in the manner of Brecht. A good example of the last form is his *Große Schmährede an der Stadtmauer* (1961; *Grand Tirade at the Town Wall,* 1961), an attack on war and militarism.

After experiments with fairy-tale theater in *Die Mohrin* (1964; the Mooress) and the street-ballad drama in *Wittek geht um* (1967; Wittek walks), Dorst found his way to a semi-documentary form that moved him away from entertainment drama and into disquieting social criticism. His first major success was *Toller* (1968; Toller), a study of the relationship between literature and politics presented in a dialogue involving the writer Ernst Toller (1893–1939). The success of *Toller* derived from Dorst's ability to depict multi-dimensional, realistic historical figures, and from the play's flawless reproduction of the contemporary socio-political atmosphere in the Federal Republic. *Eiszeit* (1973; ice age), a play about the Norwegian writer Knut Hamsun (1859–1952), is less successful than *Toller.* Dorst's attempt to show the difficulties of grappling with the past is obscured by the more superficial problems of aging and bridging the generation gap. *Die Villa* (1980; the villa) and *Merlin, oder das wüste Land* (1981; Merlin, or the wasteland) reflect Dorst's unerring ability to reproduce the spirit of the times. *Merlin* is one of his best plays, but its length defies the practical demands of stage economy.

Although Martin Walser does not employ the devices of documentary theater, his brand of realism demands a precise and active processing of historical and present reality. All of his most important plays, from *Eiche und Angora* (1962; oak and angora) through *Der schwarze Schwan* (1964; the black swan), *Die Zimmerschlacht* (1967; *Home Front*, 1972), and *Kinderspiel* (1970; child's play), present life as a struggle for mastery and dominance, whether in man–woman relations, the business world, or the political realm. The plays are successful because Walser is a master of the dynamics of self-experience. That fact is most strongly substantiated in his masterpiece, *In Goethes Hand* (1982; in Goethe's hand), a cruelly powerful analysis of psychological motivations.

Rolf Hochhuth (b. 1931) is best known for his contributions to the documentary theater. The highly controversial play *Der Stellvertreter* (1963; *The Deputy*, 1964) brought him instant notoriety with its suggestion that Pope Pius XII shared the responsibility for the Nazis' extermination of the Jews because he failed to oppose the persecutions. *Soldaten: Nekrolog auf Genf* (1967; *Soldiers: An Obituary for Geneva*, 1968) is another modern morality play. These two works are important because they influenced other writers toward political involvement and served as models for new creations of the same type, but they are not especially effective dramas. *The Deputy* is marred by shallow characterizations and cheaply sensationalistic confrontations that offset the claim to documentary objectivity. *Soldiers* offers a powerful psychological interpretation of Winston Churchill, but it suffers from artistic flaws that reduce its literary value. Hochhuth's later plays, including *Guerillas* (1970; guerrillas), *Die Hebamme* (1971; the midwife), *Lysistrate und die NATO* (1973; Lysistrata and NATO), and *Die Juristen* (1980; the legal profession), confirm the fact that his popular success is more a function of the plays' shock and agitation value than their artistry.

The documentary element in Hochhuth's dramas consists of invented texts and situations found in the appendix, in essayistic stage directions, and in source material that is generally used only indirectly. By contrast, the plays of other writers feature characters who speak directly from real documentary sources. Although this technique theoretically renounces authorial intrusion, the professed avoidance of tampering is an illusion, because arrangement, editing, and emphasis of sources poetizes and alters reality.

The extremes that typify the writings of Hochhuth, Peter Weiss, and the East German refugee Heinar Kipphardt (b. 1922) did not become the final standard for most new dramatists, but many of them adopted the documentary theater's sharply critical stance with respect to social and political problems. More important, its stimulus accelerated and intensified the productive treatment of realistic substance.

Industry and the world of work form the background for most of Gerlind Reinshagen's (b. 1926) plays, but her main concern is the position of the individual in an oppressive social context. *Doppelkopf* (1968; two-headed man) offers a satirical study of the struggle between management and labor. The play falters artistically because its second half retreats into propagandistic sloganism. Reinshagen's most documentary piece is *Leben und Tod der Marilyn Monroe* (1971; life and death of Marilyn Monroe), an unconvincing attempt to present a paradigm for the connection between the creation of myth and the destruction of individual consciousness. The equation of failing awareness with loss of control over personal destiny is also the basis for *Himmel und Erde* (1974; heaven and earth). Although its plot is weak, *Himmel und Erde* reveals Reinshagen's powerful facility with language. Subsequent plays, including *Sonntagskinder* (1976; Sunday children) and *Das Frühlingsfest* (1980; celebration of spring), have made her well known, but they are not the works of a premier dramatist.

Other socially committed playwrights include Thomas Valentin, Martin Sperr (b. 1944) and Jochen Ziem (b. 1932). Each of them employs theater to expose the hypocrisies and underlying destructive conflicts in contemporary relationships.

Thomas Valentin's strength lies in precise dialogue and language that authenticates his diagnoses of social disorders. His best play is *Die Unberatenen* (1964; the unadvised ones). It illuminates generation conflicts as results of challenges to authority and failure to communicate. The confrontation between young and old also informs *Der Hausfreund* (1969; friend of the family) and *Familienbande* (1974; family ties), in which Valentin demonstrates his mastery of characterization through careful manipulation of linguistic gestures and physical mannerisms.

Intimate knowledge of milieu, an unerring sense of social mood, and a disturbingly penetrating eye for human despicableness give Martin Sperr's unpleasant realism its caustic flavor. His *Jagdszenen aus Niederbayern* (1966; hunting scenes from Lower Bavaria) is a merciless exposure of rural narrowmindedness and viciousness. Similarly, *Landshuter Erzählungen* (1967; *Tales from Landshut,* 1969), a peculiarly evil version of *Romeo and Juliet,* offers a horribly realistic picture of human brutality, continuing prejudices, corruption, aggressiveness, and destructive ego-centered behavior. These two plays and the third part of the "Bavarian Trilogy," *Münchner Freiheit* (1971; Munich freedom), form an ugly mural of modern morality, from village ethics to city politics. Although *Münchner Freiheit* is not as convincing as the earlier plays, it contains isolated scenes that are starkly powerful. Sperr's most successful play is *Koralle Meier* (1970; Koralle Meier), a sensitive revelation of the origins of Nazi brutality and inhumanity in the attitudes and prejudices of common people.

On a different scale, Jochen Ziem's play *Nachrichten aus der Provinz* (1967; news from the province) offers a spiritual panorama of life in the Federal Republic as a whole. This work is a mirror of malice, intolerance, and cowardice, but it employs cabaret-sketch techniques that reduce the scenes to banal clichés. *Nachrichten aus der Provinz* is even less successful than Ziem's first dramatic effort, *Die Einladung* (1967; the invitation), an illumination of the East–West conflict as seen in the fractured lives of a geographically divided family. The sequel to *Die Einladung, Die Versöhnung* (1971; the reconciliation), bogs down totally in trivial conversation.

Although the West German theater was dominated by realism during the latter half of the 1960s, weak traditional plays were also created, and there were a few examples of theatrical experimentation that departed radically from popular trends. Especially visible were new open forms, such as street theater and the so-called "happenings," which attempted to draw the audience into the dramatic process. Free dramatic forms are found in the works of Bazon Brock (b. 1936) and Wolf Wondratschek (b. 1943).

The focus of Bazon Brock's efforts is the promotion of total artistic freedom. His productions are theatrical only in that they sometimes involve a mixture of live "performance," props, and spoken material. More than anything else, they are "dramatization" of pop culture, variously labeled "happenings," "actions," and "montages." Typical for his art is the "radio play" *Grundgeräusche und ein Hörraum* (1969; basic sounds and an auditorium), in which he offered a catalogue of acoustical perceptions of the environment. Although Brock has drawn attention with his concepts, he has hardly made a contribution to drama per se.

Wolf Wondratschek's radio-play experiments are somewhat less radical. His analytical style of association, his pregnant language, and his concentrated forms of expression give special character to works such as *Zufälle* (1968; chance happenings), *Zustände und Zusammenhänge* (1970; conditions and relationships), *Einsame Leichen* (1970; lonely corpses), and *Maschine Nr. 9* (1973; machine number nine). By forcing his audience to create new kinds of associations, he creates a uniquely personal dramatic art that challenges the listener's imagination while making it easy to renounce established patterns of aural perception.

The various tendencies of the 1960s all come together in the creations of Rainer Werner Fassbinder (1946–82). Everything from pop culture to semi-documentary realism found its way into his plays and films. His first play, *Katzelmacher* (1968; Katzelmacher), is an intensified, urbanized version of Sperr's *Jagdszenen aus Niederbayern,* if anything describing a more brutal, less sensitive, more primitive community than Sperr's rural village. The theme of brutalization also dominates *Pre-paradise sorry now* (1969; pre-paradise sorry now), a horrifying collage of sex, violence, sadism—and boredom. Fassbinder's most successful play is *Bremer Freiheit* (1971; Bremen freedom), a biographical study of the nineteenth-century poisoner Gesche Gottfried (d. 1831), which focuses on problems of female emancipation. Its strength lies in the psychological penetration of the central figure and her motivations. *Bremer Freiheit* was followed by plays and films that focus on the boredom, human indifference, nonparticipation in productive social relationships, and tendencies toward anarchy that are visible signs of modern society's terminal malaise. Fassbinder presented these things more successfully than any other dramatist of his generation.

Treatment of the complex dialectic between the individual's lack of social ties and contempt for others, between obedience and refusal to obey, between social and anti-social attitudes became increasingly more dominant in plays produced during the 1970s. The tension between self and the potential for violence belonged to a new theater of isolation that often portrayed life as a threatening hunt. Two important creators of this type of drama are Franz Xaver Kroetz (b. 1946) and Botho Strauß.

For Franz Xaver Kroetz, the mark of social disjointedness is inability to communicate. His successful manipulation of techniques developed originally by Ödön von Horvath (1901–38) and Marieluise Fleisser (1901–74) helped him to become one of the most popular dramatists of the 1970s. The influence of Horvath's "process of speechlessness" and Fleisser's calculated use of dialect and depiction of underprivileged characters is especially visible in *Hartnäckig* (1971; stubborn), *Heimarbeit* (1971; homework), and *Geisterbahn* (1971; ghost train). These plays aroused the public through drastic representations of sexuality, abortion, violence, and murder, and through vulgar language, but did not offer substantial strength of form or theatrical originality. Kroetz created his most extreme play in *Wunschkonzert* (1973; *Request Concert*, 1976), the story of a woman who becomes totally silent as she recognizes the senselessness of her life. In *Maria Magdalena* (1973; Mary Magdalene), *Agnes Bernauer* (1977; Agnes Bernauer), *Mensch Meier* (1978; good grief!), and *Furcht und Hoffnung der BRD* (1984; fear and hope of the Federal Republic of Germany), he abandoned his earlier direction in favor of an active political realism. The more recent works continue to emphasize problems of loneliness, oppression, and personal misery among the lower classes, but the elaboration of the conflicts is not very convincing.

Botho Strauβ is an extremely popular representative of the new folk theater. His dominant themes are identity crisis and the individual's inability to establish social connections. Failure to communicate is but one pathological manifestation of the crippling introversion that typifies his figures. In *Die Hypochonder* (1973; the hypochondriacs), a grotesquely irreal crime story, Strauβ interchanges internal and external worlds in a peculiar blending of reality and dream. *Bekannte Gesichter, gemischte Gefühle* (1974; familiar faces, mixed feelings) also meshes subjective and objective experience in portraying the triviality of middle-class existence, while *Trilogie des Wiedersehens* (1976; trilogy of reunion) stresses the impossibility of positive social relationships. Strauβ's more recent plays, *Kalldewey Farce* (1981; Kalldewey farce) and *Der Park* (1983; the park), attempt to treat the crisis of isolation in a hostile environment with greater artistry than before, but *Kalldewey Farce* is weakened by the dominance of linguistic and radical-culture stereotypes, and *Der Park* offers little novelty in its depressing exposure of the psychological vacuum that overwhelms the characters.

Michael Schneider (b. 1934) is radically political in his treatments of human isolation. His *Die Wiedergutmachung* (1977; the restoration) is an enterprising, highly stylized dramatization of capitalism's triumph over postwar socialism in West Germany. Its strength lies in the relevance of its substance. The dramatic presentation is relatively weak. *Luftschloβ unter Tage* (1982; air castle under ground) resembles Strauβ's *Trilogie des Wiedersehens* in its parade of failures in political and private relationships. Schneider's challenge to young intellectuals to renew their social and political activism is clearly stated, but the drama form provides only a medium for its communication, not an enhancement of the message's presentation.

Narcissism is one of the stronger symptoms of the psychological isolation that dominates Bodo Kirchhoff's plays. His dramatic texts emphasize psychoanalytic penetration of characters and problems of communication and language. *Das Kind oder Die Vernichtung von Neuseeland* (1978; the child, or the destruction of New Zealand), *Body-Building* (1979; body-building), and *An den Rand der Erschöpfung, weiter* (1980; on the verge of exhaustion, onward) reflect the influence of the Theater of the Absurd. *Wer sich liebt* (1981; whoever is in love) does not quite get off the ground. Although there are flashes of original humor in the play, its disjointed structure, fractured dialogues, and esoteric references to unknown fictional figures form barriers to audience comprehension.

Authorial emphasis on the victimized individual is a common manifestation in drama of gloom and doom in the early 1980s. In the works of Friederike Roth (b. 1948), characters are oppressed by traditions of behavior and language that render the individual helpless because there is no escape. For Klaus Pohl (b. 1952), the ugliness of historical and contemporary reality provides ample substance for both pathos and satire.

Friederike Roth's *Klavierspiele* (1981; piano selections) is a peculiar combination of lyricism, active feminist imagination, and trivial plot. It reflects disenchantment with conventional social relationships and the devices of communication by which they are maintained. Her most successful creation, *Ritt auf die Wartburg* (1981; ride to the Wartburg), describes the visit of four West German women to the German Democratic Republic. The tension between their expectations and the realities of their experience becomes symbolic for a despair that arises as much out of individual halfheartedness as unfavorable external circumstances.

In *Das alte Land* (1984; the old country) by Klaus Pohl examination of the final political dissolution of Prussia in 1947 and the subsequent bitter misery of the land-reform years become a sharp mirror of the unpleasant, painful, and unviable social relationships of the present. *Das alte Land* is one of the most powerful examples of grappling with the past in recent drama. Especially noteworthy are Pohl's mastery of characterization and his deft combination of historical reality and theatrical fantasy. The more recent plays, *Der Spiegel* (1985; Der Spiegel), titled after the German newsmagazine, and *La Balkona Bar* (1985; the La Balkona bar), illustrate his strong satirical gift. Both plays foster uncomfortable exposure of particularly revolting aspects of modern West German behavior.

3 ▪ THE GERMAN DEMOCRATIC REPUBLIC

FICTION

Emigrant writers who returned to the Soviet Occupied Zone quickly established specific goals for new fiction. They defined the most immediate task as illumination of the Nazi experience, its causes and effects. A proper understanding of the past could then provide a basis for determining what must be done to prevent similar political catastrophes in the future. Antifascist literature of the exile period became contemporary art in East Germany because it could not be read earlier. At the same time, it served as a model for prose of the early postwar years. Among the most strongly advocated characteristics of the new literature were fresh emphases on the German people, homeland, landscape, and the individual's relationship to family. Special attention was given to educating the coming generation toward ideals of love, friendship, and community, while stressing rejection of fascism and its defenders.

Two kinds of narrative dominated this initial period. One group of works exhibited documentary and informational characteristics. It included reports and chronicles from concentration camps, resistance activities, and the war itself.

These are sober, unembellished writings that testify about what happened, without aesthetic ambition. The other type of fiction also reported on resistance and the war, but it emphasized the portrayal of individuals who overcome acquiescence or passive resistance, who became effective anti-fascists. These creations established ideological models for the development of the new society. Some authors also expanded the focus on the past. They felt that knowledge of all German history was necessary to an understanding of Hitler's Germany.

Among the returning novelists was Anna Seghers (1900–83), an undisputed master of the portrayal of individual reality. Her famous novel *Das siebte Kreuz* (1942; *The Seventh Cross*, 1942), the account of an escape from a concentration camp, is a powerful classic of anti-fascist literature and remains one of the best artistic portrayals of the complex moods, social relationships, and political atmosphere of Nazi Germany. The postwar novels, *Die Toten bleiben jung* (1949; *The Dead Stay Young*, 1950), *Die Entscheidung* (1959; the decision), and *Das Vertrauen* (1968; trust), are all less satisfying than *The Seventh Cross*. Her attempt to braid together many narratives in *The Dead Stay Young* results in a cumbersome work that is difficult to read. Nevertheless, the intense penetration of social strata, a complete psychological portrayal of even the most negative figures, and an accurate revelation of both internal and external realities outweigh in import the stylistic weaknesses. The same cannot be said for *Die Entscheidung* and *Das Vertrauen*, which bog down in trivial complexity.

Seghers's late fiction contains interesting deviations from mainstream East German tendencies. "Sagen von Unirdischen" (tales of extraterrestrials), from *Sonderbare Begegnungen* (1972; peculiar encounters), is an artistically successful science fiction story, while the novella *Steinzeit* (1975; stone age) powerfully portrays the psychological and physical self-destruction of an American Vietnam veteran.

The postwar novels of Arnold Zweig (1887–1968) are weaker than those he produced outside the restraints of programmed literature. Zweig is best known for his indictment of militarism in *Der Streit um den Sergeanten Grischa* (1927; *The Case of Sergeant Grischa*, 1928). This first volume of his enormous cycle *Der große Krieg der weißen Männer* (the great war of the white men) was followed after 1945 by *Die Feuerpause* (1954; the ceasefire), *Die Zeit ist reif* (1959; *The Time Is Ripe,* 1962), and *Traum ist teuer* (1962; dream is costly). Of the three, only *The Time Is Ripe,* a retrospective chronicle of the years 1913 to 1915, offers any real sense of the psychological and social dynamics of the period portrayed. *Die Feuerpause* features the unconvincing portrayal of the central figure's conversion to militant socialism, while *Traum is teuer* offers only a watery variation of motifs from *The Case of Sergeant Grischa.*

The experience of World War I was also productive for Ludwig Renn (1889–1979), whose *Krieg* (1928; war) won him recognition as one of the classical authors of East German literature. Renn's postwar creations include anti-militaristic war novels and strongly autobiographical reports. Although none of them has the literary stature of *Krieg,* the autobiographical pieces *Kindheit und Jugend* (1957; childhood and youth), *Inflation* (1963; inflation), *Zu Fuß zum Orient* (1964; to the Orient on foot), and *In Mexiko* (1974; in Mexico) are at least interesting for their documentary substance. By contrast, the novel *Krieg ohne Schlacht* (1957; war without battle) is colorless, shallow, and boring.

Hans Marchwitza's (1890–1965) superficial, artlessly naive novels of political and social criticism exemplify works produced by older proletarian authors. The focus of his writing is glorification of class consciousness. His most ambitious creation, the trilogy *Die Kumiaks* (1934; the Kumiaks), *Die Heimkehr der Kumiaks* (1952; the Kumiaks' homecoming), and *Die Kumiaks und ihre Kinder* (1959; the Kumiaks and their children), describes how a family of mine workers finds its way into the new era of East German society. In these narratives, and in the industrial novel *Roheisen* (1955; raw iron), the stereotyped figures and situations drown in worn-out phrases and trite slogans.

Another proletarian writer was Willi Bredel (1901–64). His narrative prose is dominated by autobiographical elements. An unpretentious manner of presentation makes his works more realistic than those of Marchwitza, although Bredel also had difficulty with style, composition, and the artistic development of material. Bredel's most successful work is the trilogy *Verwandte und Bekannte* (relatives and acquaintances), consisting of *Die Väter* (1943; the fathers), *Die Söhne* (1949; the sons), and *Die Enkel* (1953; the grandchildren). *Verwandte und Bekannte* offers interesting and original characters and background, but lacks action and consistently developed plot lines. Bredel's shorter compositions are even less successful. They are often wooden and stiff, with contrived resolutions of conflicts and one-dimensional characters.

With *Leutnant Bertram* (1944; *Lieutenant Bertram*, 1961), Bodo Uhse (1904–63) established himself as a capable artist, although mastery of psychological portrayal and the effective treatment of contemporary themes are somewhat softened by plot weaknesses. His strongest postwar novels are *Wir Söhne* (1948; we sons) and *Die Patrioten* (1954; the patriots). *Wir Söhne* is narrated in simple, clear language that conveys convincing impressions of milieu and period, while realistically processing moral and ethical conflicts. *Die Patrioten* is less compelling, primarily because the author knew too little about the realities of resistance, concentration camps, and the political attitudes of the masses. Uhse also produced several books of short stories, including *Die heilige Kunigunde im Schnee* (1949; St. Cunigunde in the snow), *Mexikanische Erzählungen* (1957; Mexican stories), and *Reise in einem blauen Schwan* (1959; journey in a blue swan). His best tales are based on personal experience, but his short fiction exhibits significant variation in quality.

The works of Stefan Heym (b. 1913) are strongly colored by personal experience and negative political/social criticism. Some of his novels appeared in English before they were published in German. *Der Fall Glasenapp* (1958; *Hostages*, 1942) illustrates Heym's problems in dealing with contemporary themes. While the novel reflects strong insight into human psychology, the realistic effect is significantly weakened by lack of knowledge concerning the workings of the Gestapo. One of Heym's more engaging books is *Kreuzfahrer von Heute* (1950; *The Crusaders*, 1948), a story set in Germany at the end of the war and in the first year after it. The depiction of human conflicts, behaviors, corruption, and vice during the Occupation is especially compelling, although the contrived victory of justice at the end dampens the work's overall effect. Heym has also written historical novels, including *Die Papiere des Andreas Lenz* (1963; *The Lenz Papers,* 1963) and *Lasalle* (1969; *Uncertain Friend,* 1968). He uses historical fiction to treat modern problems. In a new version of the biblical King David's life, *Der König David Bericht* (1972; the King David report) he illuminates the problems of Stalinism, and in *Ahasver* (1981; *The Wandering Jew,* 1984) he examines the threat of nuclear destruction and the dangers of bureaucratic petrification. *The Wandering Jew* is Heym's most demanding novel. The more recent *Schwarzenberg* (1984; Schwarzenberg), a peculiarly naive political fairy tale, lacks depth of perception.

Very few new East German writers produced their first pieces of fiction during the late 1940s. Among those whose works had lasting significance for socialist German prose were Eduard Claudius (1911–76), Wolfgang Joho (b. 1908), and Stephan Hermlin (b. 1915).

Eduard Claudius's *Grüne Oliven und nackte Berge* (1945; green olives and bare mountains) was one of the first German novels about the Spanish Civil War. In this work and the short-story collection *Haβ* (1947; hate) Claudius presented striking images, distinctive emotionalism, and clear development of his characters' world of feeling. His industrial novel *Menschen an unserer Seite* (1951; people at our side), with its negative portrayal of East German factory conditions, is a significant attempt to examine critically real problems of the new society. Later efforts, including *Von der Liebe soll man nicht sprechen* (1957; one should not talk of love) and *Wintermärchen auf Rügen* (1965; winter tale on Rügen), combine consistently unpleasant reality with contrived problem resolutions. They are artistically questionable, even from a socialist perspective.

The works of Wolfgang Joho treat the stock plot situation of the individual's transformation from bourgeois to active communist. His creations show little originality and are shallow in language and presentation. Representative volumes, from *Die Hirtenflöte* (1948; the shepherd's flute) and *Jeanne Peyrouton* (1949; Jeanne Peyrouton) through *Die Nacht der Erinnerung* (1957; the night of memory) and *Es gibt kein Erbarmen* (1962;

there is no mercy), offer cut-and-dried stories of people who either grow into the new society, join the proletariat, or perish when they cannot adapt to prevailing conditions. Among his more enterprising endeavors are *Das Klassentreffen* (1968; the class reunion) and *Abschied von Parler* (1972; farewell to Parler), in which Joho compared situations in East and West Germany.

The most talented newcomer was Stephan Hermlin. His works combine demanding aestheticism with clear ideological commitment. The result is some of the best fiction that has come from East Germany. The surrealistic dreams and illusions of the novella *Der Leutnant Yorck von Wartenburg* (1946; Lieutenant Yorck of Wartenburg) reflect great narrative skill and psychological insight. Careful interweaving of dream and reality also contribute to the compelling presentation of *Reise eines Malers in Paris* (1947; journey of a painter in Paris). His strongest anti-fascist productions are the short prose selections in *Die Zeit der Gemeinsamkeit* (1950; *City on a Hill*, 1962). The title story offers vivid depictions of the Jewish experience in the Warsaw Ghetto, while other pieces deal sensitively with the lives of people in occupied France. *Corneliusbrücke* (1968; Cornelius bridge) is interesting for its color and its realistic projection of the atmosphere of Hermlin's childhood, but it lacks decisive political commitment.

Although anti-fascist themes and grappling with the war remained important during the 1950s, many new authors began to emphasize the problems of socialist reconstruction and the building of the new society. Reconstruction narratives often suffer from black-and-white sketching of problems, stereotyped characters, and artificiality, but the focus on contemporary reality also yields opportunities for freshness and vitality.

Erich Loest's (b. 1926) career can be divided into two distinct periods separated by years of political imprisonment. His early novels, *Jungen, die übrig blieben* (1950; boys who remained), *Die Westmark fällt weiter* (1952; the West German mark continues to fall), and *Aktion Bumerang* (1957; operation boomerang), focus on the war or its immediate aftermath. *Jungen, die übrig blieben* is his best work of the period. It portrays young men who emerge from the war psychologically old and illusionless. Later treatments of East German reality, in *Schattenboxen* (1973; shadow boxing) and *Es geht seinen Gang oder Mühen in unserer Ebene* (1978; it goes on as usual; or, efforts on our level), deal only superficially with important political or social problems. Despite plots that are shallow and melodramatic, Loest carefully controls his figures. As a result, his books are generally entertaining, even if not artistic.

One of the most successful writers of the reconstruction period was Erwin Strittmatter (b. 1912). *Der Ochsenkutscher* (1951; the oxcart driver) portrays the author's own development of a social consciousness. *Tinko* (1954; Tinko) and *Ole Bienkopp* (1963; *Ole Bienkopp,* 1966) are ideological sequels to *Der Ochsenkutscher. Tinko* emphasizes the death of the old capitalist era and the birth of the new order, while *Ole Bienkopp* demonstrates that the new society cannot be built by the individualist. Strittmatter's novellas and short stories, in such collections as *Die blaue Nachtigall; oder, Der Anfang von etwas* (1973; the blue nightingale; or, the beginning of something) and *Meine Freundin Tina Babe* (1977; my lady friend, Tina Babe), reflect an earthy honesty, a quiet homespun humor, and a degree of complex reality that lend them charm, interest, and readability. Autobiographical elements remain powerfully compelling in *Der Laden* (1983; the store), a combination of social commentary and artistic accomplishment that is very enjoyable reading.

Autobiography is also important in the novels and stories of Jurij Brězan (b. 1916), a Sorb whose German-language writings depend upon the color, attitudes, and milieu of his origins for their hearty earthiness, humor, and humanity. Brězan did not receive significant recognition until the appearance of his trilogy *Der Gymnasiast* (1958; the high school student), *Semester der verlorenen Zeit* (1960; *The Fallow Years,* 1963), and *Mannesjahre* (1964; manhood). The portrait of Felix Hanusch's development gives interesting insights into the world of the East German Sorbian minority. In later books, such as *Reise nach Krakau* (1966; journey to Cracow), *Der Mäuseturm* (1970; the mouse tower), and *Die Rattenschlacht* (1977; the rat slaughter) Brězan broadened his narrative focus while retaining the folksy, amusing, softly pedagogical tone that gives his writing its unique flavor. His *Bild des Vaters* (1982; picture of the father) is a masterpiece of regional milieu dominated by powerful, fundamental emotions and uncomplicated reflection.

Another popular regional author is Herbert Nachbar (b. 1930). The locale of his colorful narratives is Mecklenburg, with its fishing villages. In *Der Mond hat einen Hof* (1956; ring around the moon) and *Die Hochzeit von Länneken* (1960; the Länneken wedding) he demonstrated his ability to create strong, original figures, although some of them are weakened by a contrived complacency. Nachbar does not reach his full artistic potential in most of his works. Even his best creation, *Ein dunkler Stern* (1973; a dark star), suffers from superficiality and oversimplification.

The satirical short fiction of Günter Kunert (b. 1929) was an unusual literary phenomenon for the Democratic Republic of the 1950s. Most of the stories in *Der ewige Detektiv und andere Geschichten* (1954; the eternal detective and other stories) are relatively harmless, with the exception of a few barbs directed against fellow writers. In *Tagträume* (1964; daydreams), *Die Beerdigung findet in aller Stille statt* (1968; a private funeral will be held), and *Tagträume in Berlin und andernorts* (1972; daydreams in Berlin and elsewhere) the satire became more biting, more direct, more precise. Kunert has not been very successful with longer forms, but some of his experiments have opened interesting new dimensions for his writing. The recent volume *Zurück ins Paradies* (1984; back to paradise) presents Kunert at his best.

A more typical short-story writer was Franz Fühmann (1922–84). *Kameraden* (1955; comrades) set the tone for his prose. The dominant theme is German fascism, its prerequisites, early symptoms, and effects. Fühmann's narratives are simple and straightforward; authenticity is contributed by the deft processing of personally experienced, familiar material. In *Kabelkran und Blauer Peter* (1961; cable crane and Blue Peter) the stories are based on his experiences in a workers' brigade on the docks of Warnemünde. Fühmann's most personal creation is the cycle contained in *Das Judenauto* (1962; *The Car with the Yellow Star*, 1968), portraits of the stations in the life of a young man who symbolizes the entire generation that was deceived by Hitler. The theme of the betrayed generation is also strongly visible in *König Ödipus* (1966; Oedipus Rex) and *Der Jongleur im Kino oder Die Insel der Träume* (1970; the juggler in the movies; or, the island of dreams). In *Die Geliebte der Morgenröte* (1978; the dawn's beloved) Fühmann returned to questions of self-definition that were the stimulus for many earlier stories.

Specific problems of individual adjustment to the new society are a primary basis for the fiction of Brigitte Reimann (1933–73). *Die Frau am Pranger* (1956; the woman in the pillory) and *Das Geständnis* (1960; the confession) reflect both talent and immaturity in their contrived, oversimplified treatment of complex situations. *Ankunft im Alltag* (1961; arrival in the everyday world), a product of the Bitterfeld Movement, is more realistic, more natural, but it lacks polish in the development of characters and the treatment of detail. Reimann's first successful novel is *Die Geschwister* (1963; brother and sister), a penetrating study of the conflicts faced by the new generation of East German intellectuals. The fragmentary *Franziska Linkerhand* (1974; Franziska Linkerhand), with its broken mosaic style of alternating perspectives, phases, flashbacks, portraits, and memories, is a powerful psychological analysis of the maturing of a modern East German woman.

The first internationally successful postwar East German novel was Bruno Apitz's (1900–79) *Nackt unter Wölfen* (1958; *Naked Among Wolves*, 1960). Based on experiences at Buchenwald, this work derives its effect from the power of events rather than from literary form or style. Roughness of language combines with clear, simple narrative to create a gripping story, but without specific development of psychological elements. Among Apitz's later works are the novella *Esther* (1959; Esther), a different kind of treatment of concentration-camp life, and *Der Regenbogen* (1977; the rainbow), a novel about a proletarian family. *Schwelbrand* (1984; smoldering fire) is a loose sequel to *Der Regenbogen* that reflects more ideological commitment than literary mastery.

Irmtraud Morgner (b. 1933) wrote her first stories about problems of individual change in the new society. Neither *Das Signal steht auf Fahrt* (1959; the signal is set at go) nor *Ein*

Haus am Rand der Stadt (1962; a house on the edge of the city) transcends mediocrity. Morgner's real contribution to East German fiction began only when she deviated from standard approaches. *Hochzeit in Konstantinopel* (1968; wedding in Constantinople) is the first of several imaginative works that respond to East German social reality with escape into a private world of fantasy, dream, and tall tale. Later volumes, including the surrealistic fairy tale *Gauklerlegende* (1970; legend of the traveling entertainer) and *Die wunderbaren Reisen Gustavs des Weltfahrers* (1972; the wonderful journeys of Gustav the world traveler), offer subtle criticism of a land in which citizens can travel abroad only in dream and imagination. Morgner's best creations are *Leben und Abenteuer der Trobadora Beatriz nach Zeugnissen ihrer Spielfrau* (1974; life and adventures of the lady troubadour Beatrice according to the testimony of her minstrel) and its sequel, *Amanda: Ein Hexenroman* (1983; Amanda: a witch novel). Skillful weaving of fiction, nonfiction, fantasy, and social criticism yield unusually artistic treatments of women's liberation themes.

Around 1960, the tone of East German prose began to change. The question was no longer the building of socialism but, rather, the individual's situation in the socialistic community. Dominant themes of this period include the nature of the German Democratic Republic as a country, but also a continued preoccupation with the past. One visible tendency is a strong concern for the tension between individual and society.

Manfred Bieler (b. 1934) received recognition in the late 1950s as a parodist and radio playwright. His first major narrative was the picaresque novel *Bonifaz oder Der Matrose in der Flasche* (1963; *The Sailor in the Bottle,* 1965). In spite of its open satire, its tone is harmlessly humorous. The same cannot be said about *Maria Morzeck oder Das Kaninchen bin ich* (1969; Maria Morzeck; or, I am the rabbit), which Bieler published after he emigrated to the Federal Republic. *Maria Morzeck* lacks the positive hero demanded by socialist realism. Its sharply pointed criticism of the East German state and its justice system is enhanced by careful attention to realistic details. Some of Bieler's best work appears in books of short stories, especially *Märchen und Zeitungen* (1966; fairy tales and newspapers) and *Der junge Roth* (1968; young Roth). His parables of guilt, immorality, hate, murder, and punishment feature undemanding language and powerful symbolism. With his later novels, from *Der Mädchenkrieg* (1975; *The Three Daughters,* 1978), to *Der Bär* (1983; the bear), Bieler has been extremely successful in turning unreflected realism into money.

Problems of life in the postwar world and of grappling with the past are also the primary substance of Günter de Bruyn's (b. 1926) fiction. *Wiedersehen an der Spree* (1962; reunion on the Spree) is an autobiographical work that suffers from defects of style and presentation. In *Ein schwarzer, abgrundtiefer See* (1962; a black, abyss-deep lake) there are glimmerings of literary polish but also many signs of continuing narrative uncertainty. Not until *Buridans Esel* (1968; *Buridan's Ass,* 1973) did de Bruyn present a compelling picture of East German social conditions. This novel's strength lies in its wit, irony, effective use of language, and variations in style and perspective. The story itself is mundane. *Buridan's Ass* is also the pinnacle of de Bruyn's achievement. *Die Preisverleihung* (1972; the award) contains excessive character descriptions that dampen the action and conflict. *Neue Herrlichkeit* (1984; new glory) offers humor as its only redeeming feature.

Karl-Heinz Jakobs (b. 1929) and Erik Neutsch (b. 1931) approach life in the Democratic Republic from the perspective of reconstruction and its inherent conflicts. For Jakobs the point of departure is a peculiar search for adventure on East German construction sites. Neutsch also focuses on industrial contexts, but from the deliberately programmed point of view of the Bitterfeld Movement.

In Jakobs's *Das grüne Land* (1961; the green land) the "adventure" provides stimulus for decision-making. For the most part, figures and situations are neither compelling nor especially convincing. There are no serious conflicts, and the approach is primarily abbreviation and understatement. Among his early works only *Beschreibung eines Sommers* (1961; description of a summer) transcends the mediocrity of stock phrases and forced optimism. Other works, from *Eine Pyramide für mich* (1971; a pyramid for me) through *Wüste kehr wieder* (1977; desert, return), consistently reflect Jakobs's professed stance of noncritical portrayal, but the results are generally flat.

The narratives in Erik Neutsch's *Bitterfeld Geschichten* (1961; Bitterfeld stories) are typical products of the Bitterfeld Movement. They contain color, facts about specialized work processes, and milieu details, but the conflicts are superficial and contrived, while the resolution of problems is trite and artificial. Neutsch's most important creation remains *Spur der Steine* (1964; trace of the stones), an enormous, roughhewn panorama of life in the Democratic Republic from 1959 to 1961. The novel's value lies in what it reveals about East German conditions, and not in its artistry. Neutsch's later writings, including the stories in *Die anderen und ich* (1970; the others and I), the novel *Auf der Suche nach Gatt* (1973; in search of Gatt), and the trilogy *Der Friede im Osten* (1974–85; peace in the East), continue to demonstrate a failure to process interesting material into polished art.

Dieter Noll's (b. 1927) two-volume novel *Die Abenteuer des Werner Holt* (1960, 1963; the adventures of Werner Holt) approaches the past and reconstruction through a revival of the individual development novel. The work is only partially successful. Although the first book gives a relatively penetrating portrayal of problems experienced by the young generation during and after the war, the second part features worn-out clichés, stereotyped experiences, and programmatic results. A later novel, *Kippenberg* (1979; Kippenberg), fails to avoid similar weaknesses.

One of the most important reconstruction authors was Christa Wolf (b. 1929). Among the few significant novels produced by the Bitterfeld Movement was her *Der geteilte Himmel* (1963; *Divided Heaven,* 1976). Wolf's experiences in a Halle railroad-car factory provided both material and psychological realism for the novel, but its narrative strength is primarily a function of successful balance between action and reflection. *Nachdenken über Christa T.* (1969; *The Quest for Christa T.,* 1970) is more complex than *Divided Heaven* but less satisfying. Plot and action are subordinated entirely to the analytical process, with the result that narrative momentum is repeatedly lost. Wolf's writings of the 1970s reveal an intensification of her attempts to master both the problems of the times and those of literary expression. The "improbable" stories in *Unter den Linden* (1974; Unter den Linden) achieve their effect through elements of the fantastic, the grotesque, and the absurd, while *Kindheitsmuster* (1976; *A Model Childhood*, 1980), is a combination of fiction, reflected autobiography, and theoretical essay. *Kassandra* (1983; *Cassandra*, 1984) is the most recent step in Wolf's retreat into introspection and definition of her own role as a writer.

Another successful creator of reconstruction fiction is Hermann Kant (b. 1926). His novel *Die Aula* (1965; the auditorium) has become a classic of East German literature. *Die Aula* is remarkable for an engaging style that produces multiple narrative levels, flashbacks, inner monologues, and the marks of an ironic skepticism. It examines complex problems, refuses to justify the failings of the new society, offers realistic criticism, presents believable, interesting characters, and gives powerful insight into the spirit of the reconstruction era. *Das Impressum* (1972; the journal) also gives significant insights into reconstruction society, but it is more programmatic than *Die Aula,* and lacks its captivating freshness. *Der Aufenthalt* (1977; the stay), an autobiographically toned analysis of prisoner-of-war experiences, is an important document of subjectivism and grappling with the past. Kant has also published interesting short fiction in *Der dritte Nagel* (1982; the third nail) and *Schöne Elise* (1983; pretty Elise). The most attractive aspect of his stories is their witty satire.

The East German author whose works are least choked by the constraints of program or ideology was Johannes Bobrowski (1917–65). For Bobrowski, the creation of novels and short stories was a deeply personal process of atonement. His masterpiece, *Levins Mühle* (1964; Levin's Mill, 1970), uses sardonic, recondite, double-edged humor and parodistic understatement to create a powerful portrayal of basic human flaws and their bearing on the relations between peoples. Although his *Litauische Claviere* (1966; Lithuanian pianos) is artistically less satisfying than *Levin's Mill,* it offers a stronger presentation of the theme of German guilt toward Eastern

European neighbors. In these two novels and some three dozen short stories Bobrowski intertwined past and present, tradition and cultural reality, soft humor and uncomfortable satire—in pointed revelations of history's impact on modern life.

Benito Wogatzki (b. 1932) is a master of dramatic tension. His early narratives *Ein Tag und eine Nacht* (1965; a day and a night) and *Der Schmied und seine Frau* (1969; the smith and his wife) deal with the world of work in an interesting fashion. Wogatzki avoids the boredom of triviality through the successful use of dialogues and changing levels of action. His *Romanze mit Amélie* (1977; romance with Amélie) rejects standard socialist plot models in favor of picaresque wit and irony. Humor and satire also contribute to the success of *Das Narrenfell* (1982; the fool's pelt), a picaresque novel about the reconstruction period, and *Schwalbenjagd* (1985; swallow hunt), an exploration of interpersonal problems in contemporary society.

Fritz Rudolf Fries's (b. 1935) *Der Weg nach Oobliadooh* (1966; *The Road to Oobliadooh,* 1968) is another example of experimentation with the picaresque approach. Because of a pessimistic focus on East German intellectual dropouts, it was rejected for publication in the Democratic Republic. The works that have made Fries visible in East Germany, including *Der Fernsehkrieg und andere Erzählungen* (1968; the television war and other stories) and *Das Luft-Schiff* (1974; the air ship), are notable for their mediation of Spanish and Spanish-American culture, but many of his short stories are mundane and pointless. Fries's best work is perhaps *Verlegung eines mittleren Reiches* (1984; transfer of a middle empire), a satirical chronicle of future events presented as an illumination of present conditions and the disasters that threaten the world.

The narratives of Manfred Jendryschik (b. 1943) reflect significant experimentation. His short stories in *Glas und Ahorn* (1967; glass and acorn) and *Die Fackel und die Bart* (1971; the torch and the beard) emphasize precise description of everyday life in the Democratic Republic, but they also focus on problems of the past. Often the accounts are unrounded and open depictions of modern lives in which the past still plays a decisive role. The novel *Johanna oder die Wege des Dr. Kanuga* (1973; Johanna; or, the ways of Dr. Kanuga) is a deceptively complex rendition of the stock socialist transformation of the individual into a viable member of the new society. Its experiments with language are something new in the East German prose of the time. Jendryschik's increasing mastery of a complete fusion of language, form, and content is most visible in *Der feurige Gaukler auf dem Eis* (1981; the fiery entertainer on the ice), where artistic miniatures captivate the reader in a realm in which reality and fantasy are difficult to separate.

Developments in fiction during the late 1960s and the 1970s were diverse and complex. East German novelists and storytellers turned their narrative focus inward. Among the results of this increased subjectivism was a renewed preoccupation with overcoming the past. At the same time, strong emphasis was placed on the situation of children, youth, and women. Of particular interest were problems related to personal development, conflict with established order, and search for identity. Family life, education processes, public institutions, and the negative influence of the state—all these came under closer scrutiny as conformity, competition, and unhealthy strivings emerged as pathological products of current reality.

Vivid examples of the rejection of programmed literature are found in the highly successful novels of Jurek Becker (b. 1937). *Jakob der Lügner* (1968; *Jacob the Liar,* 1975) has become a unique classic of anti-fascist literature. Its peculiarity is not its Jewish-ghetto substance but its intensely human approach to the characters' situation. Although less compelling, *Irreführung der Behörden* (1973; deceiving the authorities) is a successful variation on the theme of coping with reality through creation of a mask of lies. *Der Boxer* (1976; the boxer) and *Schlaflose Tage* (1978; *Sleepless Days,* 1979) are dominated by bitter resignation in the face of society's inability to satisfy basic human needs. The stories in *Nach der ersten Zukunft* (1980; after the immediate future) and the novels *Aller Welt Freund* (1982; friend of all the world) and *Bronsteins Kinder* (1986; Bronstein's children) reflect a continuing progression toward disillusionment caused by the deterioration of basic human relationships. Becker's works exhibit literary power, originality, maturity of conception, and balance of composition that are quite rare in East German fiction.

Klaus Schlesinger (b. 1937) explores individual confrontation with past and present as part of the process of self-realization. *Michael* (1971; Michael) is his major attempt to present the difficulties of overcoming the fascist past. It is less interesting than *Alte Filme* (1975; old films) and the stories of *Berliner Traum* (1977; Berlin dream), where he offers variations on the modern individual's everyday frustrations, dreams, and attempts to escape from oppressive realities. Schlesinger's best creations feature precise language and directness of expression. His penetration to the psychological and social roots of today's alienation has made his texts very important for the progress of East German fiction.

Helga Schütz's (b. 1937) grapplings with the past in *Vorgeschichten oder Schöne Gegend Probstein* (1970; early stories; or, the beautiful Probstein area), *Das Erdbeben bei Sangershausen und andere Geschichten* (1972; the earthquake near Sangershausen and other stories), *Festbeleuchtung* (1974; festival illumination), and *Jette in Dresden* (1977; Jette in Dresden) reflect the strong influence of Johannes Bobrowski, both in style and power of observation. Her most convincing narratives are subtle, humorous interpretations of situations and characters from her native Silesia. *Julia oder Erziehung zum Chorgesang* (1981; Julia; or, education in choral singing) is one of the better recent studies of individual adjustment to modern East German conditions.

Analytical autobiography and calculated social criticism form the bases for Volker Braun's (b. 1939) *Das ungezwungene Leben Kasts* (1972; Kast's unconstrained life). What gives Braun's prose its vitality and attraction is the honest rejection of prescribed attitudes and perceptions of life under socialism. The stories clearly document the author's separate opinion about modern reality. Braun's nonconformity has made him controversial. His *Hinze-Kunze-Roman,* with its free play of sexual themes, created a scandal even before it appeared. The escalation of criticism of governmental hypocrisy and repressive exploitation is tastelessly framed, but it is all the more powerful for its uniqueness.

The short stories in Bernd Jentzsch's (b. 1940) anthologies *Jungfer im Grünen und andere Geschichten* (1973; virgin on the green and other stories) and *Ratsch und ade!* (1975; rip and adieu!) are also documents of protest, but they are softer in tone than Braun's writings. In the first volume, Jentzsch offers a plea to respect human individuality, even when it contributes to unusual behavior. Most pieces in the second collection benefit from experimentation with grotesque, fantastic, and fairy-tale elements, but one or two of them are very direct.

One writer who has emphasized feminine roles is Waldtraut Lewin (b. 1937). Known especially for her historical novels, Lewin employs history to examine the present. In her trilogy about Roman slavery, *Herr Lucius und sein Schwarzer Schwan* (1973; Lord Lucius and his black swan), *Die Ärztin von Lakros* (1977; the woman doctor of Lacros), and *Die stillen Römer* (1979; the quiet Romans), she created a remarkably differenti-ated picture of the times through skilled characterization. Her most interesting contribution to women's literature is the gro-tesque artistic fairy tale *Der Sohn des Adlers, des Müllmanns und der häßlichsten Frau der Welt* (1981; the son of the eagle, the garbage collector, and the ugliest woman in the world). With *Federico* (1984; Federico) she illuminated the life of Fred-erick II from a uniquely feminine perspective. Lewin has also experimented with short stories, but the volume *Kuckucksrufe und Ohrfeigen* (1983; cuckoo calls and slaps in the face) reveals a degree of narrative uncertainty and lack of facility with more limited forms.

The existential problems of East German youth form the basis for the fiction of Ulrich Plenzdorf (b. 1934). His *Die neuen Leiden des jungen W.* (1973; *The New Sufferings of Young W.*, 1979) is a critical commentary on the idealized reception of German classicism and a pointed statement about the younger generation's self-perception. Plenzdorf's most biting indict-ment of a society that fails to satisfy basic emotional and spiritual needs is *Legende vom Glück ohne Ende* (1979; legend of unending happiness). In masterful language it presents the idea that inner deprivation robs the individual of the power to build the future.

To some extent the sketches of Thomas Brasch (b. 1945) complement the works of Plenzdorf. Brasch's protests, in *Vor den Vätern sterben die Söhne* (1977; the sons die before the

fathers) and *Rotter und weiter* (1978; Rotter and onward), are
little more than snatches of existential thought. Very few of
them are finished pieces of art. Rather, they outline experience
with the East German political/social order, augmenting the
picture of frustration through critical exploration of the endless versions of flight from external and internal reality.

The theme of escape from normal existence is also an important aspect of Jürgen Lehmann's (b. 1934) *Strandgesellschaft*
(1979; beach party). Like the stories in *Begegnung mit einem
Zauberer* (1976; encounter with a magician), *Strandgesellschaft* features a quietly ironic undertone in descriptions
of conflicts that force the individual to search for personal identity and self-realization. *Hochzeitsbilder* (1984;
wedding pictures) offers new variations of the same themes,
but it is not very successful because the author fails to crys-
tallize his concerns amid the impressionistic images.

A popular form of exploring social alienation is illumination
of tragic historical figures, especially artists. Berndt Wagner's
(b. 1948) anthologies *Das Treffen* (1976; the meeting) and *G. in
B.* (1979; G. in B.) describe individuals in their subjection to
time and history. The second book is somewhat more political
than the first, but both works reflect a significant talent for the
psychological penetration of characters. Wagner's idea of confinement within the historical context is applied to the human
condition in East Germany in the sketches of *Reise im Kopf*
(1984; travel in the mind). By merging fantasy and reality,
conscious and unconscious experience, Wagner provides an
original approach to vicarious encounters with foreign and
exotic places.

Increased stress on fantasy is almost pathological in the
1980s. Escape into the realm of the mind culminates in insanity, resignation, and despair. Mental illness is a more and
more typical symbol for external reality and the individual's
sense of isolation and impending disaster.

In Christoph Hein's (b. 1944) *Einladung zum Lever Bourgeois* (1980; invitation to the bourgeois levee) figures such as
Jean Racine and Alexander von Humboldt's servant Johann
Seifert struggle with the tensions between physical and mental abnormality. The novella *Der fremde Freund* (1982; the

foreign friend) is a singularly disturbing but powerful portrayal of the Democratic Republic as a nation in which everyone has a wounded psyche, and where hope lies in senility.

Alcoholism, purposeless sex, and suicide are signs of parallel mental and social decay in *Schattenriß eines Liebhabers* (1980; silhouette of a lover) by Rosemarie Zeplin (b. 1939). Her treatments of the problems of achieving equality for women within socialist society do not strike a strong blow for feminism. It is as though her sickly female characters do not deserve emancipation. *Alpträume aus der Provinz* (1984; nightmares from the province) is somewhat more convincing than her earlier writings. Zeplin succeeds especially well in conveying the oppressive atmosphere of small-town life, with its pettiness, lies, and façades, but the overall result remains tedious and the reading depressing.

Fear of confrontation with self is another symptom of an individual's inability to cope with reality. Manfred Pieske's (b. 1937) novel *Schnauzer* (1980; Schnauzer) portrays the inner world of a man who has become an integrated citizen of the new society without resolving the tension between his past and present. Although Pieske's character portrayal is clear and convincing, the resolution of the psychological conflict is weak. His short stories, in *Vom viel zu kleinen Glückspfenning* (1981; about the lucky penny that was much too small), *Orpheus in Bärnau* (1983; Orpheus in Bärnau), and *Der Frühling beginnt am Abend* (1985; spring begins in the evening), reveal a progressive polishing of style but simultaneous degeneration into triviality and superficiality.

One exception to the continuingly dismal picture of existence is Karl Hermann Roehricht's (b. 1928) autobiographical trilogy *Vorstadtkindheit* (1981; suburban childhood), *Großstadtmittag* (1982; big-city midday), and *Waldsommerjahre* (1982; forest summer years). These novels focus on experiences of childhood and the problems of finding a personal reality within the new society. What makes them different from so many others is a strong sense of realistic balance, the author's masterful use of pictorial talent to present a carefully diverse group of characters, and a remarkable feeling for the vitality of the human comedy.

POETRY

The most difficult challenge for East German poets during the early postwar years was the necessity to wrestle with the Nazi legacy. Things that had to be confronted were the nationalistic ballads of fascist writers, the sterile classicism of the older generation, and the escapist nature poetry of the "inner emigration." Lyrics of the late 1940s were static and conservative. They avoided directness and concreteness. Poets often withdrew into a metaphysical sphere where fascist villains became demons. Many lyricists imitated earlier writers and each other.

Major emigrant authors struggled with postwar reality. They could not write about the beauties of nature without remaining silent about the war and its horrors. At the same time, aggressive, militant, revolutionary, agitation poetry no longer fit the circumstances of life. As a result, two kinds of verse dominated those early years; retrospective attacks on Nazism and proclamations of the bright future promised by a Marxist Germany. Poets who were unwilling or unable to conform to these patterns either quit writing or moved to other literary forms.

The dominant lyricists in the first years after the war were returned exiles. Among them were Johannes R. Becher (1891–1958), Louis Fürnberg (1909–57), and Bertolt Brecht.

In opposition to the aestheticism, isolationism, and esotericism practiced in the West, Johannes R. Becher defended reality and tradition. The collections *Heimkehr* (1946; homecoming), *Wiedergeburt* (1947; rebirth), and *Volk im Dunkel wandelnd* (1948; nation wandering in darkness) document his major theme: Germany and its people in a time of change. Later books, such as *Neue deutsche Volkslieder* (1950; new German folk songs), *Liebe ohne Ruh* (1957; love without rest), and *Schritt der Jahrhundertmitte* (1958; stride of mid-century), expanded the realm of acceptable themes to include love, nature, and the new socialist individual. Becher's poetry was treated by many younger writers as a model for emulation—which contributed enormously to the flatness, triteness, and insipidness of their productions. Most of Becher's late works lack vividness, concreteness, poetic tension, and compelling substance.

Louis Fürnberg could never quite fit his creations to the realities in which he lived. He had written agitation and propaganda poetry in the 1930s. Superficiality and political naiveté remained typical for his postwar lyrics. *Der Bruder Namenlos* (1947; brother nameless), *Wanderer in den Morgen* (1951; wanderers in the mornings), and *Das wunderbare Gesetz* (1956; the wonderful law) contain political verse that repeatedly glorifies the party, Lenin, Stalin, and the Soviet Union. His nature, love, and philosophical lyrics are of like quality. Their superficial use of language, careless form, and random flow of ideas mark his failure to transcend artistic mediocrity.

Of the returning emigrants, only Bertolt Brecht produced poetry that had strength and originality. His lyric production during the first postwar years was sparse. New collections appeared in the 1950s: *Hundert Gedichte* (1951; a hundred poems), *Gedichte* (1955; poems), *Gedichte und Lieder* (1956; poems and songs), and *Lieder und Gesänge* (1957; songs and hymns). What influenced Brecht's contemporaries most was his ability to distinguish between old and new elements in the developing society and to exercise criticism accordingly. His epic and didactic lyrics became strong models for the new poetry of social and political activism.

Brecht's creations of the period treat a broad diversity of themes. He wrote love and nature poetry, descriptions of memories, humorous and sad poems about the general human condition. The lyrics of his late years lost their emphasis on practicality and placed a new stress on beauty. The recently published *Gedichte über die Liebe* (1982; poems on love) contains many items not available earlier. They are not his best efforts, but they exemplify his consistent directness of approach.

Not all poets who returned to East Germany had been political emigrants. Peter Huchel (1903–81) had fought in the German army. *Gedichte* (1948; poems) and *Die Sternenreuse* (1967; the star basket) contain prewar poetry that formed the basis for later production. Huchel was a nature poet of the highest caliber. His early pieces set a pattern of precision, detail, and effective use of language and poetic form.

The works he created in East Germany are of two kinds.

Desolation and coldness dominate his nature studies, while other lyrics declare his enthusiastic support for the political and social changes that occurred during the early years of the new society. Huchel's eventual loss of faith in East German political policies, increasing melancholy, and feelings of isolation are extremely visible in *Chauseen Chauseen* (1963; highways highways) and *Gezählte Tage* (1972; numbered days). Pessimism is magnified to a strong preoccupation with death in *Die neunte Stunde* (1979; the ninth hour). Although he did not write a great deal, his poems are among the very best written in German since 1945.

Georg Maurer (1907–71) returned to East Germany from a Soviet prisoner of war camp. His *Gesänge der Zeit* (1948; hymns of the time) maintained the religious tone that had dominated his prewar creations. The volumes that he published during the 1950s, from *42 Sonette* (1953; 42 sonnets) and *Die Elemente* (1955; the elements) through *Lob der Venus* (1958; praise of Venus) and *Poetische Reise* (1959; poetic journey), reflect increasing artistic maturity parallel to his abandonment of religious themes in favor of other concerns. Representative volumes of his late years, *Gestalten der Liebe* (1964; figures of love), *Variationen* (1965; variations), *Gespräche* (1967; conversations), and *Kreise* (1970; circles), mirror unadorned directness that often renders his art dry and tedious.

The most important new poet of the 1940s was Stephan Hermlin. He is unusual for his eclecticism. French surrealism and German expressionism provided him with important models of form, syntax, language, imagery, mood, and theme. In his creations these elements are combined with a strong ideological commitment to communism. Some of his best poems are in *Zwölf Balladen von den großen Städten* (1944; twelve ballads of the great cities), which established the tone and themes for *Zweiundzwanzig Balladen* (1947; twenty-two ballads). Hermlin's early lyrics feature bold, often harsh imagery, conscious stylization, and the use of elaborate esoteric and technical vocabulary. Their vitality and virtuosity are painfully missing in the propagandistic *Mansfelder Oratorium* (1950: Mansfeld oratorio) and *Der Flug der Taube* (1952; the flight of the dove).

The works of Kurt Barthel (1914–67), who wrote under the pseudonym Kuba, are intended only to serve the state. His lyrics in *Gedicht vom Menschen* (1948; poem about man), *Kantate auf Stalin* (1949; cantata to Stalin), *Gedichte* (1961; poems), *Brot und Wein* (1961; bread and wine), and *Wort auf Wort wächst das Lied* (1969; the song grows word after word) lack concreteness and linguistic power. His agitation and propaganda poems and his tractor-romanticism are trivial and boring, but the hymns to Stalin are noteworthy for the unintended humor produced by their seriousness.

Early on, Armin Müller (b. 1928) was an enthusiastic singer of the new order. Creations in *Hallo, Bruder aus Krakau* (1949; hello, brother from Cracow) and *Seit jenem Mai* (1953; since that May) are uniformly optimistic in their naive descriptions of East German rural happiness, the confidence of the workers, and the beauties of the new nation. Beginning with *Das weiße Schiff* (1959; the white ship), doubts begin to appear. Elements of fear and mourning are projected in dark images, within poems that protest against events in Korea and atomic warfare while also illuminating East German reality. The tempered despair of *Reise nach S.* (1965; journey to S.) and *Auf weißen Pferden* (1983; on white horses) is an almost profound experience.

East German poetry of the 1950s is varied and diverse. Strong subjectivity appears in the productions of writers whose backgrounds and experience were significantly different. Their verse reflects marked disparity in political attitudes. The central problem of poetry during this period is the relationship of the individual to society. It is not always treated successfully or critically, and there is a strong tendency to versify new themes without examining problems and contradictions. Superficial affirmation and a feeling of being beyond fascism are very apparent in writings of the younger generation.

Two phases mark the poetry of Günter Kunert. *Wegschilder und Mauerinschriften* (1950; road signs and wall inscriptions), *Unter diesem Himmel* (1955; beneath this sky), *Tagwerke* (1960; daily work), and *Das kreuzbrave Liederbuch* (1961; the well-behaved songbook) feature a positive belief in social progress and universal human rebirth. The stance of the poems is calm and reserved. Kunert employed traditional structures successfully, but he also developed his own versions of Brecht's dialectical and epic forms. During his later period, represented in *Der ungebetene Gast* (1965; the uninvited guest), *Verkündigung des Wetters* (1966; weather forecast), *Warnung vor Spiegeln* (1970; warning against mirrors), *Unterwegs nach Utopia* (1977; on the way to utopia), *Verlangen nach Bomarzo: Reisegedichte* (1978; longing for Bomarzo: travel poems), and *Abtötungsverfahren* (1980; mortification procedures), his poems became increasingly skeptical, bitter, and sad. *Abtötungsverfahren* and *Stilleben* (1983; still life) are no less powerful for their extreme subjectivism. Kunert's private struggles with silence, lost dreams, loneliness, and death are among the most important lyric productions of the last forty years.

Erich Arendt's (b. 1903) early lyric creations mirror the influence of German expressionism, but their themes emerge from personal experience. *Trug doch die Nacht den Albatros* (1951; the night did carry the albatross) and *Bergwindballade* (1952; mountain-wind ballad) document impressions from the Spanish Civil War and grapplings with the specter of fascism. *Tolu* (1956; Tolu) is an outcry against the situation of blacks and South American Indians. In later years he expanded his substance to include classical mythology, Baltic scenes, sea, moon, and wind. Collections such as *Feuerhalm* (1973; fire straw) and *Zeitsaum* (1978; hem of time) exhibit power in describing contrasts, but they are increasingly dark and hermetic. Although his best poems belong to his early period, even his most recent creations are better than most of those produced in East Germany.

In Franz Fühmann's poetry there is a naive affirmation of the new order. *Die Fahrt nach Stalingrad* (1953; the journey to Stalingrad) and *Die Nelke Nikos* (1953; Niko's carnation) attempt to explain past events, strengthen hope for the future, and describe the differences between postwar socialist society and the West's decadence. His most original creations appear in *Aber die Schöpfung soll dauern* (1957; but creation should last) and *Die Richtung der Märchen* (1962; the direction of fairy tales). There he suggested that his own era was a time when fairy-tale wishes began to come true. In these late volumes there is a decline in blatant propaganda poetry and an increase in reflected presentation, but Fühmann never dealt effectively with the real problems of the times.

Influenced by Johannes R. Becher, Paul Wiens (1922–82) wrote agitation and propaganda poetry that promoted activism, painted optimistic pictures of the future, and glorified the prosaic concreteness of life in the new order. After *Beredte Welt* (1953; eloquent world) appeared, he ceased relying on pathos for poetic effect. In *Nachrichten aus der dritten Welt* (1957; news from the third world) he retreated from popular fashion into a more subjective poetic world, where he could focus on his own past, wishes, and fears. His best creations appear in *Dienstgeheimnis* (1968; service secret) and *Vier Linien aus meiner Hand* (1972; four lines from my hand), in which he achieved an interesting processing of feeling without crossing the border into kitsch.

Märzlicht (1954; March light), Hanns Cibulka's (b. 1920) first volume of poems, mirrors its author's affinity for classical and classicistic models. Cibulka processes nature and landscape through the filter of socialist reconstruction. Experiences of childhood, war, and confinement also inform his creations, but the emphasis is on form and condition rather than causes, effects, or processes. Later volumes, from *Zwei Silben* (1959; two syllables) through *Arioso* (1962; arioso), *Umbrische Tage* (1963; Umbrian days), and *Windrose* (1968; wind rose), reveal an uncertain vacillation between nature poetry and political lyrics. One result is a peculiar, melancholy, philosophical verse, filled with pictures of trees, springs, rural houses, and peasants. Collections like *Lebensbaum* (1977; tree of life) and *Der Rebstock* (1980; the grapevine) reflect an inclination to mask critical commentary with manipulated nature imagery. *Der Rebstock* is a poetic masterpiece.

Heinz Kahlau (b. 1931) published three volumes of mediocre political songs and propaganda lyrics: *Hoffnung lebt in den Zweigen der Caiba* (1954; hope lives in the caiba's branches), *Probe* (1956; test), and *Die Maisfibel* (1960; the corn primer). Although *Der Fluß der Dinge* (1964; the flow of things) shows an increase in poetic reflection, even there Kahlau only made observations. He did not interpret or offer direct criticism. In *Balladen* (1971; ballads), *Du* (1972; you), and *Flugbrett für Engel* (1973; flight board for angels), socialist moralizing is replaced somewhat by simple, artful reports about everyday life and work, but there is also development of themes from legend and elsewhere. *Bögen* (1981; sheets of paper) and *Fundsachen* (1984; things found) feature clever poems that transform impressions into pointed commentary about personal and public life.

Like Kahlau, Helmut Preißler (b. 1925) is a disciple of Brecht. His creations are songs, agitation and propaganda lyrics, and didactic epic poetry. Beginning with *Stimmen der Toten* (1957; voices of the dead) and *Stimmen der Lebenden* (1958; voices of the living), he created several volumes of pedestrian, programmatic lyrics about the war, socialist workers, and other heavily belabored themes. Although *Mein erstes Leben* (1983; my first life) has received rave reviews in the East, it only illustrates the strength of official support for thoughtless conformism.

Reiner Kunze (b. 1933) is more versatile, more open, more genuine in his writing than either Kahlau or Preißler. To be sure, the images in the simple, folklike poems of *Vögel über dem Tau* (1959; birds above the dew) are often somewhat overdone in their inwardness, but they reflect a clear commitment to the concept of humanity. The more mature creations in *Widmungen* (1963; dedications) and *Sensible Wege* (1969; sensitive ways) reflect an increasing diversity of theme and approach. Kunze's most productively critical poems appear in *Zimmerlautstärke* (1972; *With the Volume Turned Down, and Other Poems,* 1973) and *Brief mit blauem Siegel* (1973; letter with blue seal). *Auf eigener Hoffnung* (1981; in personal hope), published after Kunze's emigration to the Federal Republic, documents a sudden expansion of the poet's lyrical horizons to include powerful expressions of internal and external changes in his life.

Young poets who began writing in the 1960s were much more critical of their society than those who preceded them. For the first time, authors began to come together in a loose collective. There they read their works to each other, criticized them, and mutually reinforced creative effort. Their common approach to literary art included precise treatment of substance and emphasis on its characteristic elements, sharp reflection of the times with a pointed Marxist focus, and conscious renewal and promotion of classical techniques. There was a strong emphasis on the possibilities for change and improvement. An important problem was the role of the individual in the new society. Some poets attempted to reconcile the community's demands with individual needs, while others became more critically assertive. As a result of rising tension with the establishment, many of them moved to the West.

Christa Reinig (b. 1926) is one of several gifted poets whose lyrical protests precluded the publication of her books in the Democratic Republic. *Die Steine von Finisterre* (1960; the stones of Finisterre) and *Gedichte* (1963; poems) appeared in West Germany before she moved there. They contain poems that are softly ironic and seldom loud in their complaint against conformist establishment demands, restrictive responsibilities, slogans, and political roarings. Her language is laconic, her tone sometimes sarcastic and provocative. The poetry written after her emigration, contained in such books as *Schwalbe von Olevano* (1969; swallow of Olevano) and *Müssigang ist aller Liebe Anfang* (1979; idleness is the beginning of all love), exhibits the irony and humor of her earlier works, but it is more epigrammatic and apodictic.

The lyric anthologies of Johannes Bobrowski are an anomaly in the literary picture of the 1960s. They neither document the younger generation's struggles with socialist reality, nor thoughtlessly affirm the new order. Rather, they are masterfully crafted, hauntingly beautiful outpourings of human feeling. Bobrowski's most important poems appear in *Sarmatische Zeit* (1961; Sarmatian time), *Schattenland Ströme* (1962; shadowland rivers), *Wetterzeichen* (1966; storm signals), and *Im Windgesträuch* (1970; in wind-blown bushes). His works focus on the deep human tragedy that arises out of lack of understanding between individuals and social groups. They are among the very best lyric creations that have been produced in East Germany.

Alphabet des Morgens (1961; morning alphabet) illustrates

Bernd Jentzsch's artistic relationship to Johannes Bobrowski. It also reveals a mature mastery of poetic techniques. Jentzsch's purpose is to illuminate human existence in simple language. In his only other book of poems to date, *Quartiermachen* (1978; arranging quarters), he renewed the approaches of the first volume in attacks on those who have forgotten the horrors of the Nazi era, in retrospective glances at childhood, and in reflections concerning contemporary conditions in East Germany. The results are poems that are strong, carefully conceived, and effective.

Another disciple of Bobrowski is Wulf Kirsten (b. 1934). He is the only regional poet of the younger generation who has produced work of any significance. In *Poesiealbum* (1968; poetry album), *satzanfang* (1970; sentence beginning), *Ziegelbrennersprache* (1975; brickmaker language), *der landgänger* (1976; the land walker), and *Der Bleibaum* (1977; the lead tree) he presents poems from the substance of his childhood. Kirsten's art depends upon the power of sounds for its effect. The most successful elements of his work combine linguistic reflection and language experimentation in presenting natural scenes as historical landscape.

Heinz Czechowski's (b. 1935) art affirms the traditions of the older generation of poets and declines to criticize contemporary East German conditions. Even the best poems of *Nachmittag eines Liebespaares* (1962; afternoon of a pair of lovers) show traces of banality, a lack of poetic tension, and a peculiar emptiness in the use of nature imagery. In *Wasserfahrt* (1967; water journey) and *Schafe und Sterne* (1974; sheep and stars) the poems have grown more substantial, more graphic. *Was mich betrifft* (1981; concerning me) illustrates successful progress away from illusion and superficial ideology, toward a sense of awareness about problems in the relationship between individual and society.

Known for his sensitive, pensive verse, Karl Mickel (b. 1935) produced works that support progressive reforms and reject dogma and ideology. *Lobverse und Beschimpfungen* (1963; poems of praise and insult) and *Vita nova mea* (1967; my new life) reflect the influence of German expressionism and Brecht, while *Eisenzeit* (1975; iron age) and *Odysseus in Ithika* (1976;

Odysseus in Ithaca) emphasize his ties to classical mythology and the classical and baroque periods of German literature. He is especially effective in his interpretations of complex East German reality, which he presents through contrasts, earthy expression, direct description, parody, and satire.

The most notorious protestor of the 1960s was Wolf Biermann (b. 1936). An uncompromising socialist, Biermann produced poetry that attacks injustice, complacency, and the society's failure to fulfill its promises, carry out its responsibilities, and purge itself of hypocrisy, opportunism, exploitation, and other abuses. His embarrassing measurement of East German reality and practice against Marxist theory, and the resulting rejection of his work in the East, made him popular in West Germany. Books such as *Die Drahtharfe* (1965; *The Wire Harp,* 1968), *Mit Marx- und Engelszungen* (1968; with the tongues of Marx and Engels), *Für meine Genossen* (1972; for my comrades), *Deutschland. Ein Wintermärchen* (1972; Germany, a winter's tale), and *Preussischer Ikarus* (1978; Prussian Icarus) are not aesthetically pleasing works, but they contain ballads, songs, and parodies that are notable for their sharpness, clarity, drastic language, directness, and honesty. *Verdrehte Welt—das seh' ich gern* (1982; crazy world—I like to see it) confirms his stature as one of the most powerful political songwriters in Europe.

To a lesser degree, Volker Braun also became a poetic spokesman of the younger generation. *Provokation für mich* (1965; provocation for me) set the tone for several books that challenge the reader to introspection and self-examination. Braun's criticism of the new society is not as sharp as Biermann's, and he more easily walks the line between what can be tolerated in the East and what cannot. In *Wir und nicht sie* (1970; we and not they), *Gegen die symmetrische Welt* (1974; against the symmetrical world), and *Training des aufrechten Gangs* (1979; training to walk upright) polemic has been replaced by the dialectic of present and future, and analysis has become more important than making charges. Braun is especially successful in conveying the complexity of life in the modern socialist state.

Among the writers who protested against Wolf Biermann's

expatriation was Sarah Kirsch (b. 1935). Before moving to West Berlin in 1977, she had published several volumes of love and nature poetry, including *Gespräch mit dem Saurier* (1965; conversation with the saurian), co-authored with Rainer Kirsch (b. 1934), *Landaufenthalt* (1967; a stay in the country), *Zaubersprüche* (1973; magic spells), and *Rückenwind* (1976; tailwind). Some of her best creations contain fairy-tale elements, but her treatments of personal existential problems are also powerful. *La Pagerie* (1980; the pagery) illustrates a special ability to combine delicate language with cynical awareness, while *Erdreich* (1982; earth domain) places renewed emphasis on nature as a counterworld to unpleasant reality. *Katzenleben* (1984; cats' lives) contains some of her most complex works, but many of the individual pieces suffer from forced effect.

The strength of Kurt Bartsch's (b. 1937) poetry lies in its effective satirization of existential questions. In *Zugluft* (1968; draught) the poet established a pattern of precise language, strong metaphors, and ironic expression. His other collections include *Poesiealbum 13* (1968; poetry album 13), *Die Lachmaschine* (1971; the laugh machine), and *Kaderakte* (1979; specialist reports). They contain pointed criticism of petit bourgeois behavior and the dichotomy between public and private morality. Among Bartsch's most successful creations are satirical parodies of poems by other authors, contained in *Die Hölderlinie* (1983; the Hölderlin line).

As a result of the increasing tension between poets and the political establishment, almost all books of verse produced during the 1970s are dominated by a mournful, retreating, bitter poetic subjectivity. The writers attempt to deal with failure to find a place in either East or (for the exiles) West German society. Characteristic tendencies include criticism of middle-class models, alienation from natural lyric forms, rejection of balance between the individual and nature, rejection of poetics based on beauty, and calculated disruption of the communication between poet and reader through language experimentation.

Melancholy informs Harald Gerlach's (b. 1940) lyrics. The experience of scenes in Silesia and Thuringia is filled with impressions of poverty, rain, graveyards, and injustice. *Sprung ins Hafermeer* (1973; leap into the sea of oats) captures village conversations, a brook's course, work in the fields—presenting them in heavy metaphors that define landscape as human living space. Later creations project a deepening isolation while reflecting Gerlach's familiarity with the broad spectrum of cultural tradition. *Nachrichten aus Grimmelshausen* (1984; news from Grimmelshausen) offers poems that are remarkably sophisticated and original while remaining clearly accessible to the reader.

Jürgen Rennert's (b. 1943) *Poesiealbum 75* (1973; poetry album 75) contains a curious mixture of poetic encouragements and sadness. The poet uses nature to approach the relationship between the individual and reality. *Märkische Depeschen* (1976; dispatches from Brandenburg) is more abstract in its approach to such themes as aging and silence. Rennert's imagery is especially vivid. It is dominated by a darkness and pessimism that are sometimes too strong and too stark. *Hoher Mond* (1983; high moon) illustrates the increasing maturity of his language artistry and his ability to integrate successfully impulses from immediate reality and from the Judeo-Christian heritage.

Strong subjectivity is especially visible in the poetry of Eva Strittmatter (b. 1930). In *Ich mach ein Lied aus Stille* (1973; I make a song from silence), *Mondschnee liegt auf den Wiegen* (1975; moon snow lies on the cradles), and *Die eine Rose überwältigt alles* (1977; one rose overpowers everything), she presents simplistic rhymed sketches of encounters with nature and penetration of landscape in the search for an understanding of herself. Her unbroken subjectivity contributes idyllic artificiality to much of what she writes. A one-sided worldview also informs the gloomy, regretful resigned poems of *Zwiegespräch* (1980; dialogues). Alienation and despair are curiously mixed with gentleness and subtle irony in creations that seem effortless and informal. The verse of *Zwiegespräch* and *Heliotrop* (1983; heliotrope) is simple, sincere, direct, and unpretentious, and therein lies its charm.

In *Poesiealbum 89* (1975; poetry album 89) and *Der schöne 27. September* (1980; the beautiful 27th of September), Thomas

Brasch demonstrated a talent for exposing the ills of society through positive ironization. The themes of exploitation, alienation, and oppression are given especially vivid treatment in *Der schöne 27. September,* where he presents impressions of Berlin and America. Although his cynicism and brutality are often juxtaposed with a peculiar lyrical compassion for the downtrodden, the general tone of his work is one of lament at the moral bankruptcy of modern civilization.

Uwe Grüning's (b. 1942) poetry reflects a naive approach to the connections between people and things. *Fahrtmorgen im Dezember* (1977; travel morning in December) illustrates Grüning's subjectivity. The descriptions of landscapes, seasons, and personal relationships to individuals and the elements of tradition are couched in language that avoids metaphor and artificial peculiarity, while projecting private, often darkly elegiac, impressions of past experience. *Spiegelungen* (1981; reflections) and *Im Umkreis der Feuer* (1985; in the circle of fires) strengthen the general feeling of gloom through presentation of anti-utopias, visions of faces amid flower petals contrasted with rotting flesh, and stringent poetic images that offer no answers to painful existential questions. Grüning's evolving strength lies in his ability to employ the symbolic value of natural imagery as a foil for poetological reflections.

Abwesenheit (1979; absence), Wolfgang Hilbig's (b. 1941) first volume of poetry, features lyrics that progress from defiance and rebellion to submission, resignation, and morbid hopelessness. Some of the poems are linguistically playful; all of them reflect longings to belong. The tension between individual and society, and the yearning for humane existence, also dominate *stimme, stimme* (1983; voice, voice). Although the pathos of his verse is often overdone, Hilbig's approach to relationships between present, past, and future is distinctly original.

East German poetry of the 1980s, whether composed by writers still in the Democratic Republic or by exiles, is increasingly pessimistic in tone. Skepticism about the possibility of positive human action is combined with representation of individuals who are lost within society. There is a strong emphasis on death, giving up, and the revelation of spiritual and physical malaise beneath a façade of beauty and life. In the writings of both established poets and newcomers there is a general vision of failed utopia, isolation, and impending catastrophe.

Richard Pietrass's (b. 1946) *Notausgang* (1980; emergency exit) contains carefully crafted, melancholy poems that describe the basic human condition in terms of continued suffering and need. Social, political, and personal hopelessness, uncertainty, and quiet despair are presented with a sensitivity and diversity of expression. Pietrass's refreshing facility with language is especially visible in *Freiheitsmusem* (1983; freedom museum). Precisely, sometimes playfully, the poet examines problems of aging, loneliness, and unfulfillment.

Beneath the diverse nature images of *Der Wind ist auch ein Haus* (1981; the wind is also a house) and the life rhythms of *Im gläsernen Licht der Frühe* (1983; in the glassy light of early morning), by Lothar Walsdorf (b. 1950) lies a seeming indifference to political and social problems. The melancholy tone of his poems is caused by existential rather than ideological conflict. Constant transformation of the lyric ego into various animate and inanimate entities in *Der Wind ist auch ein Haus* is matched by the rampant emotion of a self in flight in the second collection. Walsdorf is not yet consistently successful in his verse, but even his least effective poems offer vitality, color, and sensual language that suggest significant promise for the future.

The poems of Steffen Mensching (b. 1958) are among the most representative recent lyric productions in the East. His *Poesiealbum* (1980; poetry album) and *Erinnerung an eine Milchglasscheibe* (1983: memory of a pane of frosted glass) reveal a significant variety in substance and form, but also a distinct commitment to portrayal of the common person's existence. It is not the passive everyday individual who interests Mensching, but the figure who exists amid contractions, fears, threats of nuclear destruction, crises, and obstacles.

DRAMA

Much of the drama that was published in East Germany during the early postwar years had been written abroad. The stage

was dominated by classics and the modern international repertoire. Anti-fascist period pieces and historical dramas were
also promoted, but most of these had been created before 1945.
There were no new East German plays that enjoyed success
comparable to that of Wolfgang Borchert's *Draußen vor der Tür*
or Carl Zuckmayer's *Des Teufels General*. Nor did any younger
dramatist produce a play during the late 1940s that had any
decisive influence on East German theater. The only members
of the older generation whose works became at all important
were Friedrich Wolf (1888–1953) and Bertolt Brecht.

Friedrich Wolf favored the closed Aristotelian approach. He
also emphasized the cathartic dimension in his art. Although
his political struggle pieces were seldom performed, his postwar plays are important as early examples of three different
types of production that evolved in East Germany. *Wie Tiere des
Waldes* (1947; like animals of the forest) is an anti-fascist
political drama, while *Bürgermeister Anna* (1950; Mayor
Anna), one of the first plays to take up contemporary conflict
material, exemplifies the drama of rural life. Wolf's last play,
Thomas Müntzer, der Mann mit der Regenbogenfahne (1953;
Thomas Müntzer, the man with the rainbow flag), is an ordinary historical piece, with substantial declamatory ballast,
little political content, and equally little dramatic attraction.

In contrast to Wolf, Brecht promoted non-Aristotelian theater. He became the most important figure of early East German drama, even though the epic theater was not yet fully
accepted. Dramatists either studied and followed his models, or
they created ineffective dramatic literature.

Brecht completed only three plays from 1945 until his death.
Der kaukasische Kreidekreis (1945; *The Caucasian Chalk Circle,* 1948) is the last of his exile masterpieces. It is a didactic
play with universal validity and substantial depth. Its theme is
the battle to survive in a world dominated by neither justice
nor reason. It also contains good illustrations of the "alienation
effect" and the other techniques for which Brecht's work is
famous. *Die Tage der Commune* (1949; *The Days of the Commune,* 1971), is a less satisfying product of preoccupation with
the situation in Germany after the liberation from fascism.
Although it projects desirable elements of the new order, it did

not fit the concepts of the anti-fascist democratic social transformation in its early stages. It was therefore not staged until 1955. Brecht's final play, *Turandot oder Der\Kongreß der Weißwäscher* (1954; *Turandot* 1974), employs the old tale of the Chinese Turandot as a parable for twentieth-century social conditions. It is one of his least successful plays, because the complex and confusing allusions in the dialogues are only partially comprehensible.

Caféhaus Payer (1945; Payer Café), Hedda Zinner's (b. 1907) first play, failed to attract any lasting attention. Under the influence of Friedrich Wolf, she wrote several other pieces about the immediate past or then-current reality. *Spiel ins Leben* (1951; play into life), *Der Teufelskreis* (1953; vicious circle), *General Landt* (1957; General Landt), and *Ravensbrücker Ballade* (1961; ballad of Ravensbrück), a vivid portrayal of life among women in a concentration camp, are typical examples of her work. Although her dramas reflect a good feeling for stage effect and a competent approach to her craft, more recent creations, from *Elisabeth Trowe* (1967; Elisabeth Trowe) through *Die Richterin* (1974; the woman judge) and *Das Abenteuer* (1976; the adventure), reflect only routine skill.

Hermann Werner Kubsch's (b. 1911) *Die ersten Schritte* (1949; the first steps) set the pattern for a series of weak, stereotyped plays dealing with the themes of rural change, socialist education, and competition in industry. Kubsch did not intend to create art in any higher sense, and the results matched his expectations.

Under the growing influence of Brecht, certain new kinds of drama became popular in East Germany during the 1950s. The rural play focused on problems of farm production and adaptation to land reform, voluntary collectivization, and mandatory communes. Parallel to the agricultural drama emerged creative works that emphasized problems of industrial production. In both cases, attempts to deal objectively with East German reality fostered severe strains between authors and the political authorities. During this period, playwrights also treated historical material and began to examine conflicts in socialist art and East–West relations.

Prozeß Wedding (1951; the Wedding trial) and *Am Ende der*

Nacht (1955; at the end of the night), Harald Hauser's (b. 1912) first two plays, are highly contrived attempts to justify the international position of the Democratic Republic. Only the political atmosphere made it possible for these and works such as *Im himmlischen Garten* (1958; in the heavenly garden), *Weisses Blut* (1959; white blood), and *Barbara* (1963; Barbara) to be staged at all. Hauser's pieces are prosaic, lacking in realistic conflict, and relatively boring.

Heinar Kipphardt's (1922–82) satirical comedy *Shakespeare dringend gesucht* (1953; Shakespeare urgently needed) is one of the few really good plays created in the Democratic Republic during the 1950s. An impressively realistic, if theatrically exaggerated, critique of contemporary cultural policy, it takes to task aspects of political practice that severely hindered the development of viable dramatic literature. Other Kipphardt plays, including *Der Aufstieg des Alois Piontek* (1956; the rise of Alois Piontek), *Die Stühle des Herrn Szmil* (1958; Mr. Szmil's chairs), and *Esel schreien im Dunkeln* (1958; asses scream in the dark), also played an important role in the development of dramatic satire in East Germany.

Kipphardt is best known for creations produced in the Federal Republic after 1959. *Der Hund des Generals* (1963; the general's dog) makes an important contribution to the literature of dealing with the past, while the internationally successful *In der Sache J. Robert Oppenheimer* (1964; *In the Matter of J. Robert Oppenheimer,* 1967) is a masterpiece of the documentary theater. Later plays, from the documentary *Joel Brand* (1965; Joel Brand) and an adaptation of Jakob Michael Reinhold Lenz's (1751–92) *Die Soldaten* (1968; the soldiers) to *März, ein Künstlerleben* (1980; März, an artist's life), were greeted with substantial acclaim for their contributions to documentary and psychological drama. *März, ein Künstlerleben* is especially notable for its sensitive treatment of mental illness, masterful use of language, and solid dramatic structure. *Bruder Eichmann* (1982; brother Eichmann) is a strong culmination of the dramatic psychoanalysis of the Nazi period that began with *Der Hund des Generals.*

Next to Friedrich Wolf's *Bürgermeister Anna,* the most important early drama about East German rural conditions is

Erwin Strittmatter's *Katzgraben* (1954; Katzgraben). Neither
Katzgraben nor *Die Holländerbraut* (1961; the Dutch bride)
was particularly successful on the stage. Yet they both contain
the realistic portrayal of the common man that has made
Strittmatter one of East Germany's most prominent writers.

One successful disciple of Brecht is Peter Hacks (b. 1928). He
has effectively employed Brecht's techniques to produce mas-
terfully constructed comedies and didactic plays that convince
through artfully applied naiveté. His early works, including
Eröffnung des indischen Zeitalters (1954; *Opening of the Indian Era,* 1970; republished as *Columbus oder die Weltidee zu
Schiffe,* 1970; Columbus; or, the world idea aboard ship), *Die
Schlacht bei Lobositz* (1956; the battle at Lobositz), and *Der
Müller von Sanssouci* (1957; the miller of Sanssouci), contrast a
Marxist view of history with myth and legends of bourgeois
tradition.

Successive stages in Hacks's development led him away from
historical substance into critical treatments of specific East
German problems, then back to politically safer materials from
cultural history and mythology. Although rejected by Marxist
critics for its negative sense of reality, *Moritz Tassow* (1961;
Moritz Tassow), a realistic, dialectically argumentative verse
comedy about a revolutionary swineherd, significantly elevated the quality of the peasant drama while satirizing land
reform and the farm commune. The play also introduced the
anti-hero into East German theater. Typical for his less directly political plays are *Omphale* (1970; *Omphale,* 1973),
which uses a Hercules legend to explore male and female social
roles, *Adam und Eva* (1973; Adam and Eve), an interpretation
of Adam's fall as a poetic allegory for man's dialectic self-
determination, and *Ein Gespräch im Hause Stein über den
abwesenden Herrn von Goethe* (1976; a conversation in the
Stein home about the absent Mr. Goethe), a hilarious satirical
monodrama that is one of Hacks's best works.

Another extremely prolific dramatist is Rolf Schneider (b.
1932). His works reflect the influence of a broad spectrum of
models, from Brecht and Hacks to the documentary theater.
Schneider is a satirist, but his social and political criticism is
directed primarily at conditions in the West. *Das Gefängnis*

von Pont-l'Évêque (1956; the prison of Pont-l'Évêque), a radio play about convicts permitted to carry out robbery expeditions for the warden, typifies Schneider's interpretations of life under capitalism. Only his *Prozeß Richard Waverly* (1961; the trial of Richard Waverly) and *Prozeß in Nürnberg* (1967; trial in Nuremberg), two contributions to the documentary theater, approach serious art, and even they are rather mediocre in quality.

Helmut Baierl's (b. 1926) dramas successfully apply Brecht's models to the treatment of problems in postwar East Germany, but they lack Brecht's power of language. *Die Feststellung* (1958; the assessment) employs epic methods and alienation effect to present the circumstances surrounding a farmer's flight from the Democratic Republic, while *Frau Flinz* (1961; Mrs. Flinz), one of East Germany's best comedies, presents the process of socialist reconstruction in realistic dialogues and convincing situations. In *Johanna von Döbeln* (1969; Joan of Döbeln), *Schlag 13* (1971; at the stroke of 13), *Die Lachtaube* (1974; the ringdove), *Der Sommerbürger* (1976; the summer citizen), and *Leo und Rosa* (1982; Leo and Rosa) his depictions of everyday life under socialism succumb to shallowness and lack of significant dramatic conflict.

Problems of reconstruction, especially in the rural setting, are also the basis for Helmut Sakowski's (b. 1924) plays. Sakowski follows a process of psychological character formation that emphasizes the relationships and interdependencies of individual and society. *Die Entscheidung des Lene Mattke* (1958; *Lene Mattke's Decision*, 1961), *Steine im Weg* (1960; stones in the way), and *Weiberzwist und Liebeslist* (1961; women's strife and love's trickery) are interesting for their treatment of village problems from the perspectives of female central characters, but they and later creations like *Letzter Sommer in Heidkau* (1965; final summer in Heidkau), *Wege übers Land* (1969; paths across the country), and *Daniel Druskat* (1976; Daniel Druskat) are weakened by oversimplification.

Psychological realism is an important aspect of Manfred Bieler's radio plays. His early works, from *Hochzeitsreise* (1959; wedding journey) and *Die achte Trübsal* (1960; the eighth sorrow) through *Nachtwache* (1963; night watch), *Ich frage* (1965; I ask), and *Dieser Herr da* (1966; that man there), reflect his aversion to experimentation and a deep interest in inner motivations for conflicts. The most effective piece is *Nachtwache,* in which Bieler illuminates the relationships between individuals in a Mecklenburg commune. His West German productions, including *Feuerzeug* (1969; cigarette lighter), *Jeronim* (1970; Jeronimo), *Der Hausaufsatz* (1972; the writing assignment), *Der Kommandant* (1973; the commander), *Oblowmows Liebe* (1977; Oblowmow's love), and *Ortswechsel* (1978; change of location), exhibit solid craftsmanship but they lack originality.

Although he is one of the most important dramatists in the Democratic Republic, Heiner Müller (b. 1929) remains a literary outsider. Much of his work has been unavailable until recently. In form, his plays continue Brecht's didactic drama and the agitprop theater of the 1920s, but they carry description of unpleasant realities further than Brecht was willing to go. *Die Korrektkur* (1957; *The Correction,* 1983) and *Der Lohndrücker* (1958; the wage cutter) were among the first East German dialectic dramas. (Dialectic theater refused to whitewash negative aspects of early socialist reconstruction, but also declined to criticize them.) When these and other creations were systematically suppressed, Müller attempted to salvage the dialectic theater in disguised form, by turning to abstractions based on classical mythology. The best of the mythological dramas is *Philoktet* (1966; Philoctetes), in which Müller transformed the traditional story into an attack on militarism. In more recent works like *Hamletmachine* (1977; *Hamletmachine,* 1983) he has used harsh and abrasive symbols to intensify the drama. *Der Auftrag* (1981; *The Task,* 1983) and *Quartett* (1981; *Quartet,* 1983) are especially graphic and brutal in their physicality.

During the 1960s, works created for the East German stage became artistically less effective. Many important plays were performed only on a limited basis; others were totally suppressed. Among the key tendencies were a loosening of Brecht's influence, the continued importance of production themes, an increased retreat into "safe" substance belonging to history or myth, growth of parable forms, proliferation of superficially dialectic entertainment plays, decline of live theater in favor of television, and reliance on conventional dramaturgy in works that are harmonious, affirmative, and uncritical. Because of restrictions imposed by the state, very few new playwrights of any significance emerged during this time.

Gerhard Rentzsch (b. 1926) made a few interesting contributions to the radio play. *Altweibersommer* (1960; old women's summer) examines the vacation concept within the socialist context, and *Nachtzug* (1962; night train) offers a psychological exploration of flight from the Democratic Republic. Creations such as *Geschichte eines Mantels* (1963; story of an overcoat), *Das Amulett* (1970; the amulet), *Der Nachlaß* (1975; the estate), *Jugendweihe* (1976; coming of age), and *Der Stein* (1977; the stone) are less compelling in their penetration of underlying aspects of everyday situations.

The dramas of Rainer Kerndl (b. 1928) are primarily stereotyped didactic pieces about contemporary reality. Kerndl emphasizes problems of human and political decision. *Schatten eines Mädchens* (1961; a girl's shadow) is a guilt play that lacks dramatic tension, while *Seine Kinder* (1963; his children) touches on important social questions without exploring them constructively. The moralistic pieces *Plädoyer für die Suchenden* (1966; plea for the seekers), *Der verratene Rebell* (1967; the betrayed rebel), and *Die seltsame Reise des Alois Fingerlein* (1967; the strange journey of Alois Fingerlein) are flat and trite. Kerndl is more successful with his comedies, *Ich bin einem Mädchen begegnet* (1969; I met a girl), and *Wann kommt Ehrlicher?* (1971; when will Ehrlicher come?), but the situations remain pat, and the spoon-fed substance is unpalatable. More recent efforts offer increasingly superficial treatments of current themes.

Unlike Kerndl and others, Armin Stolper (b. 1934) has produced a few moderately original plays. He is most successful in adapting classical models and contemporary foreign literature for the stage. In *Amphitryon* (1967; Amphitryon) he presents a Zeus who is impotent, while *Ruzante* (1967; Ruzante), *Zeitgenossen* (1969; contemporaries), and *Himmelfahrt zur Erde* (1970; ascension to the earth) offer variations of individual confrontation with social contradictions. Stolper's *Lausitzer*

Trilogie (1980; Lausitz trilogy), consisting of *Klara und der Gänserich* (1973; Klara and Gänserich), *Der Schuster und der Hahn* (1975; the shoemaker and the rooster), and *Die Vogelscheuche* (1980; the scarecrow), illustrates his spotty effectiveness with original material. All of the plays mix realism and fantasy with music and dance, but only *Klara und der Gänserich* contains characters with any psychological depth.

Another dramatist who creates works based on existing literature, as well as original pieces, is Claus Hammel (b. 1932). *Hier ist ein Neger zu lynchen* (1958; here is a Negro to lynch), *Fischerkinder* (1962; fishermen's children), *Frau Jenny Treibel oder Wo sich Herz zum Herzen find't* (1964; Mrs. Jenny Treibel; or, where heart finds its way to heart), *Ein Yankee an König Artus' Hof* (1966; a yankee at King Arthur's court), and *Der Macher oder Warten auf Godeau* (1970; the doer; or, waiting for Godot) illustrate his manipulation of German, American and French models. The most successful play is *Der Macher oder Warten auf Godeau,* a critical parody of Samuel Beckett's comedy. Hammel's own works focus ironically on the decay of bourgeois society. Representative pieces such as *Um neun an der Achterbahn* (1964; at nine o'clock at the roller coaster) and *Rom oder Die zweite Erschaffung der Welt* (1974; Rome; or, the second creation of the world) are weakened by an avoidance of confrontation with real social conflicts.

Hartmut Lange (b. 1937) began with parables that were intended to illustrate the principles of dialectical materialism. *Marski* (1965; Marski) and *Senftenberger Erzählungen oder Die Enteignung* (1967; Senftenberg stories; or, the expropriation) critically examine reconstruction situations of the early postwar period. Three of his later plays, *Der Hundsprozeß* (1968; the dog trial), *Heracles* (1968; Hercules), and *Trotzki in Coyoacan* (1971; Trotsky in Coyoacán), offer strong polemics against the Stalin cult, although *Der Hundsprozeß* is the strongest of the three. In the more recent pieces, *Vom Werden der Vernunft oder Auf der Durchreise nach Petersburg* (1976; on the development of reason; or, passing through on the way to St. Petersburg) and *Frau von Kauenhofen* (1977; Mrs. von Kauenhofen), Lange combined psychological drama with documentary elements. The resulting effects appear forced and contrived.

The most important new playwright of the period was Volker Braun. His dramas are uncomfortable for Eastern critics because of their direct and uncompromising illumination of social conflicts and contradictions. In *Kipper Paul Bauch* (1966; tipper Paul Bauch), *Freunde* (1971; friends), and *Hinze und Kunze* (1973; Hinze and Kunze) he emphasizes the tension between socialized production and the continued monotony of physical labor, between the bureaucratization of masculine productivity and the hampering of female contributions to production, and between individual needs and the external demands of the community. Comparison of these works with *Guevara oder Der Sonnenstaat* (1975; Guevara; or, the sun state), *Der große Frieden* (1979; the great peace), and *Simplex Deutsch* (1981; German simplex) reveals a maturation of tone, increasing mastery of realistic characterization, and further magnification of a special facility with sexual metaphor.

A variety of tendencies are visible in East German drama of the 1970s. In addition to superficial treatment of contemporary life, there is a renewed interest in overcoming the past and its impact on the present. The position of the individual within the society also assumes greater importance. Where drama of the 1960s often distinguished only between individuals who fail and those who succeed, the heroes of the 1970s are measured against ethical norms. The special province of new writers is the highlighting of conflicts between personal needs and the society's expectations. In their works society often becomes a negative force that destroys the individual by forcing him to adjust or revolt. Unlike the pseudo-conflicts of the 1960s, the new situations stress real crises and defend the validity of private requirements.

Strong illustrations of the conflict between individual and society are found in the plays of Stefan Schütz (b. 1944). In *Majakowski* (1971; Mayakowski) the title figure is placed in conflict with the bureaucracy, and a figure representing the aspect of his nature that cannot adapt to the establishment's expectations is destroyed. Other works, including *Odysseus*

Heimkehr (1974; Odysseus's homecoming), *Antiope und Theseus* (1976; Antiope and Theseus), *Heloise und Abalard* (1976; Héloïse and Abélard), *Fabrik im Walde* (1977; factory in the forest), *Kohlhaas* (1977; Kohlhaas), *Laokoon* (1979; Laocoön), and *Die Schweine* (1981; the swine), consistently portray unconditionally active heroes who suffer beneath the restrictions of society. The most notable aspects of Schütz's dramatic art are an extremely expressive use of language, unusual metaphors, and a carefully calculated theatrical intensity.

Unlike Schütz's figures, Edgar Wibeau, in Ulrich Plenzdorf's *Die neuen Leiden des jungen W.* (1972; *The New Sufferings of Young W.*, 1979), is an outsider drawn from modern East German society. Several factors make this play successful, among them the realistic use of language that is both flippant and honest, the carefully tight dramatic construction, and a lack of exaggeration. Plenzdorf also dramatized Günter de Bruyn's novel *Buridans Esel* in 1976, but the result is not very compelling.

Three other writers who experimented with drama during the 1970s were Karl Hermann Roehricht, Uwe Saeger (b. 1948), and Thomas Brasch. None of them made monumental contributions to the theater, but all of them produced pieces that reflect the atmosphere of the times. Roehricht's *Familie Birnchen* (1975; the Birnchen family) illustrates the structured subjectivism of regional folk theater, while Saeger's radio play *Besuch beim lieben Gott* (1976; a visit to the dear God) and the stage production *Das Vorkommnis* (1977; the incident) examine the behavior of teachers and parents with respect to youth. *Rotter* (1977; Rotter), the most important drama that Brasch published after moving to the West, describes the new individual as an opportunist who has adapted himself to continually changing circumstances. *Lieber Georg* (1980; dear Georg) is an intensely subjective confession that highlights the situation of the lonely writer in constant conflict with a senseless world. Brasch's other plays complement these two in portraying the modern individual who has lost his way.

The most talented emerging dramatist of the 1970s was Christoph Hein. In *Cromwell* (1978; Cromwell) and *Lassalle fragt Herrn Herbert nach Sonja* (1981; La Salle asks Mr. Herbert about Sonya) he employed a peculiar mixture of history and anachronism to explore situations of revolutionary change. His consistent emphasis on the conflict between individual and society reached a high point in *Schlötel oder Was solls* (1981; Schlötel; or, what's it to be), the description of an idealist who cannot adapt to mundane East German reality. Hein's plays represent a personal attempt to define a viable role for the intellectual in the new social order. His *Die wahre Geschichte des Ah Q* (1983; the true story of Ah Q) suggests that a revolutionary society inevitably destroys the intellectual by forcing him to act against it.

Hein's *Die wahre Geschichte des Ah Q* and Heiner Müller's *Quartett* are particularly symptomatic of one extreme in East German drama during the first half of the 1980s. They both reflect a sense of radical historical pessimism in which hopelessness is a dominant mood, and action for change—symbolized repeatedly in various versions of revolution—becomes a framework for death. Pessimism on a personal level accents individual inability to establish secure and lasting interpersonal connections, while the most drastic representations of alienation occur in plays that focus on the fine line between sanity and insanity.

Trampelpfad (1981; path) by Jürgen Gross (b. 1946) presents the reasons for a love affair and its collapse. In the character of one of the lovers, Gross gives an extremely human and convincing portrayal of the destructive power of preoccupation with self. The author's psychological penetration of the figures and his sensitive rendering of universal problems of social interaction achieve fascinating results.

The distance between individual and society is conveyed in more subdued symbols in Albert Wendt's (b. 1948) *Die Dachdecker* (1981; the roofers). In this play, Wendt attempts to demonstrate the responsibility of the person who can look at the society objectively. Unfortunately, he does not succeed very well. What is interesting about the play is the effective juxtaposition of figures representing the socialist commitment to plan fulfillment with others who argue in favor of a life-style that responds more directly to individual desires and needs.

One vivid example of the drastic disparity between the isolated outsider and the community is Einar Schleef's (b. 1943) *Wezel* (1983; Wezel). His rendering of the life of the writer Johann Karl Wezel (1747–1819) focuses on a time when the title figure fluctuated between rationality and mental illness. While much of the language comes across as artificial, and the dialogues fail to create any meaningful dramatic tension, the interactions between Wezel and the other characters underscore feelings of complete personal alienation.

4 ■ AUSTRIA

FICTION

The initial tendencies of postwar Austrian fiction prolonged the use of established patterns. Typical creations from the late 1940s include historical novels and other efforts to reject or ignore the implications of the immediate past. Most established authors simply began again where they had left off, and those who had remained in Austria during the war played a strong role in determining the type of works produced. For many of them, coming to grips with the decline and collapse of the old Austrian monarchy and its way of life remained a far more compelling problem than responding to events of the Nazi era.

A strong representative of traditional Austria was Alexander Lernet-Holenia (1897–1976). His most artistic narratives were written before 1945, but even his later adventure and detective novels foster the aristocratic spirit of the monarchy's upper class. At best, the works that follow *Der 27. November* (1946; the 27th of November)—from *Die Inseln unter dem Winde* (1952; the islands beneath the wind), *Der Graf Luna* (1955; *Count Luna,* 1956), *Das Finanzamt* (1955; the finance office), and *Das Goldkabinett* (1957; the gold cabinet) through *Die weiße Dame* (1965; the white lady), *Die Hexen* (1969; the witches), and *Wendekreis der Galionen* (1972; tropic of the figureheads)—can be described as elegant entertainment literature. Lernet-Holenia's novels offer a peculiar combination of action and excitement with elevated style and affected language, but they maintain the reader's interest through seemingly effortless psychological differentiation and penetration of characters.

Albert Paris Gütersloh's (1887–1973) *Eine sagenhafte Figur* (1946; a fabulous figure) is a good example of Austrian preoccupation with the years surrounding the First World War. The erotic treatment of the battle of the sexes gives the work its focus, but successful portrayal of a specific class of people contributes an important social dimension that makes up for weaknesses in other areas. Gütersloh achieved greater artistry in *Fabeln vom Eros* (1947; fables of Eros) and *Laßt uns den Menschen machen* (1962; let us make man). The symbolic "total" novel *Sonne und Mond* (1962; sun and moon) is his most important postwar creation. The stories in the two collections are notable for their power of language, while *Sonne und Mond* is a significant attempt at a summation of the spiritual, sensual, secular, and religious elements of the Austrian manner of dealing with life.

Another aspect of the retreat into Austrianness is the continued strength of regional literature.

Although she produced her most important creations before the war, Paula Grogger (b. 1892) later maintained the vitality of language, the colorful milieu description, and the sensitivity to the spirit of her Styrian homeland that had made her earlier works successful. *Unser Herr Pfarrer* (1946; our pastor), *Der Antichrist und unsere liebe Frau* (1949; the Antichrist and our dear Lady), *Die Mutter* (1958; the mother), *Späte Matura* (1975; late graduation examination), and *Die Räuberlegende* (1977; the robber legend) are among the most representative examples of postwar regionalistic prose.

The mountainous area around Bad Gastein provided the settings for the novels and novellas of Karl Heinrich Waggerl (1897–1973). Like Paula Grogger, he wrote his best books before 1945, but his postwar writings reflect the characteristic warmth, simplicity, and sensuous observation of nature and people that captivated his prewar audience. In *Fröhliche Armut* (1948; happy poverty) Waggerl portrayed with soft irony the small, closed world of his own childhood. The strength of this and later works such as *Drei Erzählungen* (1950; three stories), *Die grünen Freunde* (1955; the green friends), and *Kraut und Unkraut* (1968; vegetables and weeds) lies in the beauty of Waggerl's language, the deeply human conflicts that he illuminates, and the immediacy of his presentation.

In his historical narratives, Fritz Habeck (b. 1916) combines Ernest Hemingway's epic approach with an element of reflection. The novellas in *Verlorene Wege* (1947; lost ways) and the novels *Der Tanz der sieben Teufel* (1950; the dance of the seven devils), *Das Boot kommt nach Mitternacht* (1951; the boat comes after midnight), *Das zerbrochene Dreieck* (1953; the broken triangle), *Der Ritt auf dem Tiger* (1958; the ride on the tiger), *Der Piber* (1965; Piber), and *Der schwarze Mantel meines Vaters* (1976; my father's black overcoat) differ from Habeck's contributions to trivial literature in the seriousness of their themes and the careful handling of the language. Habeck's most imaginative novel is *Der schwarze Mantel meines Vaters*, a combination of fantasy and autobiography that grapples with the Nazi era in a unique manner.

Gertrud Fussenegger (b. 1912) is a strong explorer of Austria's past. Her epic trilogy, *Die Brüder von Lasawa* (1948; the Lasawa brothers), *Das Haus der dunklen Krüge* (1951; the house of the dark jugs), and *Das verschüttete Antlitz* (1957; the buried face), traces Bohemia's history from the seventeenth century into the modern period. The strength of these novels lies in carefully crafted symbols and penetrating psychological insights into the motivations for human action. One of Fussenegger's best creations is *Zeit des Raben, Zeit der Taube* (1960; time of the raven, time of the dove), in which she contrasted the lives of Marie Curie (1867–1934) and the French novelist Léon Bloy (1846–1917). In spite of the employment of nontraditional narrative forms, *Die Pulvermühle* (1969; the powder mill) does not reflect a significant change in her literary approach. Even here, she succeeds very well in making the case for the resolution of interpersonal conflicts through rational communication.

In the case of Franz Tumler (b. 1912), identification with the spirit of an earlier Austria is a question of artistic attitude. That Tumler is a disciple of Adalbert Stifter (1805–68) is visible in his carefully subdued style. In his postwar creations, from *Der alte Herr Lorenz* (1949; old Mr. Lorenz), *Heimfahrt* (1950; journey home), and *Ein Schloß in Österreich* (1953; a castle in Austria) through *Aufschreibung aus Trient* (1965; notebook entry from Trient) and *Pia Faller* (1973; Pia Faller), he subordinates external events to the psychology of human problems and relationships. Experiments with new narrative approaches in *Aufschreibung aus Trient* and *Pia Faller* are unsuccessful and reflect Tumler's inability to transcend rigid conventionality.

Imma von Bodmershof (b. 1895) also continued her career after the war without responding to the events of the Nazi period. Her books exhibit unusual artistry in their strongly poetic language, their carefully integrated dramatic tensions, and their reserved, yet plastic, style. The strongest elements in *Die Rosse des Urban Roithner* (1950; Urban Roithner's horses), *Solange es Tag ist* (1953; as long as it is day), *Sieben handvoll Salz* (1958; seven handfuls of salt), and *Die Bartabnahme* (1966; the beard removal) are the nature and landscape descriptions, the treatment of rural life, and the presentations of simple people in their strong ties to the natural, physical world.

Writers who had left Austria during the Nazi period were less inclined to avoid the immediate past in their works. They were also important forces for literary change, even though the movement toward modernism was relatively fragmented and slow.

Robert Neumann (1897–1975) published many of his works in English before they appeared in German. His talent for imitating diverse styles made him more famous as a parodist than as a serious novelist, but his postwar novels are certainly worthy of note. *Die Kinder von Wien* (1948; *The Children of Vienna,* 1946) illustrates his ability to pursue the psychological complexities of a situation with solid effect. Later productions, from *Die Puppen von Poshansk* (1952; *Insurrection at Poshansk,* 1952) to *Ein unmöglicher Sohn* (1972; an impossible son), reveal his gift for creating plastic, engaging political and social satire.

The early postwar narratives of Friedrich Torberg (1908–79) are less artistic than those of Neumann. In *Mein ist die Rache*

(1947; *Vengeance Is Mine,* 1943), *Hier bin ich, mein Vater* (1948; here I am, my father), and *Die zweite Begegnung* (1950; the second encounter) the artful use of language is subordinated to plot, conflict, and character development. For all of that, *Vengeance Is Mine* is a work of enormous emotional power. Torberg's later explorations of the problem of anti-Semitism in *Golems Wiederkehr* (1968; return of the golem), *Süßkind von Trimberg* (1972; Süßkind von Trimberg), *Die Tante Jolesch oder Der Untergang des Abendlandes in Anekdoten* (1975; Aunt Jolesch; or, the decline of the West in anecdotes), and *Die Erben der Tante Jolesch* (1978; the heirs of Aunt Jolesch) contain flashes of pointed imagination, stark descriptions, and even successful satire—but also an overabundance of clichés.

Next to Robert Musil (1880–1942), whose *Der Mann ohne Eigenschaften* (1930–43; *The Man without Qualities,* 1953) had far-reaching impact on the postwar novel, the most important Austrian emigrant for the development of fiction was Hermann Broch (1886–1951). His masterpiece, *Der Tod des Vergil* (1945; *The Death of Virgil,* 1945), provided other writers with a major model for employment of radically new narrative techniques, including inner monologue, destruction of continuity through essayistic intrusions, variation of style, and the application of elements from other disciplines to the creative process. Neither *Die Schuldlosen* (1950; *The Guiltless* 1974), an intense study of the spiritual prerequisites for Hitler's rise to power, nor *Der Versucher* (1953; the tempter), one version of Broch's so-called *Bergroman* (1969; mountain novel), attains the richness of *The Death of Virgil,* but both are powerful studies in mass psychology.

Hilde Spiel's (b. 1911) postwar novels are studies in resignation at the loss of a stable world. *Flöte und Trommel* (1947; flute and drum) is the over-romanticized portrayal of a European woman who follows the flute of Pan through Italy until the drum signals war. In *Lisas Zimmer* (1965; *The Darkened Room,* 1961), Spiel attempted to catch the mood of life in exile by depicting a Viennese society woman in New York. *Die Früchte des Wohlstands* (1981; the fruits of prosperity) is interesting for its projection of Vienna's atmosphere in the 1870s, but the language is old-fashioned, and the mixture of impressionism and sentimentality makes the work less appealing than *The Darkened Room.*

Several significant writers produced their first fiction during the years 1945 to 1949. Some had previously established themselves in other genres; others were newcomers. Because local publishers hesitated to print new creations, much of their work appeared in the Federal Republic.

The narrative prose of Johannes Urzidil (1896–1970) is strongly autobiographical. Even his mature works reflect continuing strong ties to his Bohemian homeland. Although *Der Trauermantel* (1945; the mourning coat) did not attract much attention, the collection *Die verlorene Geliebte* (1956; the lost beloved) established him as a creator of powerful, sensitive fiction. In *Das große Halleluja* (1959; the grand hallelujah) he unfolded a broad panorama of impressions of the United States. The novel is somewhat lacking in vitality but is important for its perceptiveness. Urzidil is at his best in the novellas of *Prager Triptychon* (1960; Prague triptych), *Magische Texte* (1961; magical texts), and *Das Elefantenblatt* (1962; the elephant leaf), in which he successfully combined elements of personal and cultural history with an overwhelming sense of life's general magic. In specific stories from *Entführung und sieben andere Ereignisse* (1964; abduction and seven other occurrences) and *Die erbeuteten Frauen* (1966; the captured women) he documented his keen feeling for the relationship between fantasy and reality.

Hans Weigel (b. 1908) published his first drama in the 1920s, but his earliest works of fiction, *Das himmlische leben* (1946; the heavenly life) and *Der grüne Stern* (1946; the green star), are pieces of exile literature. Weigel's forte is satire, and *Der grüne Stern* is an interesting satirical utopian novel in which a vision of dictatorship is reduced to elements of the irrational. Unfortunately, oversimplification of parallels between Weigel's created world and the Nazi dictatorship render the narrative ineffective as social criticism. His other postwar novel, *Unvollendete Symphonie* (1951; unfinished symphony), is somewhat more successful than *Der grüne Stern,* especially in its treatment of the general human and political problems of life in Vienna after 1945.

Unlike Urzidil and Weigel, Milo Dor (b. 1923) was a postwar newcomer to the Austrian literary scene. The stories in *Unterwegs* (1947; on the way) and the novels *Tote auf Urlaub* (1952; *Dead Men on Leave*, 1962), *Internationale Zone* (1953; international zone), *Romeo und Julia in Wien* (1954; Romeo and Juliet in Vienna), and *Othello von Salerno* (1956; Othello of Salerno), the last of which he wrote with Reinhard Federmann (1923–76), offer starkly realistic treatments of guilt, disaster, and terror. *Tote auf Urlaub* is his best early work. Although the fragmented structure of *Nichts als Erinnerung* (1959; nothing but memory) dampens its effect as a novel, sections of the work are among the best pieces of short prose created during the period. Dor's attempts to diversify his narrative approach in *Die weiße Stadt* (1969; the white city) are only partially successful. Many of the ironic and satirical beginnings are not carried out to full realization. In later works, such as *Alle meine Brüder* (1978; all my brothers), he returned to a traditional linear narrative style, but the results were mediocre at best.

One of the most promising new authors of the late 1940s was Johannes Mario Simmel (b. 1924). *Begegnung im Nebel* (1947; encounter in the fog) features stories that are notable for their originality, their flowing style and certainty of expression, and their richly poetic language. Beginning with *Das geheime Brot* (1950; the secret bread), *Ich gestehe alles* (1953; *I Confess*, 1977), and *Gott schützt die Liebenden* (1956; God protects lovers), he moved toward entertainment literature. Recent works such as *Bitte, laßt die Blumen leben* (1982; please let the flowers live), *Hurra, wir leben noch* (1983; hurrah, we are still alive), and *Die im Dunkeln sieht man nicht* (1984; one does not see the ones in the dark) maintain his position as one of the most popular authors in the German language, but his formula novels are filled with clichés and trivialities that belie the artistic promise of his beginnings.

Herbert Zand's (1923–70) works depend on realism for their effect. In *Die Sonnenstadt* (1947; the sun city) he sought to create a total epic metaphor for World War II. With its confused and confusing structure, the novel is much less effective than *Die letzte Ausfahrt* (1953; *The Last Sortie*, 1955), which describes the siege of an East German city. *The Last Sortie* exhibits metaphoric strength in its rigid, compelling style. The attempt to employ realistic material to create a poetic symbol for the isolated individual is most effective in *Der Weg nach Hassi el emel* (1956; *The Well of Hope,* 1957), the story of a downed pilot's fight to escape from the North African desert. The socially critical *Erben des Feuers* (1961; heirs of the fire) offers a less powerful variation of the same general theme in portraying young Austrians caught between remnants of the monarchy and the profit-oriented middle class.

One of the most important young Austrian novelists of the immediate postwar years was Ilse Aichinger (b. 1921). *Die grössere Hoffnung* (1948; *Herod's Children,* 1963), a parabolic statement about human alienation, is an important early product of the avant-garde. It set the pattern for her later writings, including *Der Gefesselte* (1953; *The Bound Man and Other Stories, 1955), Spiegelgeschichte* (1954; mirror story), *Wo ich wohne* (1963; where I dwell), *Eliza, Eliza* (1965; Eliza, Eliza), *Schlechte Wörter* (1976; bad words), and *Meine Sprache und ich* (1978; my language and I). Aichinger progressed from a strong early dependency on symbolism to a mature prose that fosters direct visualization of characters and landscapes. Her most successful stories are parables of large general processes, couched in the most private aspects of individual life.

Austria between the world wars is the special focus of George Emmanuel Saiko's (1892–1962) prose. His novels and novellas contained in *Auf dem Floβ* (1948; on the raft), *Der Mann im Schilf* (1955; the man in the reeds), *Giraffe unter Palmen* (1962; giraffe under palms), and *Der Opferblock* (1962; the sacrificial block), combine elements of social criticism and psychology with the devices of magical realism. Saiko's major contribution to Austrian literature lies in his detailed penetration of human motivations contributing to the dichotomy between indecisiveness and the need to act. The works themselves are weakened by a combination of enormous complexity, a dearth of action, and annoying repetition.

The element of psychology is an important general aspect of Austrian narratives during the 1950s. New writers experimented with serious prose that moved in the direction from psychological to surrealistic, while remaining within defined limits. Their creations also reflect concern for problems related to language, substance, and form. Much of the prose written during this time belongs somewhere between serious art and trivial literature, but some authors developed individual attitudes and themes. One growing tendency was artistic preoccupation with history. Interest in the Austrian past was furthered especially by posthumous republication of the works of Fritz von Herzmanovsky-Orlando (1877–1954).

The most important molding force for Austrian fiction in the 1950s was Heimito von Doderer (1896–1966). His postwar novels, beginning with *Die erleuchteten Fenster* (1950; the lit windows) and *Die Strudlhofstiege* (1951; the Strudlhof staircase), had a strong influence on younger writers. The powerful constructive energy of his prose, the stress placed on Vienna as a theme, and Doderer's anti-ideological stance all contributed to his positive reception. His treatments of Austria in the 1920s in *Die Strudlhofstiege* and *Die Dämonen* (1952; *The Demons,* 1961) combine realism and symbolism in remarkably deep representations of the many strata of the society. *Die Wasserfälle von Slunj* (1963; *The Waterfalls of Slunj,* 1966), the only completed portion of *Roman No. 7* (novel no. 7), presents a clearly and openly composed treatment of the tensions between generations. The unfinished second part of the series, *Der Grenzwald* (1967; the border forest), is notable for its consummate artistry and literary balance.

Another figure who explored the major prewar European political and social problems was Manès Sperber (1905–84). His trilogy *Wie eine Träne im Ozean* (1961; like a tear in the ocean), consisting of *Der verbrannte Dornbusch* (1950; *Burned Bramble,* 1951), *Tiefer als der Abgrund* (1961; *The Abyss,* 1952), and *Die verlorene Bucht* (1955; *Journey Without End,* 1954), examines the European communist experience of the 1930s and 1940s and culminates in the violent spectacle of Europe's collapse. The major value of *Burned Bramble* lies in its documentary portrayal of the times. As a narrative, it founders on the weight of a disjointed and confusing panorama of characters, scenes, and situations. An overemphasis on political dialectic in *The Abyss,* combined with the work's inability to stand as an independent piece of fiction, makes it even less satisfying than the first volume. By contrast, *Journey Without End* possesses a dramatic power not found in the earlier novels.

Dissective moralism and psychologically objective narration dominate the writings of Herbert Eisenreich (b. 1925). *Auch in ihrer Sünde* (1953; even in her sin) offers a symbolic representation of the contemporary individual's spiritual failure, while the stories in *Böse schöne Welt* (1957; evil beautiful world), *Sozusagen Liebesgeschichten* (1965; love stories, so to speak), *Die Freunde meiner Frau* (1966; my wife's friends), and *Ein schöner Sieg und 21 andere Mißverständnisse* (1973; a beautiful victory and 21 other misunderstandings) emphasize interpersonal relations in an ambiguous, insecure world. The spectrum of presentation ranges from humorous and frivolous to melancholy and grotesque. Among Eisenreich's best creations are the love stories of *Die blaue Distel der Romantik* (1976; the blue thistle of romanticism).

The psychology of interpersonal relations, especially regarding the modern woman's loneliness and longing for love, is the central focus of Marlen Haushofer's (1920–70) prose narratives. The female characters in her novels, from *Das fünfte Jahr* (1951; the fifth year) and *Eine Handvoll Leben* (1955; a handful of life) to *Schreckliche Treue* (1968; terrible loyalty) and *Die Mansarde* (1969; the garret), exist in varying degrees of alienation. Haushofer's prose is evenly precise, and her descriptive facility is solid and mature. Only in the final novel, *Die Mansarde,* does the process of introspection become somewhat banal.

Hans Lebert (b. 1919) focused on problems of collective guilt and individual responsibility regarding Austrian participation in events of the Nazi period. His writing career, which began with the publication of *Ausfahrt* (1952; departure) and *Das Schiff im Gebirge* (1955; the ship in the mountains), reached its peak in *Die Wolfshaut* (1960; the wolf skin). Its penetrating effect is a product of careful integration of reflection, dialogue, description, symbolism, and interpretations of situations and relationships. In *Der Feuerkreis* (1971; the fire circle), an attempt to combine Austrian realities of the late 1930s with universal mythical and religious symbols, Lebert failed to achieve his intended effect. The novel is structured like an opera, but the language does not communicate effectively the intense emotionality and the profound psychological conflicts and tensions of the substance.

In the fiction of Jeannie Ebner (b. 1918), the psychological element is often masked by fairy-tale relationships. Her early narratives, *Sie warten auf Antwort* (1954; they await an answer), *Die Wildnis früher Sommer* (1958; the wilderness of early summers), *Der Königstiger* (1959; the kingly tiger), and *Die Götter reden nicht* (1961; the gods do not speak), are dominated by mythological, allegorical, and surrealistic devices. *Die Wildnis früher Sommer* is especially interesting for its lyrically sensitive, subtle portrayal of the conflicts between innocence and guilt in young people. Ebner offered more direct treatments of contemporary social situations in *Figuren in Schwarz und Weiß* (1964; figures in black and white) and *Protokoll aus einem Zwischenreich* (1975; report from an intermediate realm), but even these works are strongly poetic. In all of her more recent works, especially *Drei Flötentöne* (1981; three flute tones) and *Aktäon* (1983; Actaeon), the characters exist in a border world between reality and dream, and the success of her writing is a function of her ability to describe accurately the search for meaning in a world of psychological alienation.

György Sebestyén (b. 1930) also explores the psychological implications of conflict between individual and society. *Die Türen schließen sich* (1957; *The Doors Are Closing,* 1958) and *Der Mann im Sattel oder Ein langer Sonntag* (1961; the man in the saddle; or, a long Sunday) are weakened by the author's lack of facility with the language, but *Die Schule der Verführung* (1964; the school of seduction), *Thennberg* (1964; Thennberg), *Berenger und Berenice* (1971; Berenger and Berenice), and *Der Faun im Park* (1972; the faun in the park) document his gradual development of linguistic discipline and mastery of modern narrative techniques. Especially successful are Sebestyén's manipulation and interweaving of memory, immediate consciousness, events, and dialogues in a powerful evocation of middle-class existence between the wars. The short novel *Albino* (1984; albino) is one of his best creations. It offers a compelling portrait of a paranoid loner who lives a nightmare life of total isolation.

Friederike Mayröcker's (b. 1924) experimental prose reflects the playful montage and variation of words and material, without regard for syntax. Her books, from *Larifari* (1956; nonsense), *Tod durch Musen* (1966; death through muses), and *Minimonsters Traum-Lexikon* (1968; mini-monster's dream encyclopedia) through *Das Licht in der Landschaft* (1975; the light in the landscape), *Fast ein Frühling des Markus M.* (1976; almost a spring of Marcus M.), *Die Abschiede* (1980; the farewells), and *Magische Blätter* (1983; magic leaves), contain colorful, glittering mosaics that are extremely difficult to decipher. Individual creations are remarkable for their associative power, their mixture of reality and fantasy, and their unusual psychological penetration of simultaneous inner experiences.

Another experimenter of the 1950s was Hans Carl Artmann (b. 1921). He produced several important volumes of prose. *Von denen Husaren und anderen Seil-Tänzern* (1959; about those hussars and other tightrope walkers) is an attempt to coordinate language with a specific interpretation of life. In *das suchen nach dem gestrigen tag oder schnee auf einem heißen brotwecken. eintragungen eines bizzaren liebhabers* (1964; the search for yesterday; or, snow on a hot bread roll: notes of a bizarre lover) and *Fleiß und Industrie* (1967; diligence and industry), but also in *Die Jagd nach Dr. U.* (1977; the hunt for Dr. U.) and *Nachrichten aus Nord und Süd* (1978; news from north and south), content is determined by grammatical form, and meaning is a product of effect. The short stories and sketches in *Die Sonne war ein grünes Ei: Von der Erschaffung der Welt und ihren Dingen* (1982; the sun was a green egg: about the creation of the world and its things) and *Im Schatten der Burenwurst: Skizzen aus Wien* (1983; in the shadow of the Polish sausage: sketches from Vienna) are renewed attempts to create a personal aesthetic reality from language. They are more significant for extravagant humor and originality than for serious literary communication.

The most significant trends in Austrian fiction during the 1960s were a polarization of conservative and progressive writers and a new magnification of national consciousness. Awareness of language and its relationship to social experience was also important. Psychological exploration of motivation, behavior, and interpersonal relationships increased, with ever heavier emphasis on the problem of alienation. New experiments with form and style were carried out, but there were also strong pressures toward conservatism and the restoration of tradition. Many authors simply did not attempt to conform to specific patterns.

Known primarily for his poetry, Erich Fried (b. 1921) has also produced successful fiction. *Ein Soldat und ein Mädchen* (1960; a soldier and a girl) is an experimental novel that permits the narrator to edit and analyze the material in the process of creating objective distance between reader and story. Fried's short stories, in *Kinder und Narren* (1965; children and fools), *Fast alles Mögliche* (1975; almost everything possible), and *Das Unmaß aller Dinge* (1982; the immoderation of all things), stress the relationship between artistic expression and literary substance. His narrative and lyrical structures are similar, offering a language of mimicry that encircles the point to be made. The modern parables of *Das Unmaß aller Dinge* are especially meaningful for their astute revelations concerning connections between words and politics.

Another writer who focuses on the interdependency of language and existence is Ingeborg Bachmann (1926–73). *Das dreißigste Jahr* (1962; *The Thirtieth Year,* 1964) stresses the idea that symbols reflect the transformation of the world. In *Malina* (1971; Malina) the presentation of observations and experiences is uncomfortably fragmented, often degenerating into confusing personal trivia. *Simultan* (1972; simultaneous) and *Gier* (1973; greed) contain stories that feature an unusual lyrical monologue approach but fail to maintain the reader's interest.

For Jakov Lind (b. 1927), literature has value only as it stimulates emotion. Accordingly, the nightmares and surrealistic visions of *Eine Seele aus Holz* (1962; *Soul of Wood and Other Stories,* 1964), *Landschaft aus Beton* (1963; *Landscape in Concrete,* 1966), *Eine bessere Welt* (1966; *Ergo,* 1967), *Der Ofen* (1973; *The Stove,* 1983), and *Reise zu den Enu* (1983; *Travels to the Enu,* 1982) mix realism with extreme symbolism. In spite of the power of his imagery, Lind's works are devoid of logical integration, and suffer from unpolished, impetuous, carelessly employed language.

With *Frost* (1963; frost), Thomas Bernhard (b. 1931), the *enfant terrible* of postwar Austrian literature, focused on the clash between the alienated individual and a decaying, defective world. The characters and situations of *Frost* and such works as *Verstörung* (1967; *Gargoyles,* 1970), *Das Kalkwerk* (1970; *Limeworks,* 1973), and *Korrektur* (1975; *Corrections,* 1979) are cold and brutal, and the narratives process in endless variation the themes of illness, insanity, death, cruelty, falsehood, and mental obsession. *Die Billigesser* (1980; the cheap eaters) is a negation of the idea of meaning in life and the intellectual's traditional role in interpreting it, while *Der Untergeher* (1983; the man going under) is a study in moral and mental decline. In *Holzfällen* (1984; chopping wood) Bernhard combined the motifs of isolation and suicide as stimuli for artistic creativity, ironically highlighting the essence of his own successful creative process.

Konrad Bayer (1932–64) employed devices of language combination, alienation, and permutation in his efforts to create literature in which the individual can become immersed. The two posthumously published volumes, *kopf des vitus bering* (1965; Vitus Bering's head) and *Der sechste Sinn* (1966; the sixth sense), reflect his search for new means of expression, his inclination toward black humor and surrealistic montage, and his endeavor to recreate a world characterized by the simultaneity of events and processes. Bayer's major contribution to prose technique is the reinterpretation of surrealism as a device to destroy the sequential nature of time.

Gerhard Rühm (b. 1930), another representative of the Wiener Gruppe, created new forms of prose expression with the so-called "texts" of *Fenster* (1968; windows) and *Die Frösche und andere texte* (1971; the frogs and other texts). Using constructivist techniques, he blended external and internal human experiences in unique fashion. The most peculiar aspect of his approach is the use of sentence montage to transform the description of an external process into a simulation of it.

A third member of the Wiener Gruppe, Oswald Wiener (b. 1935), published *Die Verbesserung von Mitteleuropa* (1969; the improvement of Central Europe) as his major contribution to avant-garde prose. Based on studies of theoretical and practical cybernetics, especially number theory, the work combines rudiments and fragments of experiments with language and thought. Continuous variation of all possible literary short forms, from aphorism and note to essay and montage, frustrates any literary expectation the reader may have, and the attempt to present language itself as social consciousness remains senseless and unconvincing.

One of the most controversial novelists who emerged in the 1960s was Peter Handke (b. 1942). The essence of his writing is language experiment and the revelation of relationships between expression and consciousness. *Die Hornissen* (1966; the hornets) mixes images and scenes from a remembered childhood with elements from a second story, in a peculiar representation of the novel's genesis. Its most important aspect is the precise detailing of reality. In *Der Hausierer* (1967; the peddler) the process of abstraction and reflection forces each reader to create a personal story. The theme of murder'that is central to *Der Hausierer* is developed in other, less effective ways is *Die Angst des Tormanns beim Elfmeter* (1970; *The Goalie's Anxiety at the Penalty Kick*, 1972) and *Die Stunde der wahren Empfindungen* (1975; *A Moment of True Feeling*, 1977). Especially successful is *Die Linkshändige Frau* (1976; *The Left-handed Woman*, 1978), the story of a person suddenly forced to cope with her own independence and disorientation. The complex tetralogy consisting of *Langsame Heimkehr* (1979; *Slow Homecoming*, 1985), *Die Lehre der Sainte-Victoire* (1980; the doctrine of Sainte-Victoire), *Kindergeschichte* (1981; children's story), and *Über die Dörfer* (1981; about the villages) stresses the positive aspects of life in a demonstration of the strong interdependency of nature and man. Handke's *Der Chinese des Schmerzes* (1983; *Across*, 1986) is a profound statement on the intrinsic dialectic between life and fiction.

Peter Marginter's (b. 1934) novels and stories exemplify the renewed interest in peculiarly Austrian figures that was stimulated by the revival of Herzmanovsky-Orlando's works. *Der Baron und die Fische* (1966; the baron and the fish), *Der tote Onkel* (1967; the dead uncle), *Leichenschmaus* (1969; funeral meal), *Königrufen* (1973; calling the king), and *Der Graf von Carabas* (1973; the count of Carabas) reflect a mixture of fantasy and realism, and comic and the macabre, in exposing the absurdities of human existence and satirizing the Austrian past.

The ironic narratives of Barbara Frischmuth (b. 1941) focus on children and young people. Her penetration of the problems of puberty in *Die Klosterschule* (1968; the convent school) stresses the tension between imposed behavior patterns and natural inclinations. Other works that successfully explore the same conflicts from new perspectives are *Amoralische Kinderklapper* (1969; amoral children's rattle), *Tage und Jahre* (1971; days and years), and *Rückkehr zum vorläufigen Ausgangspunkt* (1973; return to the provisional point of departure). The novel *Das Verschwinden des Schattens in der Sonne* (1973; the shadow's disappearance in the sun) and the four stories in *Haschen nach Wind* (1974; grabbing at the wind) present in a highly convincing manner realistic interpersonal conflicts from a feminist perspective. Her trilogy *Die Mystifikationen der Sophie Silber* (1976; the mystifications of Sophie Silber), *Amy oder Die Metamorphose* (1978; Amy; or, the metamorphosis), and *Kai und die Liebe zu den Modellen* (1979; Kai and the love for the models) develops the connection between dream and reality by portraying the real world as a product of thought and feeling. With these novels and newer works such as *Die Ferienfamilie* (1981; the vacation family), *Die Frau im Mond* (1982; the woman in the moon), *Traumgrenze* (1983; dream border), and *Kopftänzer* (1984; head dancers) Frischmuth is justifiably recognized as one of Austria's most important nondoctrinal feminist authors.

Geometrischer Heimatroman (1969; geometrical regional novel), Gert Friedrich Jonke's (b. 1946) first volume of prose, introduced a series of creations that emphasize playful ordering, repetition, and variation of idea and word strands in humorous, ironic language experiments. Although aspects of *Glashausbesichtigung* (1970; viewing a glass house), *Beginn einer Verzweiflung* (1970; beginning of a despair), *Musikgeschichte* (1970; music story), *Die Vermehrung der Leuchttürme* (1971; multiplication of lighthouses), and other similar volumes are interesting and even provocative, their repetitiveness and banality often become tiresome. With *Schule der Geläufigkeit* (1977; school of fluency) Jonke reached a new stage in his development. The narrative is now more direct and less frivolous; the dialectic between appearance and reality assumes a more tangible role in a presentation with remarkable depth. Although *Der ferne Klang* (1979; the distant sound) is more abstract than *Schule der Geläufigkeit*, Jonke's processing of the development of wish to dream is singularly effective. In *Erwachen zum großen Schlafkrieg* (1982; awakening to the great sleep war) the author completes a willful dissolution of reality in a unique flow of luxuriant language, grotesque wordplays, and extraordinary word creations.

The language experiments of the Wiener Gruppe and the nontraditional approaches of Peter Handke exerted significant influence on the prose creations of Michael Scharang (b. 1941). Unlike his models, Scharang gives his writings a practical political orientation. *Verfahren eines Verfahrens* (1969; process of a process) and *Schluß mit dem Erzählen und andere Erzählungen* (1970; an end to storytelling and other stories) are documents of the extreme left. They employ devices of concrete poetry in a dialectical attempt to capture the social extremes in everyday reality. *Charley Traktor* (1973; Charly Tractor) and *Sohn eines Landarbeiters* (1976; son of a farmworker) present precise and realistic descriptions of social tensions between the middle and lower classes. They belong to the mainstream of Austrian literature of the working world.

New writers of the 1970s experimented with fresh techniques of expression to deal with different kinds of experience. Some focused on the observation and isolation of events and situations, while others worked with satirical montage, anecdotal narrative, and the alienation of events from their context. Interpretation of reality was filtered through a new aesthetics involving the superficialities of consumer society, pop-art sentiment, trivial novel paraphrase, and the clichés of illustrated magazines. Treatment of the psychology of experience became more extreme through the employment of stream-of-consciousness techniques, the exploration of drug encounters, the application of psychoanalytical experimentation to the relationships between individual and society, and the examination of unusual mental conditions. At the same time, experiments with language continued. Conservative authors reemphasized Austrian tradition; political and social reformers stressed practical literature and a new realism.

Elfriede Jelinek's (b. 1946) fiction emphasizes manipulation of personal existence in a deindividualized society. In *Wir sind Lockvögel, Baby* (1970; we are decoys, baby) she combined linguistic and other aspects of regional literature with pornographic, comic, and horror elements. The result is a biting parody of the traditional novel. *Michael, Ein Jugendbuch für die Infantilgesellschaft* (1972; Michael, a juvenile book for the infantile society) satirizes media heroes by juxtaposing their world with that of their fans, while *Die Liebhaberinnen* (1975; the women enthusiasts) is a merciless satire about the lives and personal consciousness of two underprivileged women. *Die Klavierspielerin* (1983; the lady pianist) is an example of black comedy at its best.

The goal of Alois Brandstetter's (b. 1938) writings is ironic, humorous illumination of Austrian social and intellectual foibles. *Überwindung der Blitzangst* (1971; overcoming the fear of lightning) and *Ausfälle, Natur- und Kunstgeschichten* (1972; losses, nature and art stories) illustrate his mastery of satire and the play of language. Among his best works are *Zu lasten der Briefträger* (1974; charges against the mailmen), *Der Leumund des Löwen* (1976; the lion's reputation), and *Die Abtei* (1977; the abbey)—strong illustrations of his blustering, accusatory lamentation about everyday outrages and prejudices. *Vom Schnee der vergangenen Jahre* (1979; about the snow of past years), *Die Mühle* (1981; the mill), *Über den grünen Klee der Kindheit* (1982; on the green clover of childhood), and *Altenehrung* (1983; honoring the old people) are the solid productions of a writer who has reached literary maturity and is able to present his ideas in extremely convincing language.

The conflict between the powerful and their subordinates is treated allegorically in Alfred Kolleritsch's (b. 1931) *Die Pfirsichtöter* (1972; the peach killers). In his anti-traditional criticism, Kolleritsch attacks and parodies philosophical language and the attitudes of his childhood world. At the heart of *Die grüne Seite* (1974; the green side) is a personal treatise on the problems of identity, individual autonomy, and their loss. In the stories "Die Ebene" (1975; the plain) and "Gangaufsicht" (1976; hallway supervision), in the novel *Von der schwarzen Kappe* (1974; about the black cap), and especially in *Gespräche im Heilbad* (1985; conversations in the health spa), Kolleritsch probes with insight and artistry unresolved questions of honesty and truth, the relationship between state and citizen, and the ties between Austrians and the Nazi past.

Unlike Brandstetter's optimistic visions, Peter Rosei's (b. 1946) prose parables focus on nature as a symbol for a monstrous world with no way out. In *Landstriche* (1972; stretches of land) the topographical background of a dismal frontier symbolizes poverty and the individual misery of human existence. From a different perspective, *Bei schwebendem Verfahren* (1973; in pending action) presents modern society as a total bureaucracy in decline. Later productions, from *Wege* (1974; ways) through *Der Fluß der Gedanken durch den Kopf* (1976; the flow of thoughts through the head) and *Das schnelle Glück* (1980; quick happiness), depict in endless variation man's inhumanity and bestiality, his inner dissolution, and his increasing desperation. Rosei's strongest gift is his ability to describe. In *Komödie* (1984; comedy) that facility is powerfully manifested in a broad range of fairy-tale, surreal, and apocalyptic visions. The work that follows it, *Mann und Frau* (1984; man and wife), is a disappointment. Lack of descriptive richness, haphazard narration, and weak presentation make it Rosei's least satisfying work to date.

Psychological aspects of human isolation are central to Gerhard Roth's (b. 1942) experimental and traditional narratives. In *die autobiographie des albert einstein* (1972; the autobiography of Albert Einstein), Roth describes an insane individual who thinks he is Einstein. He experiences an inner change of consciousness, destroys his existing view of the world, and creates a new one. The three pieces in *Der Ausbruch des ersten Weltkrieges und andere Romane* (1972; the outbreak of the First World War and other novels) project a fatally ill society, while *Der Wille zur Krankheit* (1973; the will to be ill) sketches the history of a decaying consciousness. *Der große Horizont* (1974; the large horizon), *Ein neuer Morgen* (1976; a new morning), and *Winterreise* (1978; winter journey) also examine existential crises, flights from reality, and psychological dualities, but they employ more traditional techniques. Two of his best works are *Der stille Ozean* (1980; the quiet ocean), a study in isolation from civilization followed by new integration into a more primitive natural world, and *Landläufiger Tod* (1984; common death), a masterfully constructed history of the life and death of a small village society.

Jutta Schutting (b. 1937) also emphasizes the psychological element in her precise portrayals of changing thoughts and feelings, but the dominant feature of *Baum in O.* (1973; tree in O.), *Tauchübungen* (1974; diving exercises), *Parkmord* (1975; park murder), and *Sistiana* (1976; Sistiana) is grammatical experimentation. Her ability to manipulate forms of expression and create unusual effects is best demonstrated in *Am Morgen vor der Reise* (1978; on the morning before the journey), where the dynamics of the story arise out of brief sequential vignettes presented from the perspective of two children. The psychological probing of self is important in *Salzburg retour* (1978; Salzburg return) and *Der Vater* (1980; the father), which are presented with great care, clear observation, deep insight, and significant poetic power. *Liebesroman* (1983; love novel) attempts an ever deeper penetration of emotions, attitudes, and feelings. It is relatively successful in projecting mood and idea, but many of the linguistic manipulations are irritating.

A literary disciple of Michael Scharang, Helmut Zenker (b. 1949) illuminates defects in society from the perspective of depraved outsiders in *Wer hier die Fremden sind* (1973; whoever the foreigners here are) and *Froschfest* (1977; frog festival), while *Kassbach* (1974; Kassbach) interprets neo-fascist brutality and terroristic political activism. *Wer hier die Fremden sind* is directly autobiographical in tone, while *Kass-*

bach is built upon pseudo-documentary devices. In *Das Froschfest* Zenker made the transition to labor literature.

The creations of Gernot Wolfgruber (b. 1944) are also a product of the new realism. His books *Auf freiem Fuβ* (1975; on his own), *Herrenjahre* (1976; years at the top), *Die Mehrzahl* (1978; the majority), and *Neimandsland* (1978; no man's land) focus on the average hopeless existence in the provincial proletarian milieu. With unprecedented authenticity, they describe in clear, direct language elements of the postwar Austrian world of work. Wolfgruber's most powerful rendering of the individual's adjustment to the world without satisfying his own emotional and spiritual needs is *Verlauf eines Sommers* (1981; the course of a summer).

In *Die Schwerkraft der Verhältnisse* (1978; the gravity of the relationships) and *Das Kind der Gewalt und die Sterne der Romani* (1980; the child of violence and the stars of the Romany), Marianne Fritz (b. 1948) offered parts of a larger cycle, tentatively called *Die Festung* (the fortress). The project focuses on the origins and reality of Austria during the First and Second Republics. *Die Schwerkraft der Verhältnisse* is an effective modern variation of the Medea legend, while *Das Kind der Gewalt und die Sterne der Romani* deals with a peasant family's existence during the nineteenth and early twentieth centuries. With *Dessen Sprache du nicht verstehst* (1985; whose language you do not understand), the massive completion of the undertaking, Fritz created one of the most complex, most frustrating novels of modern Austrian literature. Almost 3,400 pages of language experiment challenge the reader's concentration. The result is an esoteric monument to the impenetrability of reality.

The personal Austrian experience is the essence of Josef Winkler's (b. 1953) trilogy *Menschenkind* (1979; human child), *Der Ackermann aus Kärnten* (1980; the farmer from Carinthia), and *Muttersprache* (1982; mother tongue). Winkler's narratives are autobiographical, but their meaning lies in the perceptive penetration of interpersonal relationships in a violently patriarchal society where language is used to dominate and oppress.

Fettfleck (1979; grease spot), Diana Kempff's (b. 1945) first novel, is a unique contribution to the literature of grappling with childhood and youth. Its first-person narrative style parallels the growth of the central character, appearing to mature and solidify as the narrator grows older. In the short sketches of *Der vorsichtige Zusammenbruch* (1981; the careful collapse) loneliness is carried to an extreme in which reality and fantasy cannot be separated, while *Der Wanderer* (1985; the wanderer) is an almost lyrical registration of impression and events that dominate a dreamscape of hopelessness, defeat, destruction, and evil. In processing themes and images, Kempff displays significant originality and an evocative strength of language.

Recent tendencies in Austrian fiction resemble those in other German literatures. Dominant themes include coldness, isolation, fear, and flight from the everyday world. External reality is a threatening force. Illness, insanity, decay, and death are the prominent elements of a nightmare landscape, and tensions arise from the constant confrontation with self, either in struggles with the past and its guilt or in grapplings with the senselessness of present-day life.

The full spectrum of current literary preoccupations is visible in the novels of Joseph Zoderer (b. 1935). Youthful rebellion against spiritual restrictions is the central theme of *Glück beim Händewaschen* (1982; the joy of washing one's hands), a work that combines brief, colorless scenes with an acutely perceptive narrative consciousness in penetrating the processes that threaten individual freedom. *Die Walsche* (1982; the Italian woman) is equally compelling. It explores in compact and forceful detail the specific problem of alienation arising out of a relationship between a man and a woman of different nationalities. From a different perspective, the individual's inability to be anything but an outsider is placed in unique focus in the figure of a nameless drifter in *Lotano* (1984; Lotano).

Although Inge Merkel's (b. 1922) *Das andere Gesicht* (1982; the other face) is tedious and contrived, it is a uniquely original variation on the theme of apocalypse and modern evil. In *Zypressen* (1983; cypresses), however, the ironic humor that strengthens *Das andere Gesicht* is insufficient to counteract laborious overwriting and naive psychologizing that bury whatever positive qualities her stories might otherwise have.

Inability to communicate and a feminist interpretation of the modern male–female relationship provide theme and focus for Lisa Witasek's (b. 1956) *Die Umarmung oder Das weiße Zimmer* (1983; the embrace; or, the white room). While the portrayal of the protagonist's inferiority complex, her personal frustrations, and her complicated mental responses are somewhat effective, the stock portrayal of self-centered masculinity, the frequent ambiguity of the text, and overdone female masochism combine to render the novella weak and unconvincing.

POETRY

New Austrian poetry was strongly influenced by an almost programmatic cultural policy that favored tradition. Heavy emphasis was placed on models of humane order and democratic human dignity, and on an unfettered, morally responsible art that does not demean the language. Coupled with these tendencies were thrusts that rejected themes that had been propagated by nationalistic poets. Confrontation with the spirit of the times destroyed many established writers, who never again matched their earlier productivity or lyric quality. Others were stimulated by their wartime experiences to achieve new literary heights.

Although Rudolf Henz's (b. 1897) collections *Wort in der Zeit* (1945; word in time), *Österreichische Trilogie* (1950; Austrian trilogy), and *Lobgesang auf unsere Zeit* (1956; song of praise to our time) are clouded by rhetorical extravagance and veneers of pathos, his later productions replaced artificiality with a dynamic, honest Christian humanism and a sincere commitment to Austrian origins. *Der geschlossene Kreis* (1964; the closed circle) emphasizes the tension between Henz's rural background and a developing allegiance to urban life. It also illuminates his search for meaning in his own art. Henz's masterpiece is *Neue Gedichte* (1972; new poems), a powerfully humane confession of his perceptions of the times and his relationship to them.

Alexander Lernet-Holenia's postwar anthologies, *Die Ti-tanen* (1945; the titans), *Germanien* (1946; Germania), *Die Trophäe* (1946; the trophy), and *Das Feuer* (1949; the fire), are distinctly different in language and tone from earlier works that had established him as a renewer of classical tradition. The new works are dominated by a lonely severity, sublime moroseness, melancholy, bitterness, revulsion, and elegiac meditation. His hymns of mourning for a past that is irre-trievably lost are among the most beautiful in modern German poetry.

Like the postwar creations of Rudolf Henz, Paula von Pre-radović's (1887–1951) *Ritter, Tod und Teufel* (1947; knight, death, and devil), *Gesammelte Gedichte* (1949; collected poems), *Verlorene Heimat* (1951; lost homeland), and *Schicksalsland* (1952; land of fate) reflect a strong connection between the poet, her origins, and the Catholic religion. The strength of her writing lies in landscape portrayal and an ability to combine musicality with strict form. In some instances, her substance threatens to overwhelm her imagery, and the result is a some-what hollow didactic.

Das Unbefehligte (1947; that which is not commanded), *Herz in der Kelter* (1954; heart in the winepress), and *Landnacht* (1966; country night), by Wilhelm Szabo (b. 1901), are addi-tional products of the postwar emphasis on Austrian tradition. In *Das Unbefehligte*, Szabo's concern is a reclamation of the concept of homeland, while *Herz in der Kelter* is dedicated to the nameless poor of the Austrian villages. His best creations are simple, serious, often elegiac representations of landscapes and rural experience. The inclination toward aphorism and didactic in *Landnacht* and *Schallgrenze* (1975; sound barrier) resulted in poems that are far less powerful than his descrip-tions of encounters with reality.

Especially regional in tone are the hymns to the landscape of the southern Tirol found in Joseph Georg Oberkofler's (1889–1962) *Und meine Liebe, die nicht sterben will* (1948; and my love that does not want to die) and *Verklärter Tag* (1950; trans-figured day). These collections offer combinations of impulses from history, folk and peasant life, and local Catholic tradition, but the portraits of Alpine farmers, stone silhouettes, mountain storms, and starlit skies seldom convey more than the superficial beauty that they describe.

There is a strong contrast between the poetry that Erika Mitterer (b. 1906) wrote before the war, and the offerings contained in the collections that followed *Zwölf Gedichte 1933–1945* (1946; twelve poems 1933–1945). Like Paula von Preradović, she devoted much creative energy to warnings and admonitions, but her criticisms of the times and the attacks on modern evils in *Gesammelte Gedichte* (1956; collected poems) and *Weihnacht der Einsamen* (1969; Christmas of the lonely) are hollow, banal, and insensitive. Only the more descriptive religious portraits in *Klopfsignale* (1970; knock signals) and a few items in *Entsühnung des Kain* (1974; the atonement of Cain) are musically stirring and compelling.

Another poet whose postwar productions belie the brightness and color of earlier work was Josef Leitgeb (1897–1952). His final collection, *Lebenszeichen* (1951; signs of life), mirrors a strong perception of general human guilt and decline. Exaggerated declamation against a humanity that is evil, ill, and infecting the universe with incurable disease informs a poetry of woundedness that he never again transcended.

The impact of Theodor Kramer (1897–1958) on postwar Austrian poetry is still unmeasured. *Die untere Schenke* (1946; the bottom tavern), *Die grünen Kader* (1946; the green cadres), *Lob der Verzweiflung* (1947; praise of despair), and *Vom schwarzen Wein* (1956; about black wine), the postwar collections published while he was alive, represent only a small portion of his work, and more than 10,000 poems remain unpublished. The most powerful volume is *Lob der Verzweiflung,* a document of spiritual isolation that focuses on the landscape of the modern world as a graveyard of nameless people. All of the motifs of isolation, failure to communicate, suicide, panic, and the like that are found in German literature of the 1980s are uncomfortably foreshadowed in Kramer's projections of his own alienation.

Not all Austrian poets who went into exile produced verse as pessimistic as Kramer's. Some of them maintained a view of the world based on positive, traditional ideals.

Ernst Waldinger's (1896–1970) *Die kühlen Bauernstuben*

(1946; the cool farmhouse parlours), *Musik für diese Zeit* (1946; music for this time), *Glück und Geduld* (1952; happiness and patience), *Zwischen Hudson und Donau* (1958; between the Hudson and the Danube), *Gesang vor dem Abgrund* (1961; song before the abyss), and *Ich kann mit meinem Bruder sprechen* (1965; I can talk with my brother) project belief in the invincibility of art and praise the strength of the occidental spirit. His powerful sonnets emphasize the art of life, the strength of traditional values, and the validity of human order. Although the poems are informed by his experience of America, they never lose the flavor and atmosphere of Austria.

Although Hans Leifhelm (1891–1947) was born in Germany, his poetic career began in Austria and is a product of experience in the "second homeland." The lyrics in *Lob der Vergänglichkeit* (1949; praise of transitoriness) reflect his almost magical ability to project sensitive impressions of nature and landscape.

The lasting value of Franz Theodor Csokor's (1885–1969) *Das schwarze Schiff* (1944; the black ship) and *Immer ist Anfang* (1952; there is always a beginning) lies in a facility for mutating the experience of force and suffering, violence and sacrifice, into catharsis and healing. His exile poetry is especially notable for its factually passionate style of argumentation, and its dramatic tension and power.

An encounter with classical antiquity and the processing of Christian ideas are combined in the almost timeless lyric creations of Felix Braun (1885–1973). *Viola d'amore* (1953; viola d'amore) and *Das Nelkenbeet* (1966; the carnation bed) reproduce the poet's inner life. Although tied closely to tradition, the poems do not imitate earlier models. Rather, they document the essence of their author's personal wisdom, humanity, openness, and noble convictions.

Like Felix Braun and other tradition-oriented poets, Paula Ludwig (1900–74) was strongly influenced by Rainer Maria Rilke. Her only postwar collection, *Gedichte* (1958; poems), illustrates her predilection for sensitive, fine-toned nature poetry, and for treatments of feminine themes, especially motherhood. Her best poems are hymns and rhapsodies that celebrate the beauties of nature, but she also created moving, deeply melancholy projections of loneliness, longing, and the experience of suffering. The quality of her verse is tempered only by its fragility and a certain self-tormenting shyness in its presentation.

Friedrich Torberg's *Lebenslied* (1958; song of life) also reflects the influence of Rilke, but its poetic forms are remarkably varied. Important themes are homelessness and divine judgment, love and innocence, transgression of eternal laws and immanent humanity. Although none of his poems are truly great, many of them are unique and powerful in their interpretation of the human condition.

The works of Austrian poets whose careers began after the war reflect increasing diversification. While many of these writers maintained ties to landscape, people, and traditions, others began a more direct and objective processing of postwar conditions, new social and political themes, existential problems, and the world situation.

Deutschland (1944; Germany) and *Österreich* (1946; Austria), Erich Fried's earliest collections, are marked by musical language and strong imagery. The poems have the quality of folk lyrics and are significantly different from his later, more socially and politically critical verse. Fried's artistic development, as reflected in *Gedichte* (1958; poems), *Reich der Steine* (1963; realm of the stones),*Warngedichte* (1965; warning poems), *Befreiung von der Flucht* (1968; liberation from flight), *Gegengift* (1974; antidote), and *Liebesgedichte* (1979; love poems), progresses toward the creation of dialectical works that denounce the contradictions and inhumanity of fixed ideologies. Manipulative association, play with words, epigrammatic pointedness, sharpness of perception, and an open, undogmatic Marxism are carefully honed elements in *Das Nahe suchen* (1982; seeking what is near) and *Beunruhigungen* (1984; uneasinesses). Unfortunately, the quality of the poems is uneven. These volumes contain a few of his best works but also some of his worst.

Another poet whose initial lyrics are filled with idyllic optimism and a positive relationship to nature is Vera Ferra (b. 1923). *Melodie am Morgen* (1946; melody in the morning) and other writings reflect a remarkably refreshing purity and directness of expression that is seldom found in the postwar works of older poets. During the 1950s, Ferra's poetic mood changed to one of hopelessness. In *Zeit ist mit Uhren nicht meß ar* (1962; time cannot be measured with clocks) life is an evil fairy tale. Her harsh, masculine, skeptical language attacks modern society as an incubator of murder and misery.

The war's impact is strongly visible in the expressive poems of Michael Guttenbrunner (b. 1919). *Schwarze Ruten* (1947; black switches) and *Opferholz* (1954; sacrificial wood) contain formally simple, richly symbolic lyrics that are filled with anger and sympathy, horror and protest against the modern world order. In later books, from *Ungereimte Gedichte* (1959; unrhymed poems) and *Die lange Zeit* (1965; the long time) through *Der Abstieg* (1975; the descent) and *Gesang der Schiffe* (1980; song of the ships), the classicistic forms have less vitality, although he is consistent in his opposition to oppression in any form, and to the systematic reduction of standards and values.

In contrast to works by Guttenbrunner, Franz Pühringer's (1906–77) nature poetry withdraws almost completely from the terror of the postwar world. *Die Wiesenfestung* (1947; the meadow fortress), *Das Paradies* (1949; the paradise), *Letzter Duft der Gartenfrühe* (1963; last fragrance of the morning garden), and *An den Quellen der Nebenflüsse* (1964; at the sources of the tributary streams) offer a sometimes ironic picture of nature, devoid of mysticism and myth. Pühringer's carefully detailed portraits of small events and relationships reduce problems of instinct to harmless, even ridiculous manifestations of things that are catastrophic and horribly senseless in the larger human context.

For Ernst Schönwiese (b. 1905) poetry is a vehicle for authentic human expression. The deeply thoughtful, musical poems of *Der siebenfarbige Bogen* (1947; the bow of seven colors), *Ausfahrt und Wiederkehr* (1947; departure and return), and *Nacht und Verheißung* (1950; night and promise) reflect the formal influence of classical models. The first high point of Schönwiese's art was *Das unverlorene Paradies* (1951; paradise not lost), a collection of timeless reflections on man's continuing relationship to God. Equally artistic are the painful laments of *Requiem in Versen* (1953; requiem in verse). In his mature works—*Stufen des Herzens* (1956; steps of the heart), *Traum und Verwandlung* (1959; dream and transformation), *Baum und Träne* (1962; tree and tear), *Geheimnisvolles Ballspiel* (1965; mysterious ball game), and *Odysseus und der Alchimist* (1968; Odysseus and the alchemist)—he achieved a remarkable precision of expression and a harmony of form, language, and humanistic substance.

Paul Celan (1920–70) was a mediator of French symbolist and surrealistic influences. *Der Sand aus den Urnen* (1948; the sand from the urns), *Mohn und Gedächtnis* (1952; poppy and memory), and *Von Schwelle zu Schwelle* (1955; from threshold to threshold) contain carefully crafted verse that is rich in imagery and associative elements, sonorous and sadly melodic. His keenly visionary, alogical metaphors and abstractly acoustical, dark word music later gave way to increasingly cryptic and puzzling language in *Sprachgitter* (1959; *Speech-Grille*, 1971), *Die Niemandsrose* (1963; the no man's rose), *Atemwende* (1967; breath turn), *Fadensonnen* (1968; thread suns), *Lichtzwang* (1970; light compulsion), and *Schneepart* (1970; snow part). Celan's esoteric, metaphorically coded verse remains among the very best produced in Austria since the war.

The dark side of nature informs Anna Maria Achenrainer's (1909–72) poems in *Appassionata* (1949; Appassionata), *Der zwölfblättrige Lotos* (1957; lotus with twelve leaves), *Der grüne Kristall* (1960; the green crystal), *Die Windrose* (1962; the wind rose), *Das geflügelte Licht* (1963; the winged light), and *Horizonte der Hoffnung* (1966; horizons of hope). Fear of death, the death wish, and a dreamlike knowledge of the realm of the dead overshadow any recognizable portrayals of landscape. The resulting productions depend on rhythm and sound rather than visual images for their effect and meaning.

Achenrainer's writings are darkly similar to those of Christine Lavant (1915–73), whose *Die unvollendete Liebe* (1949; the incomplete love) was greeted as the work of Austria's most important new nature poet. *Die Bettlerschale* (1956; the beggar's bowl), *Spindel im Mond* (1959; spindle in the moon), *Der Pfauenschrei* (1962; cry of the peacock), and *Gedichte* (1972; poems) are filled with a strangely morbid mysticism, in which the agony of regret and self-castigation magnifies the struggle for grace and the longing to transcend this world to a union with God. The strength of her poetry lies in the combination of transparency and intensity of expression with a uniquely personal confessional vision of suffering and lament.

The apocalyptical element is extremely typical for Austrian poetry of the 1950s, but other tendencies manifested themselves as well. Some writers moved toward the absurd, while others focused on existentialist concepts of active freedom. Experimentation led to enormously successful dialect poetry, combinations of romanticism and surrealism, word montage, sound poems, letter patterns, and other extremes. The strongest trend led toward surrealistic hermetic verse, but traditionalism and rejection of playful experimentation also remained important.

Christine Busta's (b. 1915) poems combine traditional forms with mythological and Christian themes. The tone of *Jahr um Jahr* (1950; year after year), *Der Regenbaum* (1951; the rain tree), *Lampe und Delphin* (1955; lamp and dolphin), and *Die Scheune der Vögel* (1958; the barn of the birds) is melodic but melancholy, combining a modern feeling of life with the experience of suffering and mourning. *Unterwegs zu älteren Frauen* (1965; on the way to older women), *Salzgärten* (1975; salt gardens), and *Wenn du das Wappen der Liebe malst* (1981; when you paint love's coat of arms) project impressions of journeys and childhood, insights and realizations, employing powerfully simple language in the search for peace in a nature threatened with destruction by man and his works.

In Rudolf Bayr's (b. 1919) *Der Dekalog* (1951; the ten commandments) and *Der Wolkenfisch* (1964; the cloud fish) the only path to lasting peace is a return to the covenant with God. The setting for *Der Dekalog* is an earth that remains the domain of farmers, threatened by the evils of industrialization. *Der Wolkenfisch* is a document of resignation in the face of destructive forces that can no longer be restrained. The only thing that makes his nihilism palatable is the subtle transformation of mourning into irony.

The early collections of Kurt Klinger (b. 1928), *Harmonie aus Blut* (1951; harmony from blood) and *Auf der Erde zu Gast*

(1956; a guest on the earth), feature language that is charged with emotion and combines broad dimensions with realistic detail. The strongest aspects of his verse are moving rhythms and a tension between the dramatic and philosophical elements. *Entwurf einer Festung* (1970; outline of a fortress), *Löwenköpfe* (1977; lion's heads), and *Auf dem Limes* (1980; on the limes) are more intellectual than artistic. They feature a baroque richness of vocabulary, a fullness of imagery, and substantial color, but the satirical elements and the manipulations of language fail to avoid artificiality.

Important examples of surrealistic hermetic poetry appear in the books of Jeannie Ebner. *Gesang an das Heute* (1952; song to today), *Gedichte* (1965; poems), *Prosadichtungen* (1973; prose poems), and *Sag ich* (1978; say I) document the development of a cyclical Creation mythos with poles of generation and destruction—each the inevitable outgrowth of the other. Ebner's metaphors vividly represent change and growth that interplay with death and decay in a dynamic vision of daily apocalypse.

Stimmen der Gegenwart (1951; voices of the present), *Zwischen Kirkenes und Bari* (1952; between Kirkenes and Bari), and *Lehm und Gestalt* (1954; clay and form), Gerhard Fritsch's (1924–69) early volumes of lyrics, explore a variety of themes, including nature, people, the war, the Austrian landscape, and human history. The tone of these and later collections, from *Dieses Dunkel heißt Nacht* (1955; this darkness is called night) and *Der Geisterkrug* (1958; the jug of the spirits) to *Gesammelte Gedichte* (1978; collected poems), is heavy and sad. While the verse of *Stimmen der Gegenwart* is traditional in form, subsequent efforts combine montage of pregnant details with argumentation, personal confession, and an almost journalistic didactic. Fritsch's best creations are dramatic, active, energetic nature lyrics with cathartic power, but some of the elegiac offerings in *Dieses Dunkel heißt Nacht* are also impressive.

One of the most important Austrian poets of the 1950s was Ingeborg Bachmann. Her books *Die gestundete Zeit* (1953; deferred time) and *Anrufung des Großen Bären* (1956; invocation of the Great Bear) are dominated by intellectually abstract, philosophical free rhythms. Personal diction and unique tone combine with esoteric encodings to form an art that is especially powerful in its mastery of language and immanent musicality. Although her symbols are not always convincing, Bachmann created a compelling, bizarre, personal world of images, natural melody, and manipulation of linguistic gesture that remains unexcelled in modern German poetry.

Herbert Zand's *Die Glaskugel* (1953; the glass ball) and *Aus zerschossenem Sonnengeflecht* (1973; from a bullet-ridden web of sunlight) project the beauties of peasant landscape and the creative power of nature. The poet's approach to his material is neither additive nor reflective. Zand accepts nature as an organism without symbolic implications. His verse is important for its expression of faith in the natural order's healing power, and for its fundamentally hopeful criticism of the times.

Thomas Bernhard's early poetry, in *Auf der Erde und in der Hölle* (1957; on earth and in hell), *In hora mortis* (1958; in the hour of death), and *Unter dem Eisen des Mondes* (1958; beneath the iron of the moon), is related in its dark colors, rich metaphors, and highly surrealistic effects to the verse of Georg Trakl (1887–1914). Bernhard's creations are somewhat unruly, filled with pain, melancholy, and horrible beauty, but they also exhibit a despairing hope and a longing for redemption. Their strength lies in an apocalyptic revelation of the poet's inner world.

In contrast to the heavy tone of Bernhard's poems, the lyrics of Doris Mühringer (b. 1920) are light and airy. The vitality of nature in *Gedichte I* (1957; poems I), *Gedichte II* (1969; poems II), *Gedichte III* (1976; poems III), and *Vögel, die ohne Schlaf sind* (1984; birds without sleep) is projected in a smooth flow of images that vividly highlight intimate confrontation with flowers, birds, insects, water, and trees. Although these creations are not starkly original, their musicality, simplicity, and warmth of tone convincingly convey the conviction that it is possible to experience life's sweetness and joy.

Experimentation with language is part of the basis for Andreas Okopenko's (b. 1930) poetic art, but the free rhythms of *Grüner November* (1957; green November), the skeptical protocols of *Seltsame Tage* (1963; strange days) and *Orte wechselnden Unbehagens* (1971; places of changing uneasiness), and the mockingly playful parodies of his contemporaries in *Der Akazienfresser* (1973; the acacia eater) all derive their power from a precise gift of observation and analysis. The real brilliance of Okopenko's work lies in its combination of grotesqueness and humor, and in its epigrammatic quick-wittedness. *Lockergedichte* (1983; loose poems) illustrates his unusual spectrum of theme and topics and his continuing manipulation of poetic forms.

Another Austrian experimenter is Ernst Jandl (b. 1925). His *Andere Augen* (1956; other eyes) contains ironically witty concrete offerings. One of Jandl's most important volumes, *Laut und Luise* (1966; loud and Luise), illustrates his ability to remove linguistic elements from their normal relationships and reorganize them into unexpected, yet compelling, configurations. In *Sprechblasen* (1968; speech bubbles) he offered new examples of playful dissection and ordering of words, sounds, and letters. More recent collections, from *Dingfest* (1973; arrested) and *für alle* (1974; for all) through *Die Bearbeitung der Mütze* (1978; the adaptation of the cap) and *der gelbe hund* (1980; the yellow dog), document a versatility that ranges from traditional expression to the most unorthodox, subtle, and surprising play with language. In *der gelbe hund* he convincingly develops a case for creative distortion, while *Selbstporträt des Schachspielers als trinkende Uhr* (1983; self-portrait of the chess player as a drinking clock) offers more traditional poems about death and its inescapability. Jandl's latest writings appear to have lost the lively humor that marks his best poems.

The poetic experiments of Hans Carl Artmann's *Med ana schwoazzn dintn* (1958; with black ink) are among the most successful examples of stylized Austrian dialect poetry. His later collections reveal that artificially created colloquial language is only one aspect of an extremely diverse lyric productivity. Among the elements to be found in *verbarium* (1966; verbarium), *Auf dem leib geschrieben* (1967; written on the body), *allerleirausch* (1967; the rapture of all sorts of things), *Aus meiner Botanisiertrommel* (1975; from my botanizing drum), and *Gedichte über die liebe und über die lasterhaftigkeit*

(1975; poems about love and about depravity) are a peculiar anarchy of language, surrealism, the precious, the old-fashioned, the eccentric, and the macabre. The poems of *verbarium* are rich in metaphor, and range from peculiar epitaphs and innocent "cemetery songs" to parodistic love poetry. In *allerleirausch* he presented satirical nursery rhymes filled with malice and insidiousness. Among his most effective creations are the strangely snubbing and eerie products in *Gedichte über die liebe und über die lasterhaftigkeit* and the mocking, ironic ballads and nature poems of *Aus meiner Botanisiertrommel.*

Like Artmann, Gerhard Rühm and Friedrich Achleitner (b. 1930) are best known as experimenters of the *Wiener Gruppe.* The volume *hosn, rosn, baa* (1959; pants, roses, bone), which they published jointly with Artmann, contains new contributions to the dialect poetry that Artmann had popularized in *Med ana schwoazzn dintn.*

Rühm's subsequent works, especially *Farbengedicht* (1965; poem of colors), *Gesammelte Gedichte und visuelle Texte* (1970; collected poems and visual texts), and *Wahnsinn* (1973; insanity), reflect his consistent preoccupation with the transformation of spoken language into written symbols, a process that involves a complex breaking, restructuring, and recombination of sounds, syllables, idioms, and expressions. Unlike Artmann's richly descriptive and imitative dialect verse, Rühm's colloquial lyrics reduce spoken language to programmed criticism of specific kinds of thought and expression.

Friedrich Achleitner's Upper Austrian dialect experiments in *hosn, rosn, baa* and *prosa, konstellationen, montagen, dialektgedichte, studien* (1970; prose, constellations, montages, dialect poems, studies) followed more conservative efforts. Conversion to new forms was not especially productive. His poems are verbally weak tabulations and repetitions of sounds. Only occasionally does he combine formal conciseness and dry humor in individually impressive creations.

Under the influence of Paul Celan, Klaus Demus (b. 1927) combined a purity of natural observation with surrealistic integration of images of beauty and horror. The peculiar pictures presented in *Das schwere Land* (1958; the heavy land) and *Morgennacht* (1969; morning night) are scenes of death and

silence, but also painlessness and catharsis. Later collections
are less compelling. *In der neuen Stille* (1974; in the new
silence), *Das Morgenleuchten* (1979; morning shine), and
Schatten vom Wald (1983; shadows of the forest) are dominated
by traditional landscape and nature poems that feature trite
contrasts and polarities.

In *Entstehung eines Sternbilds* (1958; genesis of a con-
stellation), *Der Doppelgänger* (1959; the double), *Nigredo*
(1962; Nigredo), *Gesicht ohne Gesicht* (1968; face without face),
and *Mare Occidentis, Das verborgene Licht, Chrysopöe* (1976;
western sea, the hidden light, Chrysopöe), Max Hölzer (b.
1915) progressed from strong surrealistic poetry to starkly
encoded transcendental verse. In the early poems, he played
with the automatism of ideas and images in an effort to dis-
solve the traditional elements of the ordered world. With the
cycles in *Mare Occidentis, Das verborgene Licht, Chrysopöe* he
completed the move from a realm of inner darkness, self-sacri-
fice, and destruction into a dreamlike, lucid sphere of momentary security, freedom, and spiritual fulfillment.

The strongest new trends of the 1960s were an increased
subjectivity, a pronounced autobiographical curiosity, and a
search for new individual experience. Unlike poets in the
Federal Republic, Austrians produced little political verse of
high quality. Even the political lyrics of Erich Fried, Vera
Ferra, and Andreas Okopenko did not have a particularly
strong focus. Among the most visible aspects of the new subjectivism were strong manifestations of sentimentality and man-
nerism, affectation in the treatment of personal experience,
strong emotionality, narcissism, personal response to external
existential forces and negative social developments, emphasis
on fantasy as private experience, and focus on the individual's
inner world. Most of the important verse produced during this
period came from already-established writers.

Although her first lyrics appeared before the war, Rose Aus-
länder's (b. 1907) reputation is a product of books published
after her return to Europe in 1965. The central themes of her
many collections, from *Blinder Sommer* (1965; blind summer)
and *Inventar* (1972; inventory) through *Andere Zeichen* (1975;
other signs), *Es ist alles anders* (1977; everything is different),

and *Ein Stück weiter* (1979; a bit further), arise out of the intimate processing of personal experience. The language of her productions is clear and unadorned, becoming more terse and dense in her later works. Newer volumes, including *Mein Atem heißt jetzt* (1981; my breath is called now), *Im Atemhaus wohnen* (1981; to dwell in the house of breath), and *Im Aschenregen die Spur deines Namens* (1984; the trace of your name in the rain of ash), reflect an increasing optimism in images that are original, compelling, and unaffected.

Friederike Mayröcker's verse moves from richly metaphoric poems of personal encounter, through surrealistic productions, to experimental, concrete texts. Her early collections—*metaphorisch* (1964; metaphorical), *texte* (1965; texts), and *Sägespäne für mein Herzbluten* (1967; sawdust for the bleeding of my heart)—are elegiac in tone, dominated by the sequencing of images. With *Blaue Erleuchtungen* (1972; blue inspirations) and *Schwarze Romanzen* (1982; black romances) she established the major aspects of her poetic phenomenology: subtle sense impressions, thoughts, memories, and imaginings that are changed and molded anew in montages of disparate aspects. In *Gute Nacht, guten Morgen* (1982; good night, good morning) close-up pictures of a discontinuous, fragmented, ambivalent reality are presented as the results of a lightly ironical processing of experience. Mayröcker's poetry is especially notable for its revelation of her discernment, imagination, and linguistic precision.

Fantasy as subjective experience is the focus of Peter Handke's lyrics, contained in *Deutsche Gedichte* (1969; German poems), *Die Innenwelt der Außenwelt der Innenwelt* (1969; the inner world of the outer world of the inner world), *Als das Wüschen noch geholfen hat* (1974; when wishing still helped), and *Das Ende des Flanierens* (1976; the end of sauntering). His approach to the poetic task is the employment of consistent self-expression as a tool to expand individual living space. Handke's poems are not always convincing, but they document the uniqueness of his artistic personality and his poetic imagination.

Aside from an increase in the polarization between innovation and convention, lyric trends in Austria during the 1970s were marked most by the search for novelty and by a productive diversity. One formal tendency that was especially apparent among younger poets was a preference for lyrical short forms. There was also a turning toward the subjective inner world of the poet for substance and stimulus.

Peter Henisch's (b. 1943) epigrams, massed together as building blocks of larger units in *Hamlet bleibt* (1971; *Hamlet, 1970*), but presented independently in *Mir selbst auf der Spur* (1977; on the trail of myself), are terse, aggressive, and critical. They are tightly related to his prose works, focusing on such problems as inherited tradition, Austrian stereotypes, the conservative patriarchal social order, and the political events of the late 1960s. The power of Henisch's writings lies more in their passionate dialectic than in their artistry.

Subjectivism and a sensitive response to conflicts between individual and society are the poles of Hermann Gail's (b. 1939) short poems. His *Exil ohne Jahreszeiten* (1972; exile without seasons), *Ich trinke mein Bier aus* (1977; I drink all my beer), *Weiter Herrschaft der weißen Mäuse* (1979; broad dominion of the white mice) explore themes as diverse as the fears and hopelessness of the poet's own prison confinement and the everyday cruelty encountered by old and lonely people. Gail's poems are not expressions of sympathy but, rather, vibrant yet unspoken accusation, mourning, bitterness, and revulsion.

In der Sprache der Inseln (1973; in the language of the islands) and *Lichtungen* (1976; clearings), Jutta Schutting's first two books of poetry, reveal an approach that is much different from that of either Henisch or Gail. Instead of creating montages of ideas, she treats her creations as separate "undiscovered" islands on an imaginary chart of the sea, focusing on language as having identifiable value. Schutting's techniques are only partially successful. In some instances her poems lack precision, and the preoccupation with language is academic and dry. Other poems achieve a unique merging of known and unrecognized meaning, and a careful balance between feeling and reality. In *Liebesgedichte* (1982; love poems) she effectively employs extremely complex language structures to accent the tension between the intensity and the impossibility of love.

Ernst Nowak's (b. 1944) *Entzifferung der Bilderschrift* (1977; deciphering of pictographs) contains impressive brief creations that mediate a disconcerted feeling of life and document the search for a less futile existence. Individual poems are not composed of images or symbols, but rather of details, episodes, and threatening moments—items that invite discovery of an interpretation that remains otherwise invisible.

Some of the best short poetry of recent years is contained in Peter Rosei's *Regentagstheorie* (1979; rainy-day theory) and *Das Lächeln des Jungen* (1979; the boy's smile). Individual poems offer charmingly naive impressionistic snatches and momentary reproductions of life. The pictures are not startling. They depict a suburban existence that is relatively sparse in objects and productive relationships. Yet what is offered is subtly striking and compelling.

Artistic discipline and traditional form govern Herbert Eisenreich's (b. 1926) *Verlorene Funde* (1976; lost findings). A specific language ethic appears in poems that stress honesty in private, social, and political action. His treatment of contemporary problems is sometimes tedious, but often the involved structures add significantly to the bite of his verse.

Einübung in das Vermeidbare (1978; practice in that which can be avoided), by Alfred Kolleritsch, exhibits traditional solidity with its softly philosophical interpretation of love. Kolleritsch's lyrics derive their strength from a combination of language mastery and the clear definition of feelings and emotions. In *Im Vorfeld der Augen* (1982; in the foreground of the eyes) and *Absturz ins Glück* (1983; fall into happiness) the poet focuses on the tension between conventional life and his own inner world. At the same time, he employs emotionally charged experience as an effective stimulus for reflection on language and personal awareness. His offerings are unique in their artisitc intensity, productive use of metaphor, and mastery of the interplay of words.

Very few new Austrian poets of note emerged during the first half of the 1980s. Nor do the themes and approaches differ greatly from those of the preceding decade. Subjectivism is still strongly visible, as are the negative, critical, fearful views of the world that appear in contemporary German literature as a whole.

Subjectivity is carried to its melancholy extreme in *Die Sprache der Salamander* (1981; the language of the salamanders) by André Heller (b. 1946). With poems and cabaret texts written in both dialect and standard German, Heller has become one of Austria's most famous songwriters. His themes include inventive portrayal of self, the search for poesy, Vienna, loneliness, and a peculiar love–hate relationship with his homeland. Many of his creations are sharply critical of the society, but their strength lies not so much in political or social message as in precise use of language and aggressive language manipulation.

Amid the gloom and fear of the 1980s, Georg Bydlinski's (b. 1956) *Die Sprache bewohnen* (1981; inhabiting language), *Distelblüte* (1982; thistle blossom), and *Hinwendung zu den Steinen* (1984; turning to the stones) are a refreshing anomaly. The tranquil, often religious world of his simple, profound poems fosters productive moods of reflection and meditation. Bydlinski does not avoid negative themes. In *Distelblüte* he portrays man as experiencing a wretched, infecund life. The important difference is that his world maintains hope. Bydlinski finds magic in natural relationships, and his well-chosen metaphors give vitality to his lyrics.

DRAMA

The immediate postwar period was not a time of substantial change in Austrian theater. Playwrights who had been productive during the 1920s and 1930s began again where they had left off. New currents and tendencies, new styles and programs were taken into Austrian plays only in softened form. Tradition was a dominant force in shaping productions for the stage. The historical Austrian emphasis on totality in drama precluded a new stress on individual aspects of presentation. The first years after 1945 were occupied with reclaiming works by older writers, and with catching up on the international reper-

toire. Cultural thrusts toward artistic autonomy caused dramatists to focus on models from the turn of the century rather
than the immediate past. Older authors attempted to bridge
the gap back to the theater of the monarchy and the First
Republic.

In his postwar comedies, Alexander Lernet-Holenia combined the standards of classical German theater with techniques and approaches developed by Hugo von Hofmannsthal
(1874–1929) and Arthur Schnitzler (1862–1931). His *Spanische Komödie* (1948; Spanish comedy) was the first of four
mediocre dramas that are more notable for the gratuitous bits
of wisdom in the dialogues than for effective theatrical construction. With *Das Finanzamt* (1969; the finance office), he
created a satirical polemical farce that is entertaining in spite
of its artistic weakness.

Richard Billinger's (1890–1965) predilection for elemental
substance is visible in *Der Zentaur* (1948; the centaur), *Traube
in der Kelter* (1951; grape in the winepress), *Das nackte leben*
(1953; the naked life), and *Bauernpassion* (1960; peasant passion). The antithesis of demonic sensuality and religious rapture is a major focus of symbolistic works that mix naturalism
and modern psychology in peculiar combinations of baroque
and peasant drama. In spite of the vitality of his language and
the power of his imagery, Billinger's dark visions and monstrous conflicts are weakened by flaws in the development of
individual roles and dramatic action.

The religious element is important in Rudolf Henz's dramaturgy. *Die Erlösung* (1949; salvation), *Die große Lüge. Ananias
und Saphira* (1949; the great lie. Ananias and Saphira), *Die
große Entscheidung* (1954; the great decision), *Die ungetreuen
Pächter* (1954; the faithless tenants), and *Der Büßer* (1955; the
penitent man) document his advocacy of a Catholic renewal of
Austria. Henz's productions are respectably consistent in their
pursuit of his didactic goals, but they are not artistically excit-
ing.

Max Mell's (1882–1971) writings also combine and stress
elements of Catholicism, old Austrian culture and legend, baroque tradition, and classical form. His most important postwar creations are *Kriemhilds Rache* (1951; Kriemhild's re-

venge), the second of two plays based on *Das Nibelungenlied* (c. 1200; *The Lay of the Nibelungs,* 1887), and *Jeanne d'Arc* (1957; *Joan of Arc,* 1961), an unconventional interpretation of the title figure's religious transformation during her imprisonment. The special success of *Kriemhilds Rache* lies in Mell's ability to focus on theatrically effective high points and to accent Christian ethics through a convincing union of mythical and religious elements. What makes *Joan of Arc* powerful are the author's mastery of dialectic dialogue and his ability to maintain a steady, consistent escalation of the dramatic tension.

Ferdinand Bruckner's (1891–1958) attempts to reclaim a position at the forefront of Austrian theater remained relatively unsuccessful. His late plays, from *Heroische Komödie* (1945; heroic comedy) and *Die Befreiten* (1946; the liberated) through *Früchte des Nichts* (1952; fruits of nothingness) and *Die Buhlschwestern* (1954; the courting sisters) to *Der Kampf mit dem Engel* (1957; the struggle with the angel), examine problems of political temptability and focus on defeated individuals as illustrations of man's respect for life. The most peculiar aspect of his postwar art was his renewal of classical theater patterns. Beginning with *Pyrrhus und Andromache* (1952; Pyrrhus and Andromache), he sought to revive both the strict forms of the verse drama and the idea of theater as a moral institution. *Der Kampf mit dem Engel* is typical of these efforts. While the piece's ethos is somewhat moving, its dramatic effect is weak.

The postwar works of Franz Theodor Csokor are somewhat more successful than Bruckner's, but they lack the power of his earlier creations. The trilogy *Olymp und Golgotha* (1956; Olympus and Golgotha), consisting of *Kalypso* (1946; Calypso), *Pilatus* (1948; Pilate), and *Cäsars Witwe* (1955; Caesar's widow), is weakened by the dissolution of action into philosophical engrossment and discussion of viewpoint. Later productions, including *Hebt den Stein ab* (1957; lift off the stone), *Treibholz* (1959; driftwood), *Die Erweckung des Zosimir* (1961; the awakening of Zosimir), *Das Zeichen an der Wand* (1962; the sign on the wall), and the three one-act plays in *Die Kaiser Zwischen den Zeiten* (1964; the emperors between the times), offer solid treatments of contemporary political and human problems, but the resolution of conflicts through humanity, tolerance, and love glosses over existing realities.

One of the most significant new Austrian plays was Hans Weigel's *Barabbas oder Der fünzigste Geburtstag* (1946; Barabbas; or, the fiftieth birthday). Billed as a "tragic revue," it set the pattern for a new dramatic form. In the context of a "solid citizen's" dream confrontation with his past failures, the author offered an ironic, critical representation of his own generation's inner experience. Later productions of the same type, notably *Angelika* (1948; Angelica) and *Die Erde* (1948; the earth), were not as well received by the public, because the central figures were existential abstractions rather than dramatically effective characters. Weigel's most successful piece is *Der eingebildete Doktor* (1956; the conceited doctor), a satirical farce that deftly picks psychoanalysis apart.

In opposition to modernist tendencies, Fritz Hochwälder (b. 1911) has remained a consistent advocate of the strict rules of classical dramaturgy and a defender of the old-fashioned idealist theater. The strength of his works lies in their polished craftsmanship. Among his most effective plays are *Das heilige Experiment* (1947; *The Strong Are Lonely,* 1980), *Der Unschuldige* (1949; the innocent man), and *Der öffentliche Ankläger* (1954; *The Public Prosecutor,* 1980), three strong variations on the theme of the misuse of power. In *Donnerstag* (1959; Thursday), *1003* (1964; 1003), *Der Himbeerpflücker* (1965; *The Raspberry Picker,* 1980), and *Der Befehl* (1967; the command) he examines contemporary themes ranging from the dehumanization of the individual to grappling with the Nazi past. One of his most interesting and original works is *Lazaretti oder Der Säbeltiger* (1975; *Lazaretti; or, the Saber-Toothed Tiger,* 1980), a strong treatment of the ruthlessness of intellectuals in their competition for status.

The verse dramas of Felix Braun, with their dissolution of dramatic action into lyricism, static images, and Christian transfiguration, are a remnant of the past, not an integral part of modern theater. Braun's primary themes in *Der Tod des Aischylos* (1946; the death of Aeschylus), *Dorothea und Theophilus* (1950; Dorothea and Theophilus), *Rudolf der Stifter*

(1953; Rudolf the founder), *Aufruf zur Tafel* (1955; call to the table), *Joseph und Maria (1956; Joseph and Mary)*, *Orpheus* (1957; Orpheus), and *Beatrice Cenci* (1958; Beatrice Cenci) come from classical mythology, biblical material, and history, but he makes little attempt to relate his substance to the contemporary world. Only in *Orpheus* did he combine lyrical language and dynamic dramatization into a successful artistic whole.

The new playwrights of the late 1940s were more inclined to come to grips with modern reality than were older authors. Two specific directions were visible in their treatments of the postwar world. Comedy and satire appeared in various forms along with revues and stylized dramatic reports as commentary on contemporary situations. The more tempered approach was the portrayal of people and their world in fables and parables.

Spaß muß sein (1948; there must be fun) and *Der Steinbruch* (1950; the quarry), Hans Friedrich Kühnelt's (b. 1918) first plays, are dramatically rough and unpolished, but the second work contains strong scenes and original ideas. His other dramas of the 1950s and 1960s were only limitedly successful. In many respects, Kühnelt reached the peak of his career with *Make up* (1950; make up), a subtle, psychological work about the question of personal identity. *Ein Tag mit Eduard* (1953; a day with Edward), a comedy about a robot, and *Geliebtes schwarzes Schaf* (1967; beloved black sheep), a rather tame farce, are somewhat effective as light entertainment, but none of his other plays deserves more than passing notice.

Helmut Schwarz (b. 1928) experimented with a variety of forms. *Das sind wir* (1948; there we are) and *Ein Mann fällt aus den Wolken* (1949; a man falls from the clouds) are effective examples of the critical revue. *Seine letzte Berufung* (1953; his last appeal), *Arbeiterpriester* (1954; workers' priest), *Die Beförderung* (1961; the promotion), and *Im Aschenregen* (1961; in the rain of ashes), a series of more traditional plays, established Schwarz's more personal theatrical style, but only *Arbeiterpriester* is completely successful as a portrayal of authentic human existence. Two dramatized reports are disparate in their effectiveness: *Das Aushängeschild* (1959; the signboard), a response to the Russian suppression of the Hungarian revolt, is pale and superficial in its accusation, while *Das Fehlurteil* (1966; the misjudgment), a documentary piece on leniency granted during Nazi war-crimes trials, stimulated significant public discussion.

The most fascinating modern Austrian satirist was Helmut Qualtinger (1928–1986). *Jugend vor den Schranken* (1948; youth before the court), a two-part "courtroom report" about how the war poisoned the younger generation, shocked the public with its negativism. During the 1950s Qualtinger collaborated with other authors in producing explosive, socially critical, highly popular cabaret sketches. *Reigen 51* (1951; round dance 51) established him as a biting critic of everyday reality. Qualtinger's most famous creation is *Herr Karl* (1962; Mr. Karl), a uniquely powerful satirical monologue in which the title figure plays down his past as a fellow traveler during social democracy, Austrian fascism, National Socialism, and the economic miracle of the Second Republic, attempting to cleanse himself from associated sins. Neither *Alles gerettet!* (1963; everything saved!), an exemplary documentary play, nor *Die Hinrichtung* (1965; the execution), a parable about love and death in the age of mass entertainment, is as artistically effective as *Herr Karl*.

Raimund Berger (1917–54) developed a theater of human weakness, devoid of didactical elements, ideology, and intellectual trappings. His theatrical parables, including *Papierblumenfrühling* (1949; paper-flower spring), *Zeitgenossen* (1951; contemporaries), *Jupiter und Jo* (1952; Jupiter and Io), *Das Reich der Melonen* (1955; the melon empire), and *Die Ballade vom nackten Mann* (1965; the ballad of the naked man), reflect the progressive firming of a sense of stage effect, but his characters are often artificial and unconvincing.

For Harald Zusanek (b. 1922), the devices of an epic, philosophical theater provided a suitable approach to art. Beginning with *Schnupfen hat Herr Cicero* (1946; Mr. Cicero has the sniffles), *Warum gräbst du, Centurio?* (1949; why are you digging, Centurio?), and *Die Straße nach Cavarcere* (1952; the road to Cavarcere), he created plays that wander between poesy and theatrics, the present and myth, affirmation of life and the victory of the spirit. The early success of *Die Straße nach Cavarcere* was not matched in his later plays. Although *Mutter Europa* (1953; mother Europe) exhibits sharp construction and technical mastery, its overall effect is banal. Strong development of the title figure in *Jean von der Tonne* (1954; Jean von der Tonne) fails to compensate for a weak story framework. Zusanek's subsequent creations, from *Des andern Kleid* (1954; the other man's clothing) to *Schloß in Europa* (1960; a castle in Europe), have never become part of the Austrian theater repertoire.

Another important representative of the parabolic theater is Rudolf Bayr (b. 1919), who believes that classical antiquity offers timeless patterns of human behavior. In addition to numerous adaptations and free renderings of ancient Greek plays, Bayr produced several works that depend on strict classical form and renewal of classical material for effect. *Königslegende* (1948; royal legend) examines the problems of human responsibility and guilt; *Sappho und Alkaios* (1952; Sappho and Alcaeus) is a parable on the destructive nature of the lust for power; *Die Liebe der Andrea* (1954; Andrea's love) emphasizes the value of order in the family. Four contemporary one-act prose plays in *Menschenliebe* (1969; love of mankind) do not exhibit the cultivated power of language and the carefully accented theatrical development of his earlier pieces.

The most visible new element in Austrian drama of the 1950s was a strong tendency toward intellectualization. Although both traditional forms and radical experiments were created, philosophical message and mastery of expression received strong emphasis as drama became a vehicle for the direct communication of ideas. The most successful newcomers could appeal to the spectator's mind while penetrating the barriers between external reality and the emotional world of the audience.

Elias Canetti (b. 1905), who received the Nobel Prize for Literature in 1981, is better known for his complex novel *Die Blendung* (1935; *Auto-da-Fé*, 1946) and his powerful essay in social psychology, *Masse und Macht* (1960; *Crowds and Power*, 1962), than for his dramas. Nevertheless, his plays are significant products of a remarkable mind. Both *Komödie der Ei-*

telkeit (1950; *Comedy of Vanity,* 1983) and *Hochzeit* (1964; *The Wedding,* 1986) are examples of Canetti's theory of "acoustical masks," which relates individual personality and moral character to speech patterns. With *Die Befristeten* (1956; *Life Terms,* 1983) they are especially powerful analyses of human motivations and mass psychology, but they are not theatrically viable.

Solid dramatic technique and careful mastery of language are the strenths of Franz Pühringer's *Der König von Torelore* (1951; the king of Torelore), *Abel Hradschek und sein Weib* (1954; Abel Hradschek and his wife), and *Die Erde ist wieder bewohnbar* (1954; the earth is habitable again). *Der König von Torelore* is a melancholy love story with tightly constructed dialogues, while *Abel Hradschek und sein Weib* is a brutally successful marriage tragedy. Although *Die Erde is wieder bewohnbar* conveys a convincing ethical message, the programmatic dialectic and corresponding aloofness of language weaken the general theatrical effect.

Kurt Becsi's (b. 1920) goal is creation of a drama of the spirit that promotes social transformation as an outgrowth of Christian revolution. His first three plays, *Deutsche Passion* (1952; German passion), *Atom vor Christus* (1952; atom before Christ), and *Das spanische Dreieck* (1952; the Spanish triangle), established him as a purveyor of startling effect, colorful scenes, cleverly juxtaposed antitheses, and solid characterization. With subsequent works, from *Der Mörder Gottes* (1955; the murderer of God) and *Der Salzmarsch* (1956; the salt fen) through *Party für Propheten* (1965; party for prophets) and *Die Nacht vor Sarajewo* (1967; the night before Sarajevo) to *Genosse Mao bittet Zum Tee* (1971; Comrade Mao invites to tea), he has remained an interesting loner, apart from the mainstream of Austrian theater.

Highly emotional, lyrical language is a strong point of Kurt Klinger's dramas. *Odysseus muß wieder reisen* (1954; Odysseus must travel again), *Der goldene Käfig* (1956; the golden cage), *Das kleine Weltkabarett* (1959; the little cabaret of the world), *Helena in Ägypten* (1968; Helen in Egypt), *Schauplätze* (1971; scenes), and *Ein Hügel in Richmond* (1973; a hill in Richmond) achieve their effect through exaggeration, sharp characterization, and a practical mastery of theatrics. In forms ranging from morality play to dark allegory, he successfully explores possibilities for touching and affecting the individual's inner world.

Realistic description of conflicts between individual and society is the defining characteristic of Oskar Zemme's (b. 1931) creations. *Die Hochzeit des Toren* (1954; the fool's wedding) is only marginally convincing in its accusations against the older generation and the contemporary world. Later works, however, including *Der Bumerang* (1956; the boomerang), *Die bessere Ernte* (1957; the better harvest), *Im Hochhaus* (1963; in the high rise), *Die Klingel* (1968; the bell), *Didi* (1968; Didi), *Die Abreise* (1969; the departure), *Die Nachtwächter* (1969; the night watchmen), and *Die Glückskonserve* (1969; canned happiness), are more successful in portraying failed attempts to break out of mundane existence. Zemme's strength is his ability to create effective roles; his weakness is a dearth of originality.

Many Austrian writers of the period created radio plays of various kinds. Among the best productions of this type are works composed by Ilse Aichinger and Ingeborg Bachmann. Individually they wrote some of the most vitally expressive dramatic works of the postwar era.

Ilse Aichinger's radio scripts are characterized by simple language and delicate sensibility. *Knöpfe* (1953; buttons), a symbolic portrayal of the dehumanization of the individual, features a clearly developed plot. Later creations, such as *Besuch im Pfarrhaus* (1961; visit to the vicarage), *Nachmittag in Ostende* (1968; afternoon in Ostende), *Die Schwestern Jouet* (1964; the Jouet sisters), *Auckland* (1969; Auckland), *Pfingstrosen* (1975; peonies), and *Gare Maritime* (1977; harbor station), juggle elements of space, time, history, wish, possibility, and reality, such that visualization depends entirely on language, while people, relationships, and landscapes simply exist without preparatory development. The results are extremely effective in their stimulation of mental associations.

The radio plays of Ingeborg Bachmann are more conventional in structure, language, and content than those of Aichinger, but some of Bachmann's works reflect experimentation with new forms of lyrical monologue. In *Ein Geschäft mit Träumen* (1952; a business with dreams) she offered a vivid mixture of daydream and reality as part of the protagonist's grappling with external circumstances. Her manipulation of language in works such as *Die Zikaden* (1955; the cicadas) and *Der gute Gott von Manhatten* (1958; the good god of Manhattan) is notable for its exposure of deepest inner feelings and emotions, its honesty and directness.

During the 1960s, a significant change in the direction of Austrian drama occurred. The most important new writers revolted against the establishment. One result was the emergence of the anti-theater. To be sure, there were also followers of tradition, but innovations favored the thematization of language as form. Portrayal of the individual was equated with representation of his language level. Conventional drama was rejected in favor of language play, often employing montage techniques in which texts from Lexica, old textbooks, and newspapers were given new order.

Just as they influenced the development of experimental prose and poetry, prominent members of the Wiener Gruppe also promoted innovation in drama. Among those participating actively in the theatrical revolution were Konrad Bayer, Hans Carl Artmann, and Gerhard Rühm. Their most important contributions to the new dramatic literature were the rediscovery of dialect and the laying of the foundation for the anti-theater.

The most significant forerunner of the anti-theater was Konrad Bayer. Most of his plays were neither published nor performed before his death. Word play—especially unusual word combinations—is the essence of *bräutigall und anonymphe* (1961; bridingale and anonymph), a peculiar experiment with poetic theater. Criticism of language and the exposure of nonsense in social communication are also the heart of *kasperl am elektrischen stuhl* (1968; Kasperl at the electric chair), *der analfabet tritt in rudeln und einzeln auf, er überfällt ausflügler* (1969; the illiterate man appears in groups and alone, he attacks people on an excursion), *die boxer* (1971; the boxers), and *die begabten zuschauer* (1973; the gifted spectators). Bayer's works are masterpieces of commentary on the fragmentary nature of human existence.

In the peculiar scripts of Hans Carl Artmann, the poet becomes his own protagonist. Stimuli from experimental expressionism, dadaism, surrealism, and other sources led Artmann to focus on the isolation of detail. He produced a substantial number of dream plays, none of which was published until they all appeared together in *die fahrt zur insel nantucket* (1969; the voyage to Nantucket Island). With only a few exceptions, such as *Kein Pfeffer für Czermak* (written 1957; no pepper for Czermak) and *la cocodrilla* (written 1954; the crocodile), Artmann's works have not been staged. They are dramas for the theater of the imagination.

The plays *rund oder oval* (1961; round or oval) and *ophelia und die wörter* (1961; Ophelia and the words), Gerhard Rühm's first theatrical productions, are attempts to apply the principles of concrete poetry to drama. In *ophelia und die wörter* Rühm dissected the complete speeches of Ophelia in Shakespeare's *Hamlet* and regrouped their elements in an effort to redefine Ophelia in terms of the words that she uses.

From works based on word constellations Rühm moved to dialect plays and dramatic montages. Montage is the most characteristic element of his stage productions. Important examples are *ein kriminalstück, kosmologie* (1961; a criminal play, cosmology) and *der fliegende holländer* (1961; the flying Dutchman), which he wrote with Konrad Bayer. Although he created several anti-theater pieces, including *Der Weg nach Bern* (1962; the way to Bern), *Unser versuch bestätigt das* (1969; our experiment confirms that), *Der Kammersänger von vorne und hinten* (1970; the chamber singer from front and back), and *Kreidekreis* (1971; chalk circle), he eventually turned away from the stage in favor of audio plays and radio scripts. With works such as *diotima hat ihre lektüre gewechselt* (1973; Diotima changed her reading material) and *von welt zu welt* (1975; from world to world) he has become a leading figure in drama of the imagination.

Another important radio playwright is Jan Rys (b. 1931). Unlike the *Wiener Gruppe,* he is a defender of the traditional audio drama as a vehicle for exploring human behavior. Works like *Grenzgänger* (1960; border crossers) and *53 Schritte* (1961; 53 steps) reveal steady consistency of expression and mastery of role development. One of Rys's most successful pieces is *Vertreibung* (1965; expulsion), a clear and simple exploration of the psychology of human adaptation to physical surroundings. Metaphysical cultural pessimism dominates *Die Letzten* (1970; the last people) and *Eine immer größere verblödete Welt* (1973; an ever larger unthinking world), while *Empfang in einem besetzten Haus* (1976; reception in an occupied house) is an especially effective rendering of the problems of outsiders.

The plays of Lotte Ingrisch (b. 1930) belong to the tradition of the Viennese folk theater. Her comedies *Vanillikipferln* (1964; vanilla croissants), *Ein Abend zu dritt* (1965; three together for an evening), *Donau so blau* (1965; Danube so blue), *Die Witwe* (1965; the widow), *Der Affe des Engels* (1971; the angel's monkey), *Letzte Rose* (1971; last rose), and *Der rote Bräutigam* (1974; the red bridegroom) are studies in shattered illusions, filled with black humor and melancholy. Although they offer entertaining combinations of humor, the macabre, and the grotesque, their greatest strength lies in their penetration of human foibles.

A more successful master of the grotesque element is Wolfgang Bauer (b. 1941). His one-act plays *Der Schweinetransport* (1962; the swine truck), *Franz Xaver Gabelsberger* (1964; Franz Xaver Gabelsberger), *Katharina Doppelkopf* (1965; Katharina Doppelkopf), and *Die Menschenfresser* (1967; the cannibals) were strongly influenced by the Theater of the Absurd. His central themes are the endangering of individual autonomy and the problems of conforming to irrational reality structures. Bauer's most successful creations portray macabre borderline situations, mixing banality with slapstick comedy and brutality with sadism. Beginning with *Party for six* (1966; *Party for Six,* 1973), he explored more realistic settings for his ideas. Both *Party for Six* and *Magic Afternoon* (1967; *Magic Afternoon,* 1973) are open dramas, without developed plot. These and later plays successfully interpret modern questions of identity in the juxtaposition of existence and role. *Change* (1969; *All Change,* 1973), *Film und Frau* (1971; film and woman), *Silvester oder Das Massaker im Hotel Sacher* (1971; New Year's Eve; or, the massacre in the Sacher Hotel), and *Gespenster* (1974; ghosts) simply offer new variations of the now-standard themes, although *Silvester oder Das Massaker im Hotel Sacher* also contains elements of the so-called "happening." Bauer's most complex,most theatrically effective piece is *Magnetküsse* (1976; magnet kisses), a grotesque moralistic creation that presents the inner world of an insane murderer.

One of the strongest representatives of the anti-theater was Peter Handke. Even more extreme than Bauer's plotless creations, Hande's famous *Publikumsbeschimpfung* (1966; *Offending the Audience,* 1969), and the less outrageous *Selbstbezichtigung* (1966; *Self-Accusation,* 1969), *Weissagung* (1966; prophecy), and *Hilferufe* (1967; *Calling for Help,* 1971), lack not only plot but also character development and dramatic construction. In these and the later works—*Kaspar* (1968; *Kaspar,* 1969), *Das Mündel will Vormund sein* (1969; *My Foot My Tutor,* 1971), *Der Ritt über den Bodensee* (1971; *The Ride Across Lake Constance,* 1972), and *Die Unvernünftigen sterben aus* (1974; *They Are Dying Out,* 1975)—he produced experiments in which language becomes the test of existence. *Kaspar* is the best of his full-length productions, while *They Are Dying Out* is his most conventional but theatrically least successful drama.

Destruction of conventional models of thought is the goal of Wilhelm Pevny's (b. 1944) plays, from *Flipper* (1968; pinball machine) and *Oedip-Entsinnung* (1969; Oedip-recollection) through *Maß für Maß* (1969; measure for measure), *Sprint-orgasmic* (1969; sprint orgasmic), and *Nur der Krieg macht es möglich* (1972; only the war makes it possible) to *Theaterleben* (1973; theater life) and *Zick Zack* (1974; zigzag). His major themes include the helplessness of the individual, the problems of emotional versus rational ties, and the power of society to mold values, attitudes, and relationships. Pevny's most successful plays, exemplified in *Rais* (1972; Rais), rely upon strictly organized language, pantomime, and artistically applied acoustical and optical media for effect.

The impact of Harald Sommer's (b. 1935) early pieces is founded in the tension between naturalistic meticulousness and the most extreme irrationality in the organization of the material. Through the use of dialect in *D'Leit* (1969; the people) and *A unhamlich schtorke Obgaung* (1970; an extremely strong departure) he established an unusual relationship between the performance of the work and its audience, but the fantastic counterpoint of a surrealistic judgment scene at the end of *A unhamlich schtorke Obgaung* also breaks the illusion of a realistic representation of the world. *Triki Traki* (1970; Triki Traki), *Die Hure Gerhild* (1970; the whore Gerhild), and *Der Sommer am Neusiedler See* (1971; the summer at Neusiedler lake) derive their stark effect from crude naturalism, while *Scheiß Napoleon* (1972; shit Napoleon), *Das Stück mit dem Hammer* (1972; the piece with the hammer), and *Ich betone, daß ich nicht das geringste an der Regierung auszusetzen habe* (1972; I emphasize that I do not find the slightest fault with the regime) employ collage, thought play, and bitter satire, respectively, as approaches to political themes. *Ich betone, daß ich nicht das geringste an der Regierung auszusetzen habe* is a powerful example of Sommer's mastery of the nuances and emptiness of modern communication and social interaction.

Tendencies in Austrian drama since 1970 do not differ greatly from those of the latter half of the 1960s. Anti-theater was especially strong during the early 1970s, placing emphasis on the grotesque treatment of contemporary problems, social parables, and language experiments. Another significant thrust that carried over was political activation and action theater. During the 1970s and early 1980s, Viennese actionism moved toward a radical renewal of theatrical art through emphasis on spontaneity. This current was also strongly influenced by surrealism.

In virtually all of his plays, including *Ein Fest für Boris* (1970; a party for Boris), *Macht der Gewohnheit* (1974; *The Force of Habit,* 1976), and *Vor dem Ruhestand* (1979; *Eve of Retirement,* 1982), Thomas Bernhard portrays existence as a nightmare. Although his plots are generally thin, Bernhard creates penetrating effects through the use of irony, comedy, and black humor. The more recent dramas—*Über allen Gipfeln ist Ruh: Ein deutscher Dichtertag um 1980* (1981; above all the peaks it is quiet: a German poet commemoration around 1980), *Der Schein trügt* (1983; appearance is deceiving), and *Ritter, Dene, Voss* (1984; Ritter, Dene, Voss)—are grotesque comedies of character that satirize German literature and thought and emphasize the hollowness and purposelessness of both life and human illusions about it. The tension between insanity and rationality in *Ritter, Dene, Voss* produces an effective statement on life as a fatal disease, but the dramatic execution is laborious and tedious.

One important extreme of the revolt against tradition is a tendency toward spoken drama that requires no stage. To that extent, the radio plays of Friederike Mayröcker are an extension of characteristic currents of the late 1960s and the 1970s. In *Zwölf Häuser—oder: Mövenpink* (1969; twelve houses; or, Mövenpink), *Anamnese. Erinnerung an eine Vorgeschichte* (1970; case history, memory of a prehistory), *Tischordnung* (1971; table order), and many others, the component of stereophonic effect is a significant aspect of the sound collages that she created. The peculiar power of these and later pieces like *Der Tod und das Mädchen* (1977; death and the girl) and *Franz Schubert oder Wetter-Zettelchen aus Wien* (1978; Franz Schubert; or, weather notes from Vienna) lies in her masterful combination of document, word, and sound association with fictional but imaginable conversations.

Peter Turrini's (b. 1944) dramas, especially *Zero Zero* (1971; zero zero), *Sauschlachten* (1972; sow slaughter), *Rozznjogd* (1973; rat hunt), and *Kindsmord* (1973; murder of a child), represent a revival of the socially critical folk play, transferred to the milieu of the modern consumer society. The success of his pieces is uneven. Provocative parabolic slices of reality are often weakened by their coarseness. The darkly satirical piece *Die Bürger* (1982; the citizens) is a starkly sad, realistic commentary on contemporary Viennese society, but it depends too much on crude sexuality and the shock value of parodistic allusion to real figures in communicating its message.

Like her fiction, Elfriede Jelinek's dramas and radio plays emphasize manipulation of the individual and depersonalization of modern society. Her special focus in *Wenn die Sonne sinkt, ist für manche auch noch Büroschluß* (1972; when the sun goes down, some still have closing time ahead), *Die Bienenkönige* (1976; the bee kings), *Was geschah, nachdem Nora ihren Mann verlassen hatte* (1979; what happened after Nora had left her husband), and *Clara S.* (1982; Clara S.) is feminist emancipation. *Clara S.* is her strongest work, but all of her didactic pieces are significant for their effective approach to a broad public.

The manipulative power of language and the problem of human isolation are key elements in the works of Gerhard Roth. *Lichtenberg* (1973; Lichtenberg) emphasizes the loss of naturalness and freedom resulting from man's tendency to order things and people under the headings of scientific categories. The strength of *Sehnsucht* (1976; longing) and *Dämmerung* (1977; twilight) lies more in the evocation of reality than its direct portrayal.

Kein Platz für Idioten (1978; no place for idiots) and the radio plays in *An den Rand des Dorfes* (1981; to the edge of the village) emphasize Feliz Mitterer's (b. 1948) concern for weak and isolated people. The power of his works lies in a finely tuned synthesis of characterizing language and realistic situations. Conflict between the abnormal individual and society is given a particularly moving interpretation in *Kein Platz für Idioten,* while the radio dramas give a poignant accent to the tragedy of inarticulate figures.

5 ▪
SWITZERLAND

FICTION

Since 1945, Swiss authors have favored fiction over poetry and drama. Their immediate postwar emphasis was a continuation of the bourgeois novel. Approaches varied from the preservation of traditional attitudes to the promotion of social progress. The most important elements of this prose are social criticism, with stress on conservative reform, and portrayal of the individual as example, victim, and bearer of responsibility.

The tension between individual and society is a critical focus of Max Frisch's novels. He explores themes ranging from the stifling effect of provincialism to alienation caused by changing values and new technology. In *J'adore ce qui me brûle oder Die Schwierigen* (1943; I adore what burns me; or, the difficult ones; republished in revised form as *Die Schwierigen oder J'adore ce qui me brûle,* 1957), the central figure finds fulfillment only vicariously, through his son. Frisch's most significant novel is *Stiller* (1954; *I'm Not Stiller,* 1958). Its artistic strength derives from a mastery of varying narrative perspectives, the ironic juxtaposition of opposing particulars, and the weaving of a deeply complex, multilayered structure. *Homo Faber* (1957; *Homo Faber,* 1959), the experimental novel *Mein Name sei Gantenbein* (1964; *Gantenbein,* 1982), and *Montauk* (1975; *Montauk,* 1976) are also complicated attempts at self-definition. *Montauk* is the most conventional and most per-

sonal of them. Autobiographical elements appear in all of
Frisch's fiction, but his first-person narrators are stylized figures. *Blaubart* (1982; *Bluebeard*, 1983) reflects a degeneration
in the quality of Frisch's prose. While it is a strong portrayal of
the tortured soul, its central idea is not convincingly presented, and the weakly projected characters are often uninteresting.

Kurt Guggenheim's (b. 1896) narrative perspective combines
praise of Switzerland, the disappointment of alienation, and
the perception that the bourgeois era is ending. His postwar
works, beginning with *Die heimliche Reise* (1945; the secret
journey) and *Wir waren unser vier* (1949; there were four of us),
are dominated by themes from middle-class life, presented in
unpretentious, cultivated prose. His most important work is
Alles in Allem (4 vols., 1952–55; all in all). This creation and
Gerufen und nicht gerufen (1973; called and not called) emphasize young people who attempt to break away from bourgeois
norms. *Gerufen und nicht gerufen* is his strongest, bitterest
statement about the problem of artistic freedom.

Man's relationship to his environment is a special aspect of
Cécile Lauber's (b. 1887) *Land deiner Mutter* (4 vols., 1946–57;
land of your mother), the panoramic story of a boy's adven-
turous journey through Switzerland. Although written for
youth, this epic is artistically important for its rich portrayal of
landscape and cultural history. It is closely related to *In der
Gewalt der Dinge* (1961; in the power of the things), which is
characteristic for Lauber's work as a whole in its fatalistic
weaving of the connections between human being, animal,
nature, objects, and general surroundings.

The narratives of Meinrad Inglin (1893–1971) belong to the
tradition of Swiss realism. Although his most important creations were written before 1945, he remained important as a
model for other writers. His later works, from *Die Lawine*
(1947; the avalanche) and *Werner Amberg* (1949; Werner Amberg) to *Besuch aus dem Jenseits* (1961; visit from the here-
after) and *Erlenbuel* (1965; Erlenbuel), emphasize Swiss folk
life with its juxtaposition of solid, earthy peasantry and root-
less civilization. Inglin's narrative approach is objective, but

many of his novellas are brittle and dry in portraying human relationships.

An especially visible theme in Swiss traditionalist prose is the problem of the artist in society. Arnold Kübler's (b. 1890) novels about Öppi Öppenau, including *Öppi von Wasenwachs* (1943; Öppi from Wasenwachs), *Öppi der Student* (1947; Öppi the student), *Öppi und Eva* (1951; Öppi and Eve), and *Öppi der Narr* (1961; Öppi the fool), detail an artistic individual's search for identity, following the pattern established by Gottfried Keller (1819–90) in *Der grüne Heinrich* (4 vols., 1854–55; *Green Henry*, 1960). The unique aspect of Kübler's novels is the fixing of the struggle for personal definition in the conflict between standard German and Swiss dialect. Playful creation and association of "Swissisms" give the novels much of their charm.

The search for identity and the individual's social responsibility are also the central concerns of Albert Jakob Welti's (1894–1965) novels *Martha und die Niemandssöhne* (1948; Martha and the sons of no man), *Die kühle Jungfrau Hannyvonne* (1954; the cool virgin Hannyvonne), and *Der Dolch der Lucretia* (1958; Lucretia's dagger). *Martha und die Niemandssöhne* is unusual for the period in its projection of feminine involvement in social problems. Although Welti advocated a moral literature, his works are not didactical. Their strength and peculiarity lie in the bold, sometimes bizarre application of fantasy to the night side of human experience.

Jakob Bührer's (1882–1975) narratives, including *Im roten Feld* (3 vols., 1938–51; in the red field) and *Yolandas Vermächtnis* (1957; Yolanda's legacy), are interesting for their uncommon themes. *Im roten Feld* deals with the French Revolution from the perspective of a need for socio-economic reform, while *Yolandas Vermächtnis* features a double suicide motivated by fear that a stock market crash would cause a world war. Such a framing of socialistic ideas in the traditional novel form is an isolated phenomenon in Swiss literature of the time.

In his novels about Zurich, *Stadt der Väter* (1941; city of the fathers), *Stadt der Freiheit* (1944; city of freedom), and *Stadt des Friedens* (1952; city of peace), Robert Faesi (1883–72) produced combinations of fiction and historical fact that are significant for their extraordinary anecdotal plasticity. His writings also document a firm grasp of traditional literary forms and techniques.

Another historian whose creative works are informed by humanistic tradition was Carl Jacob Burckhardt (1891–1974). Known more for *Richelieu* (3 vols., 1935–66; *Richelieu and His Age,* 1970) and *Gestalten und Mächte* (1941; figures and powers) than for his fiction, Burckhardt created stories that are precise and exacting in detail and language. *Drei Erzählungen* (1952; three stories), *Der Liliputaner* (1961; the Lilliputian), and *Wolfjagd* (1970; wolf hunt) reflect the same poetic mastery of subtle insight into psychological processes, and the same careful management of expression that give his essays and history books their attractive vitality.

Ludwig Hohl (1904–80) was concerned more with internal than external experience. In his *Nächtlicher Weg* (1943; night path), *Vernunft und Güte* (1956; reason and goodness), *Polykrates* (1961; Polycrates), *Daß fast alles anders ist* (1967; that almost everything is different), *Drei alte Weiber in einem Bergdorf* (1970; three old women in a mountain village), and *Bergfahrt* (1975; mountain journey) essayistic and aphoristic elements are often stronger than epic narration. Hohl's primary theme is spiritual/intellectual change viewed historically. *Drei alte Weiber in einem Bergdorf* and *Bergfahrt* are his best stories, but all of his works are significant models of a solid, penetrating, lucid prose style.

The only world-class Swiss writer who began his career in the late 1940s was Friedrich Dürrenmatt. Like his dramas, Dürrenmatt's stories and novels, including *Pilatus* (1949; Pilate), *Der Nihilist* (1950; the nihilist), *Die Stadt* (1952; the city), *Der Richter und sein Henker (1952; The Judge and His Hangman,* 1954), *Die Verdacht* (1953; *The Quarry,* 1962), *Grieche sucht Griechin* (1958; *Once a Greek,* 1965), *Das Versprechen* (1958; *The Pledge,* 1959), and *Der Sturz* (1971; the fall), concern themselves with such themes as guilt, justice, and mercy. A passionate moralist, Dürrenmatt creates tragicomic satires that are strongly inclined toward grotesque distortion, bizarre situations, cynical humor, aggressive sarcasm, and penetrating revelation of human caprice and inconsistency. The narratives in *Stoffe I–III* (1981; subjects I–III) and *Justiz* (1985; justice) reveal a process of profound interweaving of deeply private experience, reflection about life and its situations, and the application of imagination to the illumination of a personal philosophy. Dürrenmatt's strongest metaphor for existence is the labyrinth. Its most powerful development occurs in *Minotaurus* (1985; the minotaur), the depiction of a lonely being who grapples with himself in a vain attempt to understand his own nature and that of the world.

Trends in fiction by Swiss writers who emerged in the 1950s range from continued social criticism and realistic portrayal of Swiss existence to experiments with new narrative forms. The search for identity, rebellion against traditional social structures, existential introspection, fear of the future, and a variety of didactical directions are common aspects of an art that seeks to define the true relationship between the individual and society. Projections of reform are common, but there are also visible longings for a lost past.

In his socially critical novels, from *Mit F-51 überfällig* (1954; with F-51 overdue) and *Geschichten um Abel* (1960; stories about Abel) to *Aber den Kirschbaum, den gibt es* (1975; but the cherry tree, it exists) and *Der Reiche stirbt* (1977; the rich man dies), Walter Matthias Diggelmann (1927–79) examined the problems of the broken family and the corrupt business practices of capitalist power figures. The elusiveness of truth and the difficulties of penetrating superficial appearances are critical parts of his mixtures of fact and fiction. Diggelmann's artistic strength lay in transforming critical observations into direct narrations.

Der junge Os (1957; the young Os) and *Das Gerüst* (1960; the framework) established the two poles of Hans Boesch's (b. 1926) narrative art: representation of the individual's relationship to nature, and portrayal of the tension between man and the world of work. In *Die Fliegenfalle* (1968; the fly trap), a complex synthesis of the two directions, he describes the destructive clash of nature and technology. Boesch's most demanding, most significant novel is *Der Kiosk* (1978; the kiosk), a creation that carries the enmity between nature and technology to an extreme in which man becomes a subordinate factor in the world's existence.

A combination of visionary fantasy and harsh reality informs the narrative prose of Jörg Steiner (b. 1930). In *Eine Stunde vor Schlaf* (1958; an hour before sleep), *Strafarbeit* (1962; penal work), *Ein Messer für den ehrlichen Finder* (1966; a knife for the honest finder), and *Schnee bis in die Niederungen* (1973; snow down into the low places) Steiner processes the themes of fear, flight, and search for identity in a society where might makes right. One of his most important works is *Auf dem Berge Sinai sitzt der Schneider Kikriki* (1969; on Mount Sinai sits the tailor Kikriki), a cycle of stories that trace the author's own attempts at self-definition. Although liberation from inner captivity is the theme of *Das Netz zerreissen* (1982; tearing the net), its major strengths lie in successful characterizations, scenic descriptions, and effective pairing of the internal and external pilgrimage. Unfortunately, the overall effect is dampened by choppy plotting and lack of consistent focus.

Paul Nizon's (b. 1929) prose is starkly autobiographical in nature. The narrative sketches in *Die gleitenden Plätze* (1959; the gliding places) offer pointed observations about everyday events, while *Canto* (1963; canto), *Im Hause enden die Geschichten* (1971; in the house the stories end), and *Untertauchen* (1972; submerging) focus on the transformation of personal consciousness in the process of self- and world mastery. Nizon's most successful work is *Stolz* (1975; pride). It contains one of the most consistent portrayals of destructive human unconnectedness in modern German Swiss literature. *Das Jahr der Liebe* (1981; the year of love) and *Aber wo ist das Leben* (1983; but where is life) are excellent examples of his facility with vivid detail, and his lucid, flexible style.

In *Der Stumme* (1959; *The Mute,* 1962), *Herr Taurel* (1962; Mr. Taurel), *Die ersten Unruhen* (1972; the first disturbances), and *Die Verwilderung* (1977; running wild), Otto Friedrich Walter (b. 1928) employed a fictitious Swiss town as a microcosmic model for the contemporary bourgeois world. Among his strongest themes are the dichotomy of guilt and punishment, and threat to personal freedom created by industrial growth, and the need for a socialist state. Walter's prose is especially effective in its clear descriptions of regional landscapes and its definition of specific human types. Compared with earlier works, *Wie wird Beton zu Gras* (1979; how does concrete become grass), a portrayal of youthful rebellion against conservative restraints, is direct and blunt in its didacticism, while *Das Staunen der Schlafwandler am Ende der Nacht* (1983; the amazement of the sleepwalkers at the end of the night), a complex study of the conflict between writers and political powers, falters on the subordination of story to political declaration.

The works of Gertrud Wilker (b. 1924), from *Der Drachen* (1959; the dragon) and *Elegie auf die Zukunft* (1966; elegy on the future) through *Einen Vater aus Wörtern machen* (1970; making a father from words) to *Winterdorf* (1977; winter village), *Blick auf meinesgleichen* (1979; glance at someone like me), and *Nachleben* (1980; afterlife), focus on the problems of authorial self-reflection and skepticism about language as a valid medium of expression. Wilker's prose is notable for its careful integration of theme and form, its precision of language, and its strictness of composition. One of her best books is *Winterdorf,* in which language is given the task of preserving the essence of life.

The most visible development in Swiss prose during the 1960s was a new emphasis on short fiction. Manifestations took various forms, including surrealistic narratives, modifications of the American short story, novellas, plotless creations, and narrated reports. Some writers produced novels that were composites of short pieces integrated into a larger structure. Others offered writings that defy classification, but which are related to short fiction in diverse ways. Among other new tendencies in the novel were the employment of reflection, shattering and differentiation techniques, the dissolution of traditional novel form, an increase in subjectivism, and a strengthening of regionalism.

One of the first writers to work extensively with short forms after the war was Kurt Marti (b. 1921). His *Dorfgeschichten 1960* (1960; village stories 1960) features experiments with various types of prose. In this and later works, Marti offered bold, original modifications of older forms and motifs. His political pieces are especially effective in their projection of local Swiss relationships and atmosphere. In *Abratzky oder Die kleine Blockhütte* (1971; Abratzky; or, the little log cabin) he explored a different stylistic possibility for short prose, presenting a fictionalized encyclopedia as an effort to portray reality in terms of facts, numbers, definitions, and interpretations. *Das Herz der Igel* (1972; the heart of the hedgehog), *Die Riesin* (1975; the giantess), *Bürgerliche Geschichten* (1981; bourgeois stories), and *Dorfgeschichten* (1983; village stories) reflect his consistent focus on problems of social and political change. *Bürgerliche Geschichten* is especially effective in representing life's disjointedness through fragmentary bits of fiction.

The experiments of Kuno Raeber (b. 1922) document a personal process of self-liberation and transformation of existence. Raeber's purpose is self-defense against a threatening world. His most important prose works are *Mißverständnisse* (1968; misunderstandings) and *Alexius unter der Treppe* (1973; Alexius beneath the stairs). *Mißverständnisse* exemplifies the loose integration of short items of fiction into an artistic whole. Fantasies, stories, puzzles, and reflections are emphasized in the exposure of threatening, volcanic, labyrinthine elements of the current world. Although *Alexius unter der Treppe* is a novel, it is closely related to short fiction in its distinctly fragmented structure. *Das Ei* (1981; the egg), is similar to the earlier novel, but its flood of grotesque images and episodes is especially unusual with its perversities, blasphemies, and cruelties couched in highly poetic language.

Jürg Federspiel's (b. 1931) terse, matter-of-fact stories in *Orangen und Tode* (1961; oranges and deaths), *Der Mann, der Glück brachte* (1966; the man who brought happiness), and *Paratuga kehrt zurück* (1973; Paratuga returns) focus on outsiders, emphasizing criticism of bourgeois forms of existence. Their most startling feature is the presentation of concentrated moments in pictorial, but also sober and succinct, language. Federspiel's most characteristic work is *Museum des Hasses* (1969; museum of hate). In portraying his impressions of Manhattan, he defined reality as brutal, insane, decadent, and contradictory. The grotesqueness of life is also stressed in *Die beste Stadt für Blinde* (1980; the best city of the blind), which contains some of the best anti-war literature of recent years, and the horribly powerful *Die Ballade von der Typhoid Mary* (1982; *The Ballad of Typhoid Mary*, 1984). This last creation is an intense metaphor for the eternal outsider.

Variations on foreignness are the essence of Raffael Ganz's (b. 1923) stories. In *Orangentraum* (1961; dream of oranges), *Abend der Alligatoren* (1962; evening of the alligators), and *Schabir* (1966; Schabir) the exotic element is presented from the perspective of concrete observation. Ganz's best and most important work is *Im Zementgarten* (1971; in the cement garden), the first volume of modern Swiss fiction to focus directly on the situation of the migrant foreign worker. What gives Ganz's narratives their special strength is the successful penetration of the outsider motif from an inner psychological perspective.

Alienation is also a factor in *Die Wohltaten des Mondes* (1963; the moon's good deeds), Urs Jaeggi's (b. 1931) first volume of stories. His figures and themes are taken from reality, but reality is always fractured and distanced through the use of surrealistic and grotesque devices. Unlike his short stories, the novels *Die Komplicen* (1964; the accomplices) and *Ein Mann geht vorbei* (1969; a man goes by) are not especially successful. The unconvincing use of fantastic elements in the first, and the triteness of the portrayal of Jewish persecution in the second inhibit their artistic effect. Jaeggi's later novels, *Brandeis* (1978; Brandeis) and *Grundrisse* (1981; outlines), are much more compelling because of their direct, authentic approach to the present reality of life in Berlin.

The novels of Hugo Loetscher (b. 1929) are primarily parables. *Abwässer. Ein Gutachten* (1963; sewers, a report) employs discussion of a big city's sewer system as a paradigm for modern existence, while *Die Kranzflechterin* (1964; the wreath weaver) and *Noah* (1967; *Noah*, 1970) are satirical exposés of the profit-based affluent society. Loetscher's most effective work is *Der Immune* (1975; the immune man), an autobiographical exploration of a journalist's survival strategy amid continuing crises. *Der Immune* is especially notable for its stylistic variety.

Peter Bichsel's (b. 1935) narratives are among the best examples of the new Swiss short forms. *Eigentlich möchte Frau Blum den Milchmann kennenlernen* (1964; *And Really Frau Blum Would Very Much Like to Meet the Milkman,* 1968) set the pattern for a prose that is almost epigrammatic in its conciseness. These precise, deceivingly simple sketches of human loneliness and disappointment make powerful statements about current existential conditions. The novel *Die Jahreszeiten* (1967; the seasons) employs short forms to illustrate the questionable nature of storytelling. *Kindergeschichten* (1969; *Stories for Children,* 1971) is Bichsel's most successful volume. Its seven ambiguous tales examine the problem of rebellion against convention. In *Der Busant: Von Trinkern, Polizisten und der schönen Magalone* (1985; the busser: about drinkers, policemen and the beautiful Magalone) the author offers his own excellent variations on the contemporary themes of loss of identity, progressive alienation, arbitrary violence, and self-destruction.

The focus of Werner Schmidli's (b. 1939) narratives is the world of work. In *Der Junge und die toten Fische* (1966; the boy and the dead fish) and *Der alte Mann, das Bier, die Uhr und andere Geschichten* (1966; the old man, the beer, the clock, and other stories) he offered precisely detailed portrayals of working-class society from a socially critical socialistic perspective. Schmidli's most important books are *Meinetwegen soll es doch schneien* (1967; it can snow as far as I'm concerned) and *Das Schattenhaus* (1968; the shadow house), which describe with penetrating insight the collapse of a family and a young boy's unsuccessful attempts at self-realization. *Fundplätze* (1974; places where things are found) and the shorter pieces in *Gustavs Untaten* (1976; Gustav's atrocities) are also quite powerful in illuminating human intolerance and its destructive impact.

Outsiders and their conflicts with modern society are an important element in Adolf Muschg's (b. 1934) ironic and satirical novels and stories. *Im Sommer des Hasen* (1965; in the summer of the hare) reflects mastery of precise narrative presentation, substantial imagination, and a flair for humor and playful parody. *Gegenzauber* (1967; counter magic) is an especially original, delightfully funny depiction of the victory of nonconformist dropouts over a conservative social order. The strength of Muschg's aesthetic realism and his command of language are particularly visible in *Fremdkörper* (1968; foreign bodies), *Liebesgeschichten* (1972; love stories), and *Entfernte Bekannte* (1976; distant acquaintances), but his best work is *Albissers Grund* (1974; Albisser's reason), an ironic, psychoanalytical exploration of motivation toward violence. *Baiyun oder Die Freundschaftsgesellschaft* (1980; white cloud; or, the friendship society) also deals with problems of violence and relationships between individual and group in a unique and interesting fashion. The stories of *Leib und Leben* (1982; life and limb) are less compelling in their treatment of common contemporary themes.

Husten (1965; cough), *Melancholie* (1967; melancholy), *Der Vogel auf dem Tisch* (1968; the bird on the table), *Der Irre und sein Arzt* (1974; the insane man and his doctor), and *Die roten Tiere von Tsavo* (1976; the red animals of Tsavo) illustrate the skeptical irony and macabre imagination that inform Walter Vogt's (b. 1927) stories. His short creations and the novels *Wüthrich* (1966; brute) and *Der Wiesbadener Kongreß* (1973; the Wiesbaden congress) present studies from the milieu of hospitals and physicians as caricatures and travesties of an organized society. Vogt's greatest literary strength lies in his ability to couch black humor and pointed sarcasm in artistically precise language.

In the satirical and grotesquely pointed stories of *Das verlorene Gähnen und andere nutzlose Geschichten* (1967; the lost yawn and other useless stories), *Idyllen* (1970; idylls), *Der Rand von Ostermundigen* (1973; the edge of Ostermundigen), *Wegwerfgeschichten* (1974; discard stories), and *Wo?* (1975; where?), Franz Hohler (b. 1943) practices a general criticism of human weaknesses and the prevalent belief in the possibility of progress. Hohler is a master of subtlety and understatement, and the force of his writing lies in his facility with indirect, dry, quiet presentation that stimulates uncomfortable laughter. *Die Rückeroberung* (1982; the reconquest), a book devoted to the idea of a subtle, more powerful reality lying beneath the surface of the conventional world, contains some of Hohler's most imaginative, most provocative creations.

Heinrich Wiesner's (b. 1925) *Lapidare Geschichten* (1967; concise stories) forms a bridge between his earlier aphoristic writings and a progressively more narrative brand of prose. The focus of the book is pointed social criticism and the satirical unmasking of clichés and taboos. Wiesner's best works are contained in *Notennot* (1973; grade trouble) and *Das Dankschreiben* (1975; letter of thanks), both of which are based on his experiences as a teacher. In *Das verwandelte Land* (1977; the transformed land), he presented a number of extremely short stories that highlight basic elements of human existence.

One of the most versatile and promising authors to emerge in the 1960s was Urs Widmer (b. 1938). *Alois* (1968; Alois) and *Die Amsel im Regen im Garten* (1971; the blackbird in the rain in the garden) reflect his ability to weave figures and motifs of the past into an ironic, parodistic representation of contemporary reality. *Die Forschungsreise* (1974; the voyage of discovery) is especially interesting for its integration of grotesque and surrealistic devices into the fantastic portrayal of an explorer's attempt to penetrate his own identity during a dream journey. More recent works, such as *Liebesnacht* (1982; night of love) and *Indianersomme* (1985; Indian summer), have firmly established Widmer as a producer of original, rich, and highly imaginative literature.

Writers who began producing fiction in Switzerland during the 1970s and early 1980s continued many of the trends that already existed. Short forms remained popular and some authors produced extreme variations. There was also increased emphasis on the world of work in the special Swiss spectrum. Experimentation with fresh techniques, especially exploration of different language possibilities, dominated some creations, while an inward focus rendered many items strongly subjectivistic.

The narratives of Hermann Burger (b. 1942), contained in *Bork* (1970; bark), *Schilten* (1976; Schilten), *Diabelli* (1979; devils), and *Die künstliche Mutter* (1982; the artificial mother), are extreme examples of experimentation with esoteric intellectual language. The author attempts to employ his unusual formulations to penetrate the façades of conventional life. Burger's most successful creation is *Schilten,* a novel that juxtaposes the motifs of education and human mortality in a particularly macabre but gripping way. In the more recent works, he has absurdly magnified the artificiality of his language, and the resulting convoluted diction is banal and boring.

Tension between a stable present and a helpless past is the focus of Erica Pedretti's (b. 1930) deeply personal fiction. The stories in *Harmloses bitte* (1970; harmless things please) are stimulated by memories of childhood. They contrast fear of death and hopelessness with the positive aspects of contemporary life. In *Heiliger Sebastian* (1973; Saint Sebastian) the past is emphasized more strongly in a protest against modern indifference to history, while *Veränderung oder Die Zertrümmerung von dem Kind Karl und anderen Personen* (1977; change; or, the demolition of the child Karl and other people) employs documentary techniques that place heavier stress on the present. Pedretti's artistic power and stylistic range are especially visible in the vignettes of *Sonnenaufgänge, Sonnenuntergänge* (1984; sunrises, sunsets), where stream of consciousness alternates with collage and direct narration, and the fluctation between reality and the imaginary world in surreal images, landscapes, and other constructs forces the reader to make private associations.

Gerold Späth (b. 1939) produces exaggerated picaresque narratives that combine elements of the traditional novel of educational development with social criticism. *Unschlecht* (1970; *A Prelude to the Long Happy Life of Maximilian Goodman,* 1975), *Stimmgänge* (1972; voice movements), *Die heile Hölle* (1974; the healthy hell), and *Balzapf oder Als ich auftauchte* (1977; Balzapf; or, when I surfaced) are notable for their power of language and their subtle critiques of bourgeois attitudes, provincialism, and materialism. *Commedia* (1980; comedy), a strange version of Dante's famous masterpiece, is an especially effective portrait of the unconnectedness of modern individuals. Späth's collections of stories, from *Zwölf Geschichten* (1973; twelve stories) to *Sindbadland* (1984; Sindbad land), reveal in even more singular detail the breaks in the surface of today's existence.

At the center of Silvio Blatter's (b. 1946) works, including *Schaltfehler* (1972; switching mistakes), *Mary Long* (1973; Mary Long), *Verschüttete Tage, genormte Zeit* (1976; buried days, standardized time), and *Zunehmendes Heimweh* (1978; increasing homesickness), are an emphasis on the world of work and an almost idyllic representation of the Swiss milieu. The individual portraits of factory workers in *Schaltfehler* are the products of penetrating observation, but the subjective tone is positive rather than sharply critical. The strength of Blatter's narrative art is most visible in *Kein schöner Land* (1983; no more beautiful land), a saga of the author's home region. *Kein schöner Land* is especially notable for its lucid language and its solid interweaving of fictional elements.

The writings of Peter Meyer (b. 1946), who publishes as E. Y. Meyer, combine detailed, realistic reproduction of strictly limited domains with uncompromising and consistent anti-idyllic criticism. *Ein Reisender in Sachen Umsturz* (1972; a traveler in the causes of upheavel), *In Trubschachen* (1973; in Trubschachen), and *Die Rückfahrt* (1977; the return trip) exemplify a unique style that favors seemingly endless convoluted sentences, indirect discourse, and exaggerated linguistic precision. Mundane, banal situations are employed as symbols for the complex, uncertain, mysterious, hopeless elements of life. Meyer's narrative strength derives from his particular sensitivity to the fine shadings and nuances of personal experience.

Like Silvio Blatter, Elisabeth Meylan (b. 1937) focuses her fiction on the world of work. The special value of *Räume unmöbliert* (1972; unfurnished rooms) and *Die Dauer der Fassaden* (1975; the duration of the façades) lies in her ability to capture precisely the atmosphere of the described milieu. *Räume unmöbliert* highlights an existence in which the individual suffocates in thoughtlessness and senselessness, while *Die Dauer der Fassaden* illuminates in harsh tones a realm where creativity is impossible, resistance collapses quickly, and individuals retreat into inactive observation.

Lukas Hartmann's (b. 1944) *Madeleine, Martha und Pia:*

Protokolle vom Rand (1974; Madeleine, Martha, and Pia: records from the edge), *Mozart im Hurenhaus* (1975; Mozart in the brothel), and *Pestalozzis Berg* (1978; Pestalozzi's mountain) are remarkable for their portrayal of tangible, rounded human figures and their reflection of a solid facility with language. *Pestalozzis Berg*, a historical novel, is the best illustration of Hartmann's command of productive linguistic structures.

The problem of dealing with history is treated more actively in the works of Walther Kauer (b. 1935). *Schachteltraum* (1974; box dream), an unusual treatment of the individual's grapplings with the Nazi past, is written from the perspective of a politically committed worker and presented on varying temporal levels. *Spätholz* (1976; late wood), Kauer's most successful creation, offers a penetrating illumination of the clash between the old, traditional Swiss peasant life and the contemporary world of technology and tourism. His more recent volumes, *Abseitsfalle* (1977; offside trap), a trivial soccer novel, and *Tellereisen* (1979; wolf trap), an allegory for the conflict between individual and society, are disappointing in the light of earlier achievements.

In his first short prose pieces, Jürg Laederach (b. 1945) achieved a consistency and tightness of narration that is sometimes missing in his novels. Although the figures in *Einfall der Dämmerung* (1974; twilight falls) are artificial and imaginary, they reflect effectively a peculiar interplay of humor and cruelty. *Im Verlauf einer langen Erinnerung* (1977; in the course of a long recollection) and *Das ganze Leben* (1978; all of life) offer a piercing scrutiny of everyday experience, but their substance generates only a forced and contrived presentation of ideas. The later volumes of stories, *Das Buch der Klagen* (1980; the book of laments), *Nach Einfall der Dämmerung* (1982; after twilight falls), and *69 Arten den Blues zu spielen* (1984; 69 ways to play the blues), document a decline in artistic effectiveness. *Das Buch der Klagen* is difficult to read because of arcane symbolism and language that is stretched to extremes, while the isolated clever vignettes of *69 Arten den blues zu spielen* are obscured by other pieces that are vacuous and banal.

Strong contributions to recent Swiss fiction have been made by Gerhard Meier (b. 1928). His short novels, *Der andere Tag*

(1974; the other day), *Papierrosen* (1976; paper roses), *Der Besuch* (1976; the visit), *Der schnurgerade Kanal* (1977; the perfectly straight canal), *Toteninsel* (1979; island of the dead), and *Borodino* (1982; Borodino), are frameworks of tension between opposites. They offer combinations of precise details and intoxicated visions, direct grasping of reality and reflection on abstractions and intellectual values. Particularly characteristic is *Toteninsel,* an almost plotless, meditative conversation between two old men whose profound observations and reflections about life are woven together with lyrically sensitive, richly colorful language.

The works of Gertrud Leutenegger (b. 1948) are deeply subjective, the product of both internal and external experience. In *Vorabend* (1975; the evening before) she blends extremely private memories of childhood, travel, work, and love. *Ninive* (1977; Nineveh) projects reflections about interpersonal relationships against the background of an excursion to see a dead whale. The novels *Gouverneur* (1981; governor) and *Komm ins Schiff* (1983; come into the ship) reveal that Leutenegger's art depends upon her ability to transform emotions into tangible images. In some instances the events that she depicts are absurd, but her constructions are strong revelations of an intense inner life.

Verena Stefan's (b. 1947) *Häutungen* (1975; *Shedding,* 1979) is recognized as an important contribution to the literature of the women's movement. Its controversial treatment of sexuality as a focus of social power relationships is presented in compelling autobiographical notes, dreams, and analyses of a personal struggle toward feminine identity.

New evaluation of human connections from a feminist viewpoint is also the focus of Margit Schriber's (b. 1939) *Aussicht gerahmt* (1976; framed view) and *Kartenhaus* (1978; house of cards). In *Aussicht gerahmt* she emphasizes the distance between individuals through portrayal of a woman who retreats from society to live alone in a house where she writes her impressions of what she sees from her window. The intensely private childhood memories of *Kartenhaus* derive their narrative power from precise, disciplined description rather than retrospective introspection. *Vogel flieg* (1980; fly, bird) is

Schriber's best work. Its presentation of the central character and the society that alienates her is notable for its exactness, authenticity, and wit.

Grünsee (1978; green lake), by Christoph Geiser (b. 1949), is another very subjective novel, but it is not as oppressive in tone as other works of the period. Geiser presents his material in simple sentences, and the psychological penetration of the protagonist is clearly defined. Themes of isolation, guilt, and death are mixed with the problems of decaying family relationships, but negative elements are balanced by signs of life and a hope that alienation can be overcome.

Among the most interesting products of the focus inward are the writings of Hanna Johansen (b. 1939). *Die stehende Uhr* (1978; the stopped clock) employs externally perceived objects and the context of an enigmatic train trip into the realm of death as ambiguous symbols for inner experience. In *Die Analphabetin* (1982; the illiterate girl) Johansen presents her personal grapplings with the Nazi past. The stories of *Über den Wunsch, sich wohlzufühlen* (1985; on the wish to feel comfortable) are especially characteristic of Johansen's fiction. They mingle realistic and surrealistic elements with illumination of puzzling aspects of simple, even trite situations.

The stories of Rahel Hutmacher (b. 1944) in *Wettergarten* (1980; weather garden) and *Dona* (1982; Dona) are examples of the return to timeless fantasy, fairy tale, and depictions of primitive life. Hutmacher's talent is most visible in the weaving together of abstract principles, emotions, and mysterious occurrences into structures that lack rational connections. Her best development of natural images is presented in the loosely related stories of *Tochter* (1983; daughter).

Matthias Zschokke (b. 1954) uses a variety of modern stylistic devices, ranging from reflection and monologue to dramatic dialogue, in his painfully humorous, satirical narratives. The peculiar anti-novel *Max* (1982; Max), the prose and drama text *Prinz Hans* (1984; Prince Hans), and the parody of transsexuality *ErSieEs* (1985; he/she/it) form a loose trilogy expressly devoted to the destruction of traditional literature in both form and substance. *ErSieEs* is a witty treatment of the emptiness of language as a symptom for the fragmented relationships between the sexes.

POETRY

Poetry is a central creative focus for only a few Swiss writers. During the early years after 1945, some of them employed lyric productions as an escape from the times. For the most part, they formulated verse that represented a secure middle-class world. Private reflections and retreats from contemporary events and politics are especially visible. Where war and other less comfortable topics are explored, the poetic point of view is typically private and subjective. Heavy emphasis is placed on religious experience, sensitivity to nature, and personal perceptions of stability. Exceptions to a strong traditionalism are distinctly isolated among poets who had established themselves before the war's end.

The primary concern of Max Rychner's (1897–1965) poems is the preservation of Western cultural and literary values. *Glut und Asche* (1946; fire and ash) and *Die Ersten* (1949; the first ones) reveal solid mastery of creative language and a cultivated sense of aesthetic discipline. *Glut und Asche* is particularly remarkable for its illumination of the human spirit's constancy, even amid the agitation, confusion, and strife of life. In *Die Ersten* he offers unique visions of the creation story in dialogues between Adam, Eve, and the serpent.

Albert Ehrismann's (b. 1908) verse—in *In dieser Nacht* (1946; in this night), *Das Stundenglas* (1948; the hour glass), *Ein ganz gewöhnlicher Tag* (1954; a completely ordinary day), *Riesenrad der Sterne* (1960; giant wheel of the stars), and *Wetterhahn altmodisch* (1968; weathercock, old-fashioned)—combines a traditional focus on love, death, and nature with a more personal relatedness to humanity and the world. Self-irony, sad humor, and a love for the beauties of the earth are clearly visible. Unlike other poets, Ehrismann did not avoid contemporary problems. His late works, *Die Gedichte des Pessimisten und Moralisten Albert Ehrismann* (1972; the poems of the pessimist and moralist Albert Ehrismann), *Eine Art Bilanz*

Switzerland

Switzerland

(1973; a kind of balance), *Mich wundert, daß ich fröhlich bin* (1973; I am amazed that I am cheerful), and *Später, Äonen später* (1975; later, eons later), exhibit sharpness and clearness of tone that amplify uncompromising political statements.

In *Lyrik* (1946; poetry), *Lyrische Texte* (1953; lyrical texts), *Die Wandelsterne* (1955; the wandering stars), and *Signaturen, Klangfiguren* (1964; signaturcs, sound patterns), Urs Martin Strub (b. 1910) published expressive, sensitive poems about nature and the world. The books form an interesting cycle. *Lyrik* presents light-filled, harmonious poems about a healthy world, while both *Lyrische Texte* and *Die Wandelsterne* depict a cosmos that is falling apart. In *Signaturen, Klangfiguren* the poet returned to musicality of form as an expression of renewed harmony.

Neo-romantic tendencies are visible in the poems of Erwin Jaeckle (b. 1909). His collections, from *Schattenlos* (1947; shadowless) and *Gedichte aus allen Winden* (1956; poems from all directions) to *Der Ochsenritt* (1967; the ox ride), *Eineckgedichte* (1974; one-angle poems), and *Das wachsende Gedicht* (1976; the growing poem), are dominated by personal experience. In bold language Jaeckle offers nature, landscape, and love poems that mythicize nature and expose elements of the past contained in the present. The strength of his lyrics lies in the consistent emphasis of cultivated form and original language as the mainstays of poetic art.

Timelessness and commitment to traditional forms are the most visible characteristics of Silja Walter's (b. 1919) poetry. *Die ersten Gedichte* (1944; the first poems; expanded as *Gedichte,* 1950; poems) and *Gesammelte Gedichte* (1972; collected poems) reflect a musicality and sensitivity to tone that augment a profound fulfillment of romantic possibilities. At the same time, individual poems transcend convention in their reaching out to touch the impossible and their pointed self-observation.

Werner Zemp's (1906–59) lyrics were the product of classical and neo-romantic literary perceptions. *Gedichte* (1943; poems; expanded, 1955) and *Das Hochtal* (1956; the high valley) feature verse that has no other purpose than magnification of the pure artistic ideal. Zemp's approach involved strict and careful cultivation of word usage to produce what he saw as rare jewels that embodied the concepts of value and beauty.

Very few significant Swiss poets published their first lyrics during the late 1940s. Two of the more important exceptions are Rainer Brambach (1917–83) and Hans Rudolf Hilty (b. 1925). Brambach's works resemble those of Werner Zemp in avoiding political or social commitment, while Hilty stresses artistic objectification of confessional elements.

In *7* (1947; 7), *Tagwerk* (1959; day's work), and *Ich fand keinen Namen dafür* (1969; I found no name for it) Rainer Brambach presented poems of remarkable vitality and nearness to nature. His best pieces are poetic photographs that promote reflection. The themes are taken from experience, observations, and an inner sense of mistrust about expressions of pure feeling. The magnitude of Brambach's artistic power is most visible in *Auch im April* (1983; also in April). Dominated by a remarkable simplicity and timeless naturalness, these lyrics exhibit wistfulness, an appreciation for beauty and life, and a charming sense of musicality and tone.

The most visible characteristic of Hans Rudolf Hilty's poetry is diversity. *Nachtgesang* (1948; night songs), *Eingebrannt in den Schnee* (1956; burned into the snow), *Daß die Erde uns leicht sei* (1959; that the earth may rest lightly upon us), and *Zu erfahren* (1969; to experience) reflect experimentation with many of the new directions taken by German poetry. Hilty specifically rejected symbols taken from mundane experience and language, but he explored alternatives offered by dialect. Some of his most effective creations are in *Zu erfahren,* where he employed the techniques of direct political statement with force and authenticity.

A new beginning for Swiss poetry occurred in the 1950s, when it achieved international prominence in three areas: concrete poetry; radical, socially critical activist verse; and refined nature lyrics. Many authors who later turned to other forms produced significant amounts of poetry during this time. One important stimulus was the periodical *hortulus,* which focused on art in a context extending beyond the borders of Switzerland. Among the more characteristic tendencies of the period were emphasis on imagery from everyday language, rejection of tradition, magnification of surrealistic elements, changes in language, focus on the domains of proletarian and peasant life, and illumination of the changing world.

Alexander Zaver Gwerder's (1923–52) creations are melancholy portraits of life as imprisonment in a small nation. The first postwar German-Swiss poet of radical social activism, Gwerder documented his personal suffering in *Blauer Eisenhut* (1951; blue iron hat), *Dämmerklee* (1955; twilight clover), and *Land über Dächer* (1959; land over roofs). His most effective poems are expressionistic explorations of the mood of death, patterned after the forms of Gottfried Benn.

Themes from antiquity are combined with experimental forms in the poems of Urs Oberlin (b. 1919). In *Eos* (1951; Eos), *Gedichte* (1956; poems), *Zuwürfe* (1964; thrown things), and *Alle sind niemand* (1972; all are nobody) ancient Greek images are employed as symbols for the modern world and its experiences. The individual pieces vary significantly in quality. Some are artificial and formalistic, while others are powerfully moving.

Progress toward laconicism is also the direction taken by Heinrich Wiesner's poetry. Wiesner began with traditional verse in *Der innere Wanderer* (1951; the inner wanderer) and *Leichte Boote* (1958; light boats), then moved to ever shorter, terser creations in *Lakonische Zeilen* (1965; laconic lines) and *Neue Lakonische Zeilen* (1972; new laconic lines). The end results of his development are brief aphoristic utterances, compressed together to exclude everything unnecessary. They often consist only of key words, ellipses, and word plays that effectively define the outcome of a story or the sketch of a portrait.

In the poems of Erika Burkart (b. 1922), from *Der dunkle Vogel* (1953; the dark bird), *Sterngefährten* (1955; star companions), and *Geist der Fluren* (1958; spirit of the meadows) through *Ich liebe* (1964; I love) and *Die weichenden Ufer* (1967; the retreating shores) to *Fernkristall* (1972; far crystal) and *Die Transparenz der Scherben* (1973; the transparency of broken pieces), bitter melancholy is couched in simple, natural, traditional forms. The most striking thing about her works is the projection of a personal, original experience of interchange between humanity and nature, in language that is remarkably musical and rhythmic.

The most significant poet to emerge in Switzerland during the 1950s was Eugen Gomringer. Recognized as the father of concrete poetry, he exerted strong influence on many writers. The strength of such books as *Konstellationen* (1953; constellations), *33 Konstellationen* (1960; 33 constellations), *Die Konstellationen* (1964; *Constellations,* 1968), and *Das Stundenbuch* (1965; *The Book of Hours* 1968) lay in reducing metaphor to word, and in combining material in repetition and change to illuminate new linguistic relationships. More than anything else, Gomringer successfully defended the idea that the creation of poetry requires analytical, rational treatment of language in the process of transcending irrationalism and individualism. Since the peak period of his influence, Swiss literature has been more hesitant to accept extremist tendencies.

Another poet who favors laconic forms is Peter Lehner (b. 1922). The poems in *rot-grün* (1955; red-green), *Asphalt im Zwielicht* (1956; asphalt in twilight), *Ausfallstraße* (1959; breakdown street), *ein bißchen miß im kredit* (1967; a bit of dis in credit), and *wehrmännchens abschied* (1973; little soldier's farewell) are consistent in their social commitment, progressing to the elaboration of strongly political themes in the later volumes. Lehner's writings are marked by a reserved but thoroughly effective employment of modern technological and industrial terminology.

Walter Gross's (b. 1924) poems are related to those of Urs Oberlin in their focus on the Mediterranean region, but, unlike Oberlin, Gross emphasizes modern landscape rather than antiquity. Typical pieces in *Die Taube* (1956; the dove), *Botschaften noch im Staub* (1957; messages still in the dust), and *Antworten* (1964; answers) reflect the influence of Johannes Bobrowski in their rhythmical forms, lightly archaic vocabulary, themes, and treatment of the relationship between human beings and nature. An especially interesting aspect of Gross's poetic act is the attempt to transform nature lyrics into social comments on the times.

The socially committed verse of Jörg Steiner progresses from colorful imagery to terse, sharply pointed directness in *Epi-*

soden aus Rabenland (1956; episodes from raven land), *Der schwarze Kasten* (1965; the black box), and *Als es noch Grenzen gab* (1976; when there were still borders). In *Der schwarze Kasten* Steiner ties banalities together in order to promote insights and viewpoints that are not banal. The offerings in *Als es noch Grenzen gab* are especially unique in their projections of views of the present from a perspective in the future.

One other important experimentalist is Kurt Marti. He did not limit himself to concrete forms, but explored the possibilities of dialect and colloquial language. In *Republikanische Gedichte* (1959; republican poems), *Gedichte am Rand* (1963; poems at the edge), and *Leichenreden* (1969; funeral orations) he effectively combined language and form experiments with elements of social and political criticism and religious sermonizing. His most successful dialect volume is *Rosa Loui* (1967; Rosa Loui), with its sensitive, finely wrought offerings. Even more original are the poems of *Leichenreden*. Patterned after conventional obituaries, they shatter the clichés surrounding the concepts of death and dying, permitting a new kind of illumination from a Christian humanistic perspective. Important changes occur in later volumes. In *meergedichte alpengedichte* (1975; sea poems, Alp poems) he presented examples of a strikingly elliptic, even cryptic, style, while *abendland* (1980; evening land) contains some of the most profoundly stirring religious verse of recent years.

The literary success of Marti's *Rosa Loui* was one manifestation of the strong renewal of dialect poetry during the 1960s. For some poets, the vernacular represented a personal poetic homeland. Others used it as a vehicle for socially critical commentary or the expression of deeply private feelings of loneliness and sadness. The use of dialect did not inhibit the use of standard German or reduce the focus on traditional forms and continuing lyrical currents, but it added depth and richness to the spectrum of poetic endeavor.

Beat Brechbühl (b. 1939) does not promote dialect. His lyric development, as mirrored in *Spiele um Pan* (1962; games around Pan), *Lakonische Reden* (1964; laconic speeches), *Gesunde Predigt eines Dorfbewohners* (1966; healthy sermon of a villager), *Die Bilder und ich* (1968; the pictures and I), *Die*

Litanei von den Bremsklötzen (1969; the litany of the brake chocks), *Auf der Suche nach den Enden des Regenbogens* (1970; in search of the ends of the rainbow), and others, has followed a course from brooding reflection, sermon, observation, and description to a more relaxed, more concise, linguistically precise utterance. His extraordinary breadth is illustrated especially well in *Temperatursturz* (1984; temperature plunge), where the power of contrast between superficial externals and subjective depth gives profound meaning to anti-establishment pronouncements about landscapes, sex, language, injustice, fear, isolation, death, and numerous other topics.

In the works of Gerhard Meier, *Das Gras grünt* (1964; the grass grows green), *Kübelpalmen traümen von Oasen* (1969; tub palms dream of oases), and *Einige Häuser nebenan* (1973; some houses next door) experience of the author's local region forms the starting point for creations that relate private circumstances to the broad world. His poems are especially interesting for the way they rupture the bonds of space and time. Ironic attempts to master mundane life and pointed articulation of the confrontation with death are among the strongest manifestations of his talent. Meier's best offerings are the prose poems of *Kübelpalmen träumen von Oasen* and *Es regnet in meinem Dorf* (1971; it is raining in my village).

The productions of Ernst Eggimann (b. 1936) are among the most original poems in Swiss dialect. As exemplified in *henusode* (1968; outward ode), they focus almost entirely on sound patterns, removing expressions and words from normal syntactical context. The result is a peculiar combination of alienation of familiar things and a new visualization of language on a different level. Besides his dialect poems, Eggimann has produced significant religious lyrics. His *Psalmen* (1967; psalms) are interesting documentation of a faith that seeks God in man and his material existence. *Jesus-Texte* (1972; Jesus texts), on the other hand, are convincing in their visual imagery but weakened by overdone confessionality.

Dieter Fringeli (b. 1942) is another Swiss poet who has successfully employed dialect in his works, but many of his poems are in standard German. His major collections, from *Zwischen den Orten* (1965; between the places) and *Was auf der*

Hand lag (1968; whatever lay in one's hand) to *Ich bin nicht mehr zählbar* (1978; I am no longer countable) and *Ohnmachtwechsel* (1981; change of powerlessness), offer pointedly aphoristic variations on themes such as language, language criticism, and speaking. Viewed as a whole, his epigrammatically concentrated verse is skeptically sarcastic commentary on the insecurity of human existence in modern society.

Subjectivity is the dominant characteristic of Christoph Geiser's poems in *Bessere Zeiten* (1968; better times) and *Mitteilung an Mitgefangene* (1971; message to fellow prisoners). The more personal his creations are, the stronger and more valid they seem. Geiser's best individual pieces are terse notes that pinpoint his own alienation without coming across as either too private or indiscreet.

Where Gomringer's tendency was to remove the word from its normal surroundings to emphasize its individuality, the direction of writers who have appeared since 1970 is the reverse. Within the context of a continuing laconicism, younger poets focus on the use of words in their accustomed milieu. Recent Swiss verse documents an increase in subjectivism and significant diversity in grappling with problems of the present day. A particularly interesting phenomenon is the expansion of socially and politically committed lyrics beyond the dichotomy of left versus right to include an evaluation of other conflicts.

Beat Weber's (b. 1947) poetry in *Halbfreiheit* (1974; half freedom) examines unusual themes connected with handicapped children. The strongest, most impressive pieces are contained in the cycle "Heilpädagogische Notizen" (pedagogical health notes), where Weber illuminates the questionability of commonly accepted social norms from the perspective of individuals who cannot comply. His terse, powerful observations offer strong indictments of conventional society, employing clear and uncompromising language.

In *Entwurf zu einer Ebene* (1975; pattern for a plain) and *Im Verlauf eines einzigen Tages* (1978; in the course of a single day) Elisabeth Meylan presented samples of a very personal lyric style that is characterized especially by extreme restraint and caution. Individual poems reflect tendencies toward rejection of linguistic artificiality, formulae, sharp outlines, and forms that simulate consistency. Meylan's most profound creations are deeply subjective dialogues with the self.

Among the most subjective lyrics in recent Swiss literature are the poems in Gertrud Leutenegger's *Wie in Salomons Garten* (1981; as in Solomon's garden). Specific items juxtapose elements such as fantasies, impressions, dreams, thoughts, sensations, and intuitions. Images are connected in strange, richly personal relationships, placed together in associative rather than logical progressions. The subtle constructions are especially powerful revelations of complicated interweavings of forces held in balance by a remarkable imagination.

DRAMA

Although Switzerland has produced two of the strongest voices in postwar German theater, drama remains the weakest of the country's literary forms. The success of Max Frisch and Friedrich Dürrenmatt has completely overshadowed and dampened the efforts of other dramatists, and none of the younger playwrights has achieved broad acclaim. Moreover, in recent years both Frisch and Dürrenmatt have created less and less material for the stage, and the void had not been filled by works of substantial quality.

Of the writers who had established themselves before 1945, very few made meaningful contributions to Swiss drama after the war. Even the exceptions were unable to retain the positions of prominence that they had occupied earlier. Their works consist mainly of traditional forms, with special emphasis on commemorative and historical pieces.

Albert Jakob Welti was one of the first authors to enter the postwar theatrical scene. His *Helfende Kräfte* (1945; helping powers), *Der Paß* (1948; the passport), *Sie aber hats nicht leicht* (1950; she, however, does not have it easy), and *Hiob der Sieger* (1954; Job the victor) remain tied to conventional structures such as the festival drama. None of them is especially remarkable, and none has the strength and vitality of Welti's earlier dialect plays.

The most important older playwright was Cäsar von Arx

(1895–1949). He produced only three plays after 1945: *Brüder in Christo* (1947; brothers in Christ), *Festakt zur Enthüllung des Schlachtdenkmals in Dornach* (1949; ceremony for the unveiling of the battle monument in Dornach), and *Das Solothurner Gedenkspiel* (1949; the Solothurn memorial play). Arx's major dramas are historical and festival pieces that focus strongly on Swiss tradition. He established the festival play as a modern national form. Although none of his late creations had lasting impact, they all reflect solid mastery of staging and precision of language and scene.

One of the most prolific writers of historical drama is Max Gertsch (b. 1894). Among his better plays are *Menschenrechte* (1937; human rights), *Napoleon vor Gericht* (1956; Napoleon on trial), and *Donna Juana, Infantin von Spanien* (1959; Donna Juana, Infanta of Spain). Even these works are weakened by lack of originality and overemphasis of themes and conflicts that are neither compelling nor currently relevant.

Max Frisch's dramas examine both private and general concerns. *Nun singen sie wieder* (1946; now they sing again) is a powerful requiem that juxtaposes the suffering and death of the war with the possibilities of external existence and fulfillment. *Santa Cruz* (1947; Santa Cruz), on the other hand, is a deeply subjective dream play that focuses on inner longings generated by tension between reality and a vision of the past.

Frisch's most significant dramatic creations are *Die chinesische Mauer* (1947; revised, 1955; *The Chinese Wall*, 1961), *Biedermann und die Brandstifter* (1958; *The Firebugs*, 1959), and *Andorra* (1961; *Andorra, 1962). The Chinese Wall* reflects the influence of Bertolt Brecht in its parabolism and its employment of alienation devices, but the piece is not altogether coherent, and its farcical tone obscures the didactical message. The strength of *The Firebugs,* Frisch's most successful play, lies in its tight construction, the effective use of black humor, and the uniquely original parody of Greek tragedy. Although *Andorra* offers a compelling treatment of the problem of racial prejudice, it is weakened by the stress placed on the question of personal image.

Two plays that offer interesting explorations of private, existential themes are *Don Juan oder Die Liebe zur Geometrie*

(1953; *Don Juan; or, The Love of Geometry,* 1967) and *Biografie; Ein Spiel* (1967; *Biography: A Game,* 1969). Both works examine the problem of freedom of choice, but *Don Juan* is especially compelling in its representation of the conflict between the realms of reality and the ideal. In *Triptychon* (1978; *Triptych,* 1981) Frisch effectively combined once more the elements that have given his works their special character: compassionate, subtle penetration of existential fears, sharp consciousness of human transitoriness, stylistic originality, richness of form, and humanness of substance.

The dramas of Friedrich Dürrenmatt are also related in form to those of Brecht. Dürrenmatt specializes in historical parables with grotesque characteristics and theological themes. He emphasizes problems of universal guilt and the immutability of the human condition in the early plays *Es steht geschrieben* (1946; it is written), *Der Blinde* (1947; the blind man), *Die Ehe des Herrn Mississippi* (1952; *The Marriage of Mr. Mississippi,* 1964), and *Ein Engel kommt nach Babylon* (1952; *An Angel Comes to Babylon,* 1962). Their strength lies in the peculiarly effective combination of macabre elements and the techniques of comedy.

Dürrenmatt's best plays are *Der Besuch der alten Dame* (1956; *The Visit,* 1962), *Romulus der Große* (1956; *Romulus the Great,* 1956), and *Die Physiker* (1962; *The Physicists,* 1964). *The Visit* offers a powerful balance between development of theme and grotesque theatricality, whereas the tragicomedy *Romulus the Great* successfully plays off ribald humor against a generally pessimistic view of the human condition. In *The Physicists* Dürrenmatt presents a compelling treatment of the insanity of destructive tendencies in modern political machinations.

Among Dürrenmatt's other contributions to dramatic literature are several significant radio plays, including *Die Panne* (1956; *The Deadly Game,* 1960), *Abendstunde im Spätherbst* (1957; evening hour in late autumn), and *Der Doppelgänger* (1960; the double). Each of these works offers a uniquely original variation on the theme of inescapable guilt.

Not all of Dürrenmatt's pieces are successful. *Portrait eines Planeten* (1970; portrait of a planet), *Der Mitmacher* (1976; the conformist), and *Die Frist* (1977; the deadline) are flawed by insufficient development of major ideas, dialogues filled with platitudes, and simple tastelessness. *Achterloo* (1983; Achterloo) is an even more disappointing rehash of old themes. It lacks coherence and the effective integration of historical substance and characters.

Playwrights who began writing during the 1950s later responded to the models of Frisch and Dürrenmatt in different ways. Many rejected Dürrenmatt in particular and created works that clearly reflected their opposition. Although there were some attempts to examine new themes, the material typically remained bound to overworked forms, and the resulting dramas were relatively unsuccessful.

The plays of Rudolf Jakob Humm (1895–1977), including *Der Pfau muß gehen* (1950; the peacock must go), *Tristan da Cunha* (1950; Tristan da Cunha), and *Robespierre spielt mit Gott* (unpublished, written 1972; Robespierre plays with God), reflect his inability to produce theatrical works that are consistently coherent. *Der Pfau muß gehen,* a weak historical piece, lacks dramatic action and tension, and contains an overabundance of irrelevant speeches. Unevenness is the primary flaw in *Tristan da Cunha,* which begins with relatively effective characterization and dialogues but fails to maintain a compelling presentation. In *Robespierre spielt mit Gott* Humm forcefully demonstrated his lack of talent for presenting effective social criticism.

Herbert Meier's (b. 1928) dramas, from *Die Barke von Gawdos* (1954; the barque of Gawdos) and *Jonas und der Nerz* (1957; Jonas and the mink) to *Rabenspiele* (1971; raven games) and *Carlotta, Kaiserin* (1977; Carlotta, empress), are more viable than those of Humm. In an effort to distance himself from Dürrenmatt, Meier emphasizes theater of language and avoids grotesqueness and ideology. Although much of his work is reasonably solid, it is often weakened by an unconvincing mixture of poetic theater and social criticism.

Increasing international acclaim for Frisch and Dürrenmatt during the 1960s did not make Swiss drama as a whole more visible. Provincialism and conservatism prevented playwrights with controversial material from reaching a broad audience.

Criticism of the society was tolerated only in comedy. In spite of attempts to avoid narrowness and broaden the perspective of Swiss theater, dramatists had difficulty in meeting the expectations of the public. One inhibiting factor was language. Given the tension between dialect and standard written German, many writers found it hard to achieve a productive balance. Dialogues created in proper German projected an artificiality that hampered their dramatic effectiveness. On the other hand, excessive use of dialect reinforced the barriers that kept Swiss plays out of the international repertoire. Conservative inertia prevented strong development of the documentary theater in Switzerland and favored poetic and absurdist forms.

In their focus on the search for guilt, the dramas of Manfred Schwarz (b. 1930) are superficially related to those of Dürrenmatt. Schwarz does not create parables but couches his theme of tribunal in the framework of realistic problem pieces. His *Angeklagte Madeleine T.* (1961; the accused, Madeleine T.) is an interesting monodrama in which a murderess illuminates the guilt of her victim husband. *Das andere Gericht* (1964; the other court) offers a psychologically penetrating exploration of the personal trial that occurs in a murderer's mind. One of Schwarz's best pieces is *Um ein bißchen Rauch* (1964; for a bit of smoke). It combines a realistic situation with elements of the absurd to accent the conflicts between two soldiers who fight over a last cigarette. *Ein Mann des Möglichen* (1975; a man of possibility), Schwarz's least convincing play, fails to achieve clarity of presentation or sharpness of development.

Elio oder Eine fröhliche Gesellschaft (1965; Elio; or, a cheerful society) and *Die Katze* (1967; the cat), by Otto F. Walter, are attempts to penetrate the changing relationships between human beings and their surroundings. *Elio oder Eine fröhliche Gesellschaft* focuses on the conflict between experience and longing, while *Die Katze* stresses the individual nature of all grappling with the past. Neither work is particularly successful in treating the disparity between reality and the mental conceptions of the characters.

Walter Vogt's plays resemble those of Dürrenmatt in their use of unexpected grotesque elements, their preference for criminal themes, and their reliance on the power of idea.

Nevertheless, Vogt's productions are more restricted in scope. Instead of a "theater of the world," he offers microcosmic symbolism. Although his satirical treatment of medicine and doctors in *Höhenluft* (1966; mountain air) was a theatrical failure, *Spiele der Macht* (1970; games of power), *Typhos* (1973; typhoid), and *Pilatus vor dem schweigenden Christus* (1974; Pilate before the silent Christ) document significant dramatic talent. The three later plays are especially notable for their sensitive revelation of the dynamics of human interaction.

The major plays of Adolf Muschg, *Rumpelstilz* (1968; Rumpelstiltskin), *Die Aufgeregten von Goethe* (1971; Goethe's agitated ones), and *Kellers Abend* (1975; Keller's evening), explore the general problem of the individual's relationship to his times. In *Rumpelstilz,* Muschg presents a dynamic interpretation of modern social problems. *Die Aufgeregten von Goethe* is a successful ironic satire that is remarkable for its multiple layers of meaning. Muschg's most ambitious play is *Keller's Abend,* a psychological study that derives its dramatic impact from the tension between the protagonist's silence and what is spoken by the people around him. Unfortunately, the work fails to illuminate the central character's inner world, and the interpretive demands placed on the audience can only be met with great difficulty.

Three features are especially evident in the dramas of Swiss authors who produced their first theatrical works after 1970. In some plays there is powerful social criticism. Other pieces are dominated by manipulations of language, ranging from use of dialect to intellectual linguistic experiment. The strongest, most visible characteristic of recent drama is a distinctly eschatological mood.

In the creations of Heinrich Henkel (b. 1937)—including *Eisenwichser* (1970; *The Painters,* 1973), *Frühstückspause* (1971; breakfast break), *Spiele um Geld* (1971; games for money), *Olaf und Albert* (1973; Olaf and Albert), and *Die Betriebsschließung* (1975; the plant closure)—the world of work and the dehumanization of the individual are emphasized. *Eisenwichser* is the first postwar play in German to portray the monotony of labor directly in the theater. It is also Henkel's most successful piece. The special strengths of his dramaturgy are its simplicity, authenticity, and sensitivity, but not all of the plays are as effective as *Eisenwichser.* In *Spiele um Geld,* for example, the presentation of reality in a casino degenerates into banality and triviality.

Hans-Peter Geschwend's (b. 1945) radio plays are devoted to the criticism of existing institutions. Instead of attacking his target from outside, he presents figures who come to grips with their own participation in questionable activities. The best example of his approach is *Feldgraue Scheiben* (1971; field-gray disks), in which a young, committed lieutenant must deal with the contradiction inherent in the notion of training efficient soldiers for a military body that is "in the service of peace."

An interesting example of the dialect play is Hansjörg Schneider's (b. 1938) *Der Erfinder oder Schpäck und Bohne* (1973; the inventor; or, bacon and beans). In this work Schneider employs dialect on two levels. As the language of the common people, it becomes an ironic vehicle of criticism directed against the peasantry. At the same time, it is employed as the outsider's mark of alienation.

The four plays in Jürg Laederach's *Fahles Ende kleiner Begierden* (1979; pale end of small desires) are radical linguistic experiments that imitate musical composition techniques of repetition and variation. In surrealistic and absurd situations, without action or plot, Laederach offers combinations of comedy and despair. Each of the plays ends in destruction and death. The world view is totally pessimistic, and the only redeeming feature of the plays is an occasional flash of black humor.

Lebe wohl, Gute Reise: Ein dramatisches Poem (1980; farewell, have a good trip: a dramatic poem), Gertrud Leutenegger's first play, is also eschatological in tone. Presented from a feminist viewpoint, it blends aspects of the modern world with the past, transforming the theme of human agitation and destructiveness into a statement on the conflict between male and female aspects of existence. In spite of the skillful projections of the tension between decay and beauty, some figures remain indistinct and underdeveloped. As a result, the play loses much of its potential power.

SELECTED BIBLIOGRAPHY

GENERAL STUDIES

Albrecht, Günter, Kurt Böttcher, Herbert Greiner-Mai, and Paul Günter Krohn, eds. *Lexikon deutschsprachiger Schriftsteller*. Kronberg: Skriptor, 1974.

Arnold, Heinz Ludwig, ed. *Kritisches Lexikon zur deutschsprachigen Gegenwartsliteratur*. Munich: Text und Kritik, 1978–present.

Brauneck, Manfred, ed. *Autorenlexikon deutschsprachiger Literatur des zwanzigsten Jahrhunderts*. Reinbeck: Rowohlt, 1984.

Demetz, Peter. *Postwar German Literature*. New York: Western, 1970.

Domandi, Agnes Körner. *Modern German Literature*. New York: Ungar, 1972.

Durzak, Manfred. *Deutsche Gegenwartsliteratur*. Stuttgart: Reclam, 1981.

Heckmann, Herbert, ed. *Literatur aus dem Leben*. Munich. Hanser, 1984.

Koebner, Thomas, ed. *Tendenzen der deutschen literatur seit 1945*. Stuttgart: Kröner, 1971.

Kunisch, Hermann, ed. *Handbuch der deutschen Gegenwartsliteratur*, 2nd ed. Munich: Nymphenburger, 1969.

Lennarz, Franz. *Deutsche Schriftsteller des 20. Jahrhunderts im Spiegel der Kritik*. Stuttgart: Kröner, 1984.

Martini, Fritz. *Deutsche Literaturgeschichte*. Stuttgart: Kröner, 1984.

Raddatz, Fritz J. *Die Nachgeborenen*. Frankfurt am Main: Fischer, 1983.

Weber, Dietrich, ed. *Deutsche Literatur der Gegenwart*. Stuttgart: Kröner, 1976.

Wiese, Benno von, ed. *Deutsche Dichter der Gegenwart*. Berlin: E. Schmidt, 1973.

Zmegač, Viktor. *Kleine Geschichte der deutschen literatur von den Anfängen bis zur Gegenwart*. Königstein: Athenäum, 1984.

FEDERAL REPUBLIC OF GERMANY

Bance, Alan. *The German Novel 1945–60.* Stuttgart: Heinz, 1980.

Batt, Kurt. *Die Exekution des Erzählers.* Frankfurt am Main: Fischer, 1974.

———. *Revolte intern.* Munich: Beck, 1975.

Bernhard, Hans Joachim, ed. *Geschichte der literatur der Bundesrepublik Deutschland.* Berlin: Volk und Wissen, 1983.

Brettschneider, Werner. *Zorn und Trauer.* Berlin, Bielefeld, and Munich: E. Schmidt, 1979.

Endres, Elisabeth. *Die literatur der Adenauerzeit.* Munich: Steinhausen, 1980.

Glenn, Jerry. *Deutsches Schrifttum der Gegenwart.* Berlin and Munich: Francke, 1971.

Hahn, Ulla. *Literatur in der Aktion.* Wiesbaden: Athension, 1978.

Hartung, Harald. *Experimentelle literatur und konkrete Poesie.* Göttingen: Vandenhoeck und Ruprecht, 1975.

Kurz, Paul Konrad. *Über moderne literatur,* 7 vols. Frankfurt am Main: Knecht, 1967–80.

Lattmann, Dieter, ed. *Die literatur der Bundesrepublik Deutschland.* Frankfurt am Main: Fischer, 1980.

Lettau, Reinhard, ed. *Die Gruppe 47.* Neuwied: Luchterhand, 1967.

Lüdke, Werner Martin. *Nach dem Protest.* Frankfurt am Main: Suhrkamp, 1979.

Lützeler, Paul Michael, and Egon Schwarz. *Deutsche literatur in der Bundesrepublik seit 1965.* Königstein: Athenäum, 1980.

Mannack, Eberhard. *Zwei deutsche literaturen.* Kronberg: Athenäum, 1977.

Mayer, Hans. *Deutsche literatur seit Thomas Mann.* Reinbek: Rowohlt, 1968.

Oberhauser, Fred and Gabi. *Literarischer Führer durch die Bundesrepublik Deutschland.* Frankfurt am Main: Insel, 1974.

Pongs, Hermann. *Dichtung im gespaltenen Deutschland.* Stuttgart: Union, 1966.

Reich-Ranicki, Marcel. *Deutsche literatur in West und Ost.* Munich: Piper, 1963.

Schwarz, Egon. *Deutsche literatur in der Bundesrepublik seit 1965.* Königstein: Athenäum, 1980.

GERMAN DEMOCRATIC REPUBLIC

Albrecht, Günter, ed. *Schriftsteller der DDR.* Leipzig: Bibliographisches Institut, 1975.

Caspar, Günter. *Im Umgang.* Berlin and Weimar: Aufbau, 1984.

Diersch, Manfred and Werner Hartinger. *Literatur und Geschichtsbewußtsein.* Berlin and Weimar: Aufbau, 1976.

Einhorn, Brigitte. *Der Roman in der DDR 1946–1969.* Kronberg: Skriptor, 1978.

Emmerich, Wolfgang. *Kleine literaturgeschichte der DDR.* Darmstadt and Neuwied: Luchterhand, 1981.

Feitknecht, Thomas. *Die sozialistische Heimat.* Bern and Frankfurt am Main: Lang, 1971.

Flores, John. *Poetry in East Germany.* New Haven and London: Yale University Press, 1971.

Franke, Konrad, ed. *Die literatur der Deutschen Demokratischen Republik.* Frankfurt am Main: Fischer, 1980.

Funke, Christoph. *Theaterbilanz.* Berlin: Henschel, 1974.

Geerdts, Hans Jürgen, and Heinz Neugebauer, eds. *Literatur der Deutschen Demokratischen Republik.* Berlin: Volk und Wissen, 1979.

Gerlach, Ingeborg. *Bitterfeld.* Kronberg: Skriptor, 1974.

Haase, Horst, and Hans Jürgen Geerdts, eds. *Literatur der Deutschen Demokratischen Republik.* Berlin: Volk und Wissen, 1976.

Hohendahl, Peter Uwe, and Peter Herminghouse, eds. *Literatur und Literaturtheorie in der DDR.* Frankfurt am Main: Suhrkamp, 1976.

Huebener, Theodore. *The Literature of East Germany.* New York: Ungar, 1970.

Jarmatz, Klaus. *Kritik in der Zeit.* Halle: Mitteldeutscher, 1970.

Klunker, Heinz. *Zeitstücke und Zeitgenossen.* Munich: Deutscher Taschenbuchverlag, 1975.

Köhler-Hausmann, Reinhild. *Literaturbetrieb in der DDR.* Stuttgart: Metzler, 1984.

Labroisse, Gerd, ed. *Zur literatur und Literaturwissenschaft in der DDR.* Amsterdam: Rodopi, 1978.

Laschen, Gregor, ed. *Lyrik in der DDR.* Frankfurt am Main: Athenäum, 1971.

Maczewski, Johannes. *Der adaptierte Held.* Bern and Frankfurt am Main: Lang, 1978.

Nalewski, Horst, and Klaus Schuhmann, eds. *Selbsterfahrung als Welterfahrung.* Berlin and Weimar: Aufbau, 1981.

Raddatz, Fritz J. *Traditionen und Tendenzen.* Frankfurt am Main: Suhrkamp, 1978.

Reich-Ranicki, Marcel. *Zur literatur der DDR.* Munich: Piper, 1974.

Rossade, Werner. *Literatur im Systemwandel.* Bern and Frankfurt am Main: Lang, 1982.

Sander, Hans-Dietrich. *Geschichte der schönen literatur in der DDR*. Freiburg: Rombach, 1972.

Schivelbusch, Wolfgang. *Sozialistisches Drama nach Brecht*. Darmstadt and Neuwied: Luchterhand, 1974.

Schlenstedt, Dieter. *Die neuere DDR-Literatur und ihre Leser*. Berlin: Akademie, 1979.

Tate, Dennis. *The East German Novel*. Bath: Bath University Press, 1984.

Weisbach, Reinhard. *Menschenbild, Dichter und Gedicht*. Berlin and Weimar: Aufbau, 1972.

Weisbrod, Peter. *Literarischer Wandel in der DDR*. Heidelberg: Groos, 1980.

AUSTRIA

Adel, Kurt. *Aufbruch und Tradition*. Vienna: Braumüller, 1982.

Basil, Otto. *Das große Erbe*. Graz and Vienna: Stiasny, 1962.

Best, Alan D., ed. *Modern Austrian Writing*. London: Wolff, 1980.

Blauhut, Robert. *Österreichische Novellistik des 20. Jahrhunderts*. Vienna: Braumüller, 1966.

Breicha, Otto, and Gerhard Fritsch, eds. *Aufforderung zum Misstrauen*. Salzburg: Residenz, 1967.

Ernst, Gustav, and Klaus Wagenbach, eds. *Rot ich weiß Rot*. Berlin: Wagenbach, 1979.

Heger, Roland, *Das österreichische Hörspiel*. Vienna: Braumüller, 1977.

———. *Der österreichische Roman des 20. Jahrhunderts*. Vienna: Braumüller, 1971.

Jung, Jochen, ed. *Glückliches Österreich*. Salzburg: Residenz, 1978.

Rieder, Heinz. *Österreichische Moderne*. Bonn: Bouvier, 1969.

Rühm, Gerhard, ed. *Die Wiener Gruppe*. Reinbek: Rowohlt, 1969.

Schmidt, Adalbert. *Dichtung und Dichter Österreichs im 19. und 20. Jahrhundert*. Salzburg: Bergland-Buch, 1964.

Schönwiese, Ernst. *Literatur in Wien 1930 und 1980*. Munich: Amalthea, 1980.

Spiel, Hilde, ed. *Die zeitgenössische Literatur Österreichs*. Frankfurt am Main: Fischer, 1980.

Suchy, Viktor. *Literatur in Österreich von 1945 bis 1970*. Vienna: Dokumentationsstelle für neuere österreichische Literatur, 1973.

Twaroch, Johannes. *Literatur aus Niederösterreich von Frau Ava bis*

Helmut Zenker. St. Pölten: Niederösterreichisches Pressehaus, 1984.

Ungar, Frederick, ed. *Handbook of Austrian Literature.* New York: Ungar, 1973.

Vogelsang, Hans. *Österreichische Dramatik des 20, Jahrhunderts.* Vienna: Braumüller, 1981.

Wimmer, Paul. *Wegweiser durch die Literatur Tirols seit 1945.* Darmstadt: Bläschke, 1978.

SWITZERLAND

Bachmann, Dieter, ed. *Fortschreiben.* Zurich and Munich: Artemis, 1978.

Bloch, Peter André. ed. *Der Schriftsteller in unserer Zeit.* Bern: Francke, 1972.

Bräm, Emil Max. *Dichterporträts aus dem heutigen Schweizer Schrifttum.* Bern: Francke, 1963.

Bucher, Werner, and Georges Ammann, eds. *Schweizer Schriftsteller im Gespräch.* Basel: Reinhardt, 1970–71.

Burkhard, Marianne, and Gerd Labroisse, eds. *Zur Literatur der deutschsprachigen Schweiz.* Amsterdam: Rodopi, 1979.

Buschenhofer, Paul F. *Switzerland's Dramatists in the Shadow of Frisch and Dürrenmatt.* Bern and New York: Lang, 1984.

Flood, John L., ed. *Modern Swiss Literature.* New York: St. Martins, 1985.

Fringeli, Dieter, ed. *Gut zum Druck.* Zurich and Munich: Artemis, 1972.

———, ed. *Literatur der deutschen Schweiz seit 1964.* Zurich and Munich: Artemis, 1972.

Gsteiger, Manfred. *Literatur des Übergangs.* Bern: Francke, 1963.

———, ed. *Die zeitgenössische Literatur der Schweiz.* Frankfurt am Main: Fischer, 1980.

Günther, Werner. *Dichter der neueren Schweiz,* 2 vols. Bern: Francke, 1963–68.

Hilty, Hans Rudolf, and Max Schmid, eds. *Modernes Schweizer Theater.* Egnach: Clou, 1964.

Jauslin, Christian. *Dramatiker der deutschen Schweiz.* Zurich: Atlantis, 1973.

Lengborn, Thorbjörn. *Schriftsteller und Gesellschaft in der Schweiz.* Frankfurt am Main: Athenäum, 1972.

Marti, Kurt. *Die Schweiz und ihre Schriftsteller—Die Schriftsteller und ihre Schweiz.* Zurich: EVZ-Verlag, 1966.

Schwengeler, Arnold Hans. *Vom Geist und Wesen der Schweizer Dichtung.* St. Gallen: Tschudy, 1964.

Steiner-Kuhn, Susanne. *Schreiben im Dazwischen-Sein.* Bern: Haupt, 1982.

Wiese, Ursula von, ed. *Schweiz.* Bern: Verbandsdruckerei, 1978.

Zeltner, Gerda. *Das Ich ohne Gewähr.* Zurich: Suhrkamp, 1980.

Index

GERMAN WRITING SINCE 1945

A Critical Survey

LOWELL A. BANGERTER

German Writing Since 1945 is the most comprehensive survey available on German literature in the postwar era.

Following a concise but information-filled introduction on the historical and political dimensions of German writing from the May 1945 ceasefire to the present, the book goes on to examine the authors, works, literary movements, and direction of German writing in The Federal Republic of Germany, The German Democratic Republic, Austria, and Switzerland. More than 400 novelists, poets, and dramatists are covered, including Günter Grass, Heinrich Böll, Hans Carl Artmann, Uwe Johnson, Friedrich Dürrenmatt, Max Frisch, Peter Handke, Ulrich Plenzdorf, and Peter Weiss among many others.

Readers of this encyclopedic critical survey of the German writing scene will gain insight into the literary as well as political dimensions and trends of German literature over the past forty years, and will come away with an enhanced view of these vital authors and their wide-ranging works.